Steps to the Future

Christopher Sauer
Philip W. Yetton
and Associates

Steps to the Future

Fresh Thinking on the Management of IT-Based Organizational Transformation

Jossey-Bass Publishers
San Francisco

Copyright © 1997 by Jossey-Bass Inc., Publishers, 350 Sansome Street, San Francisco, California 94104.

Substantial discounts on bulk quantities of Jossey-Bass books are available to corporations, professional associations, and other organizations. For details and discount information, contact the special sales department at Jossey-Bass Inc., Publishers (415) 433–1740; Fax (800) 605–2665.

For sales outside the United States, please contact your local Simon & Schuster International Office.

Jossey-Bass Web address: http://www.josseybass.com

Credits appear on page 321.

 Manufactured in the United States of America on Lyons Falls Turin Book. This paper is acid-free and 100 percent totally chlorine-free.

Library of Congress Cataloging-in-Publication Data

Sauer, Christopher, date.
    Steps to the future : fresh thinking on the management of IT-based
organizational transformation / Christopher Sauer, Philip W. Yetton,
and associates.
      p. cm. — (The Jossey-Bass business & management series)
    Includes bibliographical references and index.
    ISBN 0–7879–0358–2
    1. Management information systems. 2. Information technology.
3. Organizational change. I. Yetton, Philip W., date.
II. Title. III. Series.
HD30.213.S276   1997
658.4'038'011—dc21   96–51899

FIRST EDITION
HB Printing 10 9 8 7 6 5 4 3 2 1

The Jossey-Bass
Business & Management Series

Contents

Preface   xv

The Authors   xxi

1. The Right Stuff: An Introduction to
   New Thinking About IT Management   1
   Christopher Sauer, Philip W. Yetton

Part One: The Traditional Solutions   23

2. False Prophecies, Successful Practice,
   and Future Directions in IT Management   27
   Philip W. Yetton

3. A Professional Balancing Act: Walking the
   Tightrope of Strategic Alignment   55
   Janice M. Burn

4. The Pathology of Strategic Alignment   89
   Christopher Sauer, Janice M. Burn

Part Two: Competencies for IT-Enabled Organizational Change   113

5. IT-Enabled Organizational Change:
   New Developments for IT Specialists   115
   M. Lynne Markus, Robert Benjamin

6. At the Heart of Success: Organizationwide
    Management Competencies   143
    V. Sambamurthy, Robert W. Zmud

Part Three: Process Change   165

7. Against Obliteration: Reducing Risk in
    Business Process Change   169
    Robert D. Galliers

8. The Real Event of Reengineering   187
    Jane Craig, Philip W. Yetton

Part Four: New Interpretations   205

9. The Paradoxes of Transformation   209
    Daniel Robey

10. Joint Outcomes: The Coproduction of IT and
    Organizational Change   231
    Rod Coombs

11. Improvising in the Shapeless Organization
    of the Future   257
    Claudio U. Ciborra

12. The Paths Ahead   279
    Philip W. Yetton, Christopher Sauer

Index   305

Figures, Tables, and Exhibits

Figures

1.1	IT Strategic Planning	7
1.2	Strategic Alignment in the Federal Structure	8
2.1	Model of Strategic Change and Fit	35
2.2	Conventional Model of Strategic Dynamics	36
2.3	Current IT Management: The Federal Solution	38
2.4	Strategic Dynamics at Flower and Samios	45
3.1	Alignment Model	59
3.2	Organizational Cultural Audit Framework	62
3.3	External Business Strategy Model	63
3.4	External IT Strategy Model	65
3.5	Organizational Infrastructure Model	68
3.6	IT Infrastructure Model	70
3.7	Business Planning Model	72
3.8	IT Planning Model	73
3.9	Strategic-Alignment Model	77
3.10	Organicity and Entrepreneurship	83
3.11	Model for IT Innovation and Entrepreneurship	85

4.1   Industry Life Cycle   99

4.2   Cycles of IT-Business Alignment   100

4.3   Stagnation in Cycles of IT-Business Alignment   101

4.4   Innovation-Consolidation Cycle
       for an Integrated Firm   107

6.1   Role of IT Management Competencies   148

7.1   Approaches to Business Strategy   172

7.2   Variation of Leavitt's Model   176

7.3   A Systemic Approach to
       Business Innovation and IT   181

8.1   MIT90s Model   189

8.2   Different Focuses of BPR Literature
       and BPR Activity   193

12.1   Model of Strategic Change and Fit   281

12.2   Conventional Model of Strategic Dynamics   284

12.3   Model of Technological Determinism   285

12.4   Strategic Dynamics at an Architectural Firm   286

12.5   Lead-Lag Model of Change   287

12.6   Organizational-Development Model of Change   291

12.7   Two Line-Leadership Competencies   292

12.8   Positioning-Versus-Core-Competency
       Model of Change   295

12.9   Influence of Culture and Strategic
       Information-Systems Planning on Change   296

Tables

1.1   Comparison of Traditional and New Mind-Sets   19

3.1   IT Planning Style   75

3.2   Organizational Planning Styles   76

5.1   Comparison of Two Worldviews on Change   120

5.2   Credibility Crunches in IT Work and
       When They Occur   136
6.1   Success with IT Deployment Across the
       Clusters of IT Management Competencies   155
9.1   Summary of Theories Used to Explain
       Organizational Transformation   217
9.2   Managerial Implications of Four
       Theoretical Perspectives   225

Exhibits

6.1   IT Management Competencies   150
6.2   Descriptions of IT Management
       Competency Clusters   154

Preface

To face the facts squarely, traditional thinking has not delivered a solution to the problem of consistently gaining business value from information technology (IT). How else to explain American Airlines's resounding failure with its CONFIRM project after the spectacular success of SABRE? (SABRE is the reservations system American placed on the desks of travel agents, which has yielded it many strategic advantages, including additional sales and information about its own and competitors' performance. CONFIRM was an attempt to build a tourism reservations system to incorporate air travel, hotels, and car rentals, which was abandoned after three-and-a-half years at a cost of $125 million.) Traditional thinking has run the gamut of rational management, from methodologies and disciplines for systems development and project management to IT planning and strategic alignment. What more fitting finale to an era than Business Process Reengineering (BPR), which epitomizes the dominant tradition's obsessive belief in the mechanistic rationality of organizations, and what more eloquent testimony to the end of that era than the admissions of its proponents that BPR has failed to deliver the turnarounds it promised?

The need for a real alternative, for a fresh approach, could scarcely be greater. Since the mid-1960s IT has diffused through most businesses to become a part of everyday working life. Today, it is a major investment and a core component in most large organizations. The increasing recognition of its strategic, competitive value emphasizes the business importance of rethinking IT management.

This book is the first formal statement of a new alternative. It is based in a new realism both about the limits of the industry's achievements in gaining business value from IT and about the true dynamics of business organizations. The book has grown out of a recognition by the contributors of the importance of IT in enabling new ways of competing through organizational transformation and out of a shared concern for how such organizational change should be managed. The various chapters give the reader compelling reasons why the conventional wisdom has not been successful. The authors tell us what not to do if we want to avoid the classic problems of gaining business value from IT. In rejecting the predictability of formal technical processes in producing organizational benefits, the new way of thinking about IT management embraces the value of deep-seated competencies and capabilities. It rejects the primacy of planned processes to achieve designed outcomes in favor of a cocktail of knowledge, skills, experiences combined with strategies, structures, and processes; together these elements permit the unpredictable to be managed. In the new thinking, success is defined not as ending up where you want to be but as wanting to be where you end up. Success lies in having what it takes to improvise successfully to achieve a desirable outcome. Thus, the new thinking makes a clear break with the past, and the implications for practice are enormous.

Unfortunately, it typically takes years for the best ideas to diffuse from their birthplace into a wider community. It takes even longer to ascertain which are the most promising lines of thought from among all the ideas that emerge. This book has eliminated the usual delays by bringing together at an early stage the latest thinking by leading researchers from four continents who themselves regularly collaborate with the best and brightest managers and consultants in the most advanced companies.

The ideas developed in this book can be expected to have enduring value for several reasons. The contributors have international reputations for leading the field. They are profoundly dissatisfied with traditional thinking; they do not criticize it superficially but demonstrate its fundamental weaknesses and hence its ultimate sterility. This is the characteristic behavior of revolutionary scientists acknowledging a crisis in their discipline. The convergence in this book on common ideas and assumptions indicates that the contributors have taken the first steps away from the crisis toward a new intellectual paradigm or tradition. These ideas and assumptions constitute an entirely new and consistent mind-set from which to approach IT.

This book spells out the fundamental reasons why traditional thinking should be abandoned and hence why the new thinking is required. It articulates the key elements of the new thinking and provides specific examples of how it is used. In addition, throughout the book the implications of specific ideas are developed, with the managerial implications being pulled together in Chapter Twelve.

The book is the only available starting point for learning how to rethink IT management. It therefore speaks to general managers, IT managers, and students of management who want to understand new developments ahead of everyone else and to have the right mind-set to shape the coming changes. It aims to be accessible to thinking managers whether they be generalists or IT specialists. Although these two groups have traditionally had different interests in IT, one of the common themes in the new thinking is the damaging nature of the traditional separation between business and IT. This is a message for both general and IT managers.

The new thinking directs general managers away from viewing IT as a complex technical specialty, responsibility for which they can hand off to technical managers. It directs them to the organization-wide competencies required to manage IT. There is an underlying message too that enjoins general managers to trust their managerial and business instincts and to be wary of technological promotions that they do not understand. IT is different in some respects from other organizational components, but this difference does not mean that it cannot be managed by intelligent attention to the standard concerns of decision making and operational management.

The new thinking has a complementary message for IT managers who recognize the need for change and are prepared to join forces with general managers in the wider interests of the business. For them, this book provides some specific conclusions about existing IT management practice and future developments in IT's role.

The new thinking is of special interest to MBA students because it challenges the conventional wisdom they find in textbooks. The cases described in this book are far closer to the messy realities new managers encounter on first entering the workplace. Unburdened by the baggage of the past, new managers can turn to their organization's IT problems with a fresh eye. Equipped with the fundamentals of a new kind of thinking they will be well positioned to successfully approach IT management. We believe that use of this book in seminars will make for stimulating discussions. Because this book is designed to be accessible to a wide audience, we believe that it will be of general interest to managers curious about how IT might be managed in their organization.

This book has a logic to its organization. Chapter One articulates the essentials of the new way of thinking. Chapters Two to Four concentrate on the shortcomings of existing solutions to managing IT for organizational transformation. Chapters Five and Six focus on management and change management competencies. Chapters Seven and Eight look at process change. Chapters Nine to Eleven explore new interpretations of and creative ways of thinking about IT-based change and how it is produced. Chapter Twelve spells out some of the implications for managing IT in the future. It is not critical that the chapters be read in order. Like a good art exhibition, where it is possible to view the works out of sequence, the reader can pick and choose. Chapters One and Twelve are like the exhibition catalogue; they provide the structure into which the body of the works fits. It may therefore pay to read them first and last.

This book has grown out of the core agenda of the Fujitsu Centre for Managing Information Technology in Organisations at the Australian Graduate School of Management, where we work. The Centre's distinctive orientation has been primarily to address general management issues relating to IT. We have found a number of colleagues around the world whose orientation is consistent with ours. During the course of 1995 they joined with us in presenting their work at international conferences in Athens, Vancouver, and Amsterdam. They are very much our fellow travelers! The latest developments in the work they presented to those conferences are included in this book.

In order to ensure that this book would contain the latest and best thinking and that it would be accessible to a wide audience, we made certain specifications. We wanted fresh work in the sense of its being novel and not already easily available to a wide audience of managers. The ideas presented have not been much aired before. We asked our contributors to present their ideas and their findings without worrying about their rigorous derivation. Detailed description of research methods and intricate statistical analysis have been set to one side. We have also been content to settle for a monolithic view of IT. We accept that IT's many forms may need different management. Application of electronic data interchange technologies that support interorganizational networks can be expected to require different management from stand-alone, in-house, commercial systems. In introducing a new mind-set we are abstracting from the detail of particular technologies to develop assumptions and principles. At this early stage, it seems better to buy clarity at the cost of oversimplification rather than accuracy at the cost of clarity.

We also encouraged our contributors to be stimulating and provocative even if some of their conclusions are speculative. We shall be quite satisfied if readers are stopped in their tracks by what they read here. We do not expect total agreement from our readers, but we do hope that the ideas presented will stimulate them to review their current thinking.

As editors we should like to thank a number of people whose names do not appear here but whose support has been crucial. The Fujitsu Centre is supported by Fujitsu (Australia) Limited and by the Commonwealth Bank of Australia. Without their foresight and continuing support we should not have been able to undertake the research that has led us to this book. In particular we thank Neville Roach, chief executive of Fujitsu (Australia), and Peter Andrews, previously general manager for information technology services and now general manager for direct banking at the Commonwealth Bank. At the Australian Graduate School of Management we have been helped in preparing the figures by Anne Davis and the staff of the Studio, and in much of the detailed preparation of the manuscript by Barbara Potter in the Fujitsu Centre. At Jossey-Bass, Larry Alexander immediately saw the book's potential and as editor has supported its development and production; Carrie Castillon has assisted him; Dave Horne has guided us through the production process. We are grateful to them all.

February 1997   Christopher Sauer
Sydney, Australia   Philip W. Yetton

The Authors

Christopher Sauer researches general management issues in organizational transformation, in particular issues relating to information technology (IT) and the dynamics of organizational change. He has a continuing interest in information-systems development and failure. His book *Why Information Systems Fail: A Case Study Approach* was published in 1993. He has also authored and coauthored a variety of papers on his research and on IT educational issues. He is associate editor for IT management for the *Australian Journal of Management* and a member of the editorial board of the *Information Systems Journal*. He is secretary for the International Federation of Information Processing Working Group 8.6 on Technology Transfer and Diffusion and is a member of the Australian Computer Society. Currently, Sauer is a senior research fellow at the Fujitsu Centre for Managing Information Technology in Organisations at the Australian Graduate School of Management in Sydney. He has been involved in groundbreaking work in IT education in both the United Kingdom and Australia. Previously, he was an IT practitioner. He has worked closely with firms in a number of industries and has been a consultant to the public sector. A graduate of Oxford University, he was awarded a doctorate in management by the University of Western Australia.

Philip W. Yetton teaches strategic leadership, organizational behavior, and the management of IT and has major research interests in leadership style, decision making, and IT. He has extensive consulting experience in Australia, Europe, the United Kingdom, and the United States in industries as diverse as computers, chemicals, textiles, and banking, and in health, prison services, and the military. He has been a consultant on strategic leadership to the ANZ Banking Group, Pearl Assurance (United Kingdom), and San Miguel (the Philippines). He is best known as coauthor with Professor Victor Vroom of the internationally acclaimed text *Leadership and Decision Making*. He is also coauthor of the leading textbook *Management in Australia* and has written numerous research papers. Yetton is on the editorial board of *Leadership Quarterly* and *Organizational Science*. He is a graduate of Cambridge University, Liverpool University, and Carnegie-Mellon University. He is the Commonwealth Bank Professor of Management and the executive director of the Fujitsu Centre for Managing Information Technology in Organisations at the Australian Graduate School of Management in Sydney.

Robert Benjamin is professor at the School of Information Studies, Syracuse University, and visiting research affiliate at the MIT Sloan School of Management's Center for Information Systems Research. He retired from a senior management role in information systems with Xerox at the end of 1988 and now has a consulting practice in the strategic management of IT. As well as being actively involved in the IT industry, Benjamin is widely published. Author of *Control of Information Systems Development*, he has contributed articles to the *Harvard Business Review*, the *Sloan Management Review*, and *MIS Quarterly*. He is associate editor of *MIS Quarterly*.

Janice M. Burn is associate professor at Hong Kong Polytechnic University and has held similar posts in the United Kingdom and

Canada. She has recently been appointed Foundation Professor of Information Systems at Edith Cowan University. Her research interests include the use and abuse of IT in Hong Kong, strategic planning for effective exploitation of IT, the management of information-systems resources, and professional and ethical practices in information-systems education. Burn has published extensively and has presented papers at numerous conferences around the world. She is coauthor of three books on information systems and is editor of a forthcoming book on the use of IT in Asia.

Claudio U. Ciborra is professor of organization theory and information systems at the University of Bologna, Italy, and at Theseus Institute in France. He received his degree in engineering at the Politecnico in Milan. He has published a major work on the economics of organizations and IT (*Teams, Markets and Systems*). He is currently involved in research projects on groupware and teamwork in large organizations and on corporate memory.

Rod Coombs is professor of technology management at the Manchester School of Management at the University of Manchester Institute of Science and Technology. He has researched and published widely on all aspects of the process of technological change. From 1987 to 1995 he directed the Manchester component of the United Kingdom's national research program on the economic and social implications of IT. He is currently working with several large companies on the strategic management of research and development and of technological innovation. Prior to earning a Ph.D. from Manchester University in the economics of innovation, Coombs was in biophysics, having completed a first degree in physics.

Jane Craig is a lecturer in general management at the Australian Graduate School of Management in the University of New South Wales. Her research interests include managing IT-based change, business process redesign, international management structures, group decision making, and leadership. Craig has published in *Sloan Management Review,* has had papers selected for presentation at the International Conference on Information Systems, the Academy of Management, and the Strategic Management Society Conference, and is coauthor of a leading Australian management text. She has also been a diplomat, a policy analyst, and a management consultant in the United States and Australia.

Robert D. Galliers is chair and professor of information management at Warwick Business School, University of Warwick, United Kingdom. Previously he headed the school's doctoral program in information systems and its Information Systems Research Unit. At Curtin University in Perth, Western Australia, he developed a master's program that emphasized management issues associated with the introduction and utilization of IT in organizations—the first of its kind in Australia. Galliers has published widely on aspects of information systems management, and has authored and coauthored several books. He is editor-in-chief of the *Journal of Strategic Information Systems.*

M. Lynne Markus is professor of information science and management at the Peter F. Drucker Management Center, Claremont Graduate School. She has also taught at leading business schools in Europe, Southeast Asia, and the United States. She has consulted with Arthur D. Little, Inc., and the RAND Corporation. Markus is the author of *Systems in Organizations: Bugs and Features* and has contributed articles to leading IT and management journals. She is a former member of the *MIS Quarterly* editorial board and is coediting a special issue of *MIS Quarterly* on intensive research methods. She currently holds office with SIM International and the Association for Information Systems.

Daniel Robey is professor of computer information systems at Georgia State University. He earned his doctorate in 1973 from Kent

State University and has served on the faculties of the University of Pittsburgh, Marquette University, Gannon University, and Florida International University. He is the author of three books and numerous articles in such journals as *Management Science, Organization Science, Information Systems Research, MIS Quarterly, Communications of the ACM, Human Relations, ACM Transactions on Information Systems, Academy of Management Review, Academy of Management Journal,* and *Decision Sciences.*

V. Sambamurthy earned his doctorate from the University of Minnesota and is associate professor of the management of information systems at Florida State University. His research focuses broadly on the design of organizations for effective use of technologies in business strategy and operations, IT coordination mechanisms, and organizational transformation. He has also researched the impact of IT on group work. His papers have appeared in top information systems journals; currently, he serves on the editorial boards of *MIS Quarterly* and the *Journal of Market-Focused Management.* Sambamurthy has participated in, and managed, major conferences including programs for the International Conference on Information Systems and the Academy of Management.

Robert W. Zmud is professor and Thomas L. Williams, Jr., Eminent Scholar in Management Information Systems at the College of Business, Florida State University. His current research interests include the impact of IT on organizational behavior and organizational efforts in planning, managing, and diffusing IT. In addition to numerous scholarly articles on these topics, he has coauthored four research monographs. Zmud is editor-in-chief of *MIS Quarterly* and serves on the editorial boards of *Management Science* and *Information Systems Research.* Both his Ph.D. (University of Arizona) and his M.S. (MIT) degrees are in management.

Steps to the Future

The Right Stuff

An Introduction to New Thinking About IT Management

Christopher Sauer and Philip W. Yetton

Today, to be successful in a global competitive environment, organizations have to compete and win across the board. Not only do they need to deliver simultaneously both high quality and low cost, which were once regarded as tradeoffs, but they also need to be innovative, flexible, and fast to market on a continuing basis. The bundling of internal resources called for by this prevailing environment of heightened competitiveness is potentially very different from the organizational configurations that allowed businesses to be successful in previous eras. Organizational transformation is usually required to achieve this new style of operating.

The significant shifts in the nature of competition highlight the need to reconsider the role of information technology (IT) in broad organizational and strategic terms and, particularly, to focus on its consequences for organizational transformation. In the 1970s and 1980s, business emphasis was on market segmentation as the strategic focus and on internal differentiation/divisionalization as the organizing response. It is not difficult to understand why IT was not part of the central debates around managing multidivisional firms. Economies of scale and other technical factors provided a compelling argument for centralizing mainframe activities. Thus IT was not part of the world of independent, bottom-line-accountable, strategic business units (SBUs). Instead, in that context, IT posed a problem: How could SBUs make IT responsive and effective and control its costs? The answer was not readily apparent. Most solutions proved to be unstable. The issue was perennially how to cope with IT, not how could IT be the source or basis of a competitive advantage.

However, in the 1990s and for the foreseeable future, the demands placed on organizations by the advent of, for example, just-in-time management are different. IT now comes to center stage. Corporations are no longer merely dependent on IT as a medium through which work is conducted; rather IT defines the way they do business. Integration rather than differentiation of activities is emphasized. We cannot expect ideas, including models and theories, derived from an era of differentiation to provide useful insights into transformations based on integrating activities.

IT is not now and never has been a competitive silver bullet. Its value depends on making changes to all parts of the organization so that strategy, structure, management processes, roles, and skills are consistent with the technology. A major obstacle to gaining IT's full value is the nonapplicability of the available ideas for doing so. The current main theories of organizational effectiveness and transformation do not incorporate a role for IT. Moreover, the literature on IT-based strategic change, although it sees IT as the principal enabler, still casts IT in a support role rather than treating it as a critical driver. Both practitioners and researchers have accepted the seductive argument that has dominated organizational thinking: we should know where we are going (strategic vision), we should organize to get there (restructure), and then we should align our IT to this strategy-structure design.

Most corporations have found it hard enough to manage IT when its role has been to support the business. Few are equipped to cope with the management challenge of the technology's new, strategic role. If IT is to live up to its business potential, therefore, managers will need a new approach to the problem of IT-enabled transformation. This book brings together the work of twelve researchers who for several years have been developing the new ideas managers need.

This introduction presents the essentials of this new approach to IT management thought. An overview is necessary to draw together all the elements common to this approach because each chapter has its own focus and perspective and makes a distinctive contribution. We therefore describe both traditional and new ideas about IT management to highlight the fundamental assumptions on which each is based. We then show that the traditional approach is barren and is likely to remain so, whereas the new approach is different and will be more fruitful.

This chapter is helpful to managers in two ways. First, it unbundles traditional thinking into its constituent assumptions and thereby reveals its limitations. The inappropriateness of these assumptions is a persuasive reason why we should consider radically new management ideas. Second, it spells out the fundamentals of new IT thinking in the form of an alternative set of assumptions or principles. This approach is particularly appropriate because the new thinking is less deterministic than traditional thinking and more oriented to situation-specific problem solving. In Chapter Twelve we build on these fundamentals to provide a set of twelve rules of thumb for managing according to the new principles.

Traditional Thinking

The problem of how to manage IT effectively has been the focus of much effort on the part of managers, consultants, and academics since the technology's first application to business in the 1950s. Ideas about the appropriate role for IT have evolved over that period from the technology's being seen as purely a support for business to its being considered a crucial weapon in competitive strategy (Ives and Learmonth, 1984; Porter and Millar, 1985). At the same time, management thinking has progressed from seeing IT as an entirely separate technical function to requiring close links between IT and the core business.

Support Role of IT

Until the mid-1980s, proponents saw IT's chief attribute as its ability to automate existing procedures. IT's value lay in its ability to do the same things faster, cheaper, and more accurately than when the same tasks were undertaken manually. In most companies, automation meant that electronic messages followed the same organizational tracks along which paper had previously been pushed. Typically, noncritical, back-office processes were the ones that were automated. Even where IT was applied to core business activities, its use in automating existing procedures left the business itself unchanged. The role of IT was to support the business.

By focusing on automation and support, traditional thinking has assumed that IT application involves little or no organizational change. The IT system is seen as a black box that can be clicked into place without the organization's missing a beat. Experience has taught us that this is an unduly optimistic view and that usually some degree of organizational change is required to accommodate a new, automated system. However, although automation has often involved organizational change, it has typically not changed the competitive structure of the firm or the industry but rather has been restricted to changing the medium through which work is performed.

Strategic Role of IT

As companies have gained experience with the technology, they have discovered that IT's capabilities extend well beyond mere automation. In fact, automation has proved to be something of a Trojan horse. It conceals more potent capabilities. As Zuboff (1988) has remarked, IT has the capacity to *informate* processes—that is, in automating information flows IT permits the capture and analysis of data that can be used to refine, improve, and redesign the basic business process underlying the automated system. The informating potential of IT can lead a corporation to review and reform the way it conducts its business. Thus, in its strategic role IT enables the corporation to change the way it competes so as to significantly improve bottom-line performance.

Since the mid-1980s, the importance of strategic information systems (SIS) has been confirmed by a number of high-profile successes. It is widely acknowledged that American Airlines's SABRE reservation system gave that airline dominance in the U.S. domestic market (Copeland and McKenney, 1988; Hopper, 1990). However, the potential for such success is widely accessible even to smaller, less technologically advanced companies, as the experience of the Australian architectural practice Flower and Samios has demonstrated. By not merely using computer-based architectural packages but totally integrating its business practice through the use of IT, this company was able to expand fivefold in a recessionary market when many of its competitors were laying off staff and closing their doors (Yetton, Johnston, and Craig, 1994; see also Chapter Two).

Managing IT

In the 1970s and 1980s IT was managed mostly as a technical function because its core activities were seen as systems development. Management of IT centered on capital, human, and knowledge resources. Acquisition of capital resources was a major issue. It involved large funding decisions, and selection of the equipment had significant implications for future development of the technology base. Human resource management was critical because so much technical knowledge was individual-dependent, skilled individuals were in short supply, and the technology advanced so rapidly that a large investment in training became necessary. Knowledge was critical because of the technical nature of IT work and also because skilled and knowledgeable individuals were scarce. Resources such as formal techniques, methods, and methodologies for planning, developing, and managing IT systems assisted in the transfer of knowledge and the development of less-skilled staff. The other major management issue was control, in particular the management and control of development projects. The management focus therefore was principally on IT technical activities.

The focus on IT as a technical specialism has meant that it has also traditionally been managed as a separate organizational function—a natural response to IT's being seen as playing a support role. Because managers have assumed that it is possible to develop systems that can slot seamlessly into place with minimal input from the business, IT has been left to manage its own activities separately from the rest of the organization. Sometimes IT has been given a separate place in the organizational structure; often it has been made part of another support function—for example, being placed under the chief financial officer. Inevitably IT has become distanced from the core business.

The distance between IT and the business has resulted in IT's often not acting in accordance with corporate priorities. IT has been criticized for pursuing its own agendas in, for example, developing technological infrastructures, not responding to urgent requests, working with a much longer time frame than the core business, and tolerating application backlogs sometimes amounting to several years' worth of work. Although managers have complained about IT's lack of responsiveness, organizations have typically not had in place adequate management processes to compensate for the structural separation of IT. For example, human resource policies have rarely encouraged the interchange of IT and business managers. As corporations have become more aware of the potential business value of IT, their interest in managing IT effectively has increased, and the approach has begun to change. Since the mid-1980s, two particular approaches to managing IT have become popular. The first is IT strategic planning (Ward, Griffiths, and Whitmore, 1990). The thrust of this approach has been to ensure that IT plans match strategic plans for the business and hence that what IT does is consistent with core-business priorities and initiatives (Figure 1.1). Such planning reduces the likelihood that IT will pursue an independent agenda.

The second approach has been based on organizing to achieve strategic alignment (Henderson and Venkatraman, 1992). Alignment is a persuasive idea that has been highly influential in determining the way corporations have chosen to manage IT since the mid-1980s. It is a potentially more powerful approach than strategic planning in that it tries to tie IT performance more closely to business needs throughout the corporation by addressing the structural separation of the IT function. Instead of relying on planning processes that are only loosely coupled to performance, strategic alignment involves configuring the organization so that IT is strategically, structurally, and managerially aligned to the business strategy, structure, and management processes. The basic principle of strategic alignment is that IT should be managed in a way that mirrors management of the business.

Strategic alignment may be best understood in the context of the federal structure (Zmud, Boynton, and Jacobs, 1986). Figure 1.2 depicts this structure for a multidivisional organization. In the federal design, there is a structural fit between IT and the business because IT is located at all levels of the organization close to the business units it serves. In addition to structural fit, strategic alignment also requires that IT be managed according to processes that

Figure 1.1. IT Strategic Planning.

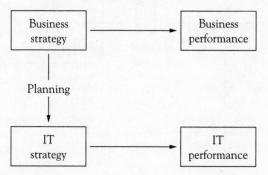

Figure 1.2. Strategic Alignment in the Federal Structure.

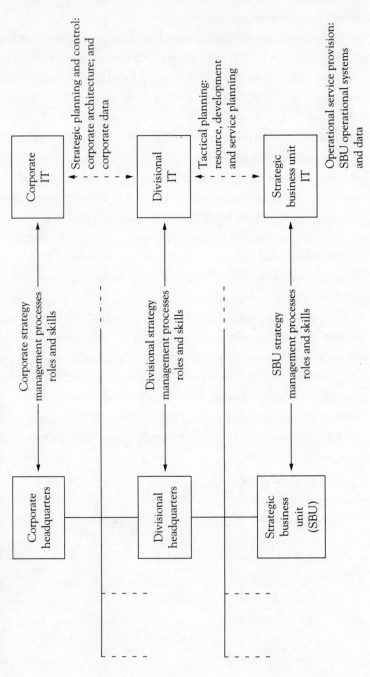

ensure consistency in corporate priorities and IT priorities at all levels and between all levels. Alignment thus aims to eliminate the problems resulting from the traditional separation of IT and the business.

The Problem of Performance

Changes in IT management thinking have been necessary because of the dissatisfaction of business managers with the performance of IT. A number of criticisms have been common. Managers have questioned the business value of the services they receive. How much of IT effort, they ask, has a direct return for the business? IT so often appears to be unresponsive, keeping step only to its own drummer. Business managers have also found the costs for IT to be high, and so they have not been satisfied with the return on their investment (Strassmann, 1985). When IT attempts to provide systems the business wants, there is a significant risk that the systems will not be delivered at the agreed cost and on the agreed schedule. Failure rates between one in three and two in three have consistently been quoted (Sauer, 1997). Even where systems have been successfully implemented, automation has only delivered business benefits when supported by active management interventions; for example, staff savings have not typically been achieved unless managers have taken positive action because employees have found alternative uses for their time.

Traditional thinking about IT management has not resolved the principal problems business managers face. The newer approaches, such as IT strategic planning and strategic alignment, have looked like plausible solutions and have encouraged some optimism that IT could be brought under control. But the vast majority of companies will admit, in private if not in public, that they still suffer from IT performance problems. If any of the accepted IT-management approaches, new or old, worked well, there would be many more satisfied companies. Rather, the secret of the success of the few must lie elsewhere—in ideas and thinking that are not widely recognized or understood.

The Challenge of IT-Based Organizational Transformation

Since the mid-1980s advances in industry understanding of the strategic role of IT together with increased competitive pressures on business have highlighted the need for IT-based organizational transformation. This organizational transformation is usually undertaken in the search for a sustainable competitive advantage or to catch up with the competition. It involves change in the organization's strategy, structure, technologies, management processes, roles, and skills (Scott Morton, 1991). IT-based organizational transformation is centered on IT's potential to change business processes and to lead to new ways of competing.

The best-known approach to IT-based organizational transformation is Business Process Reengineering (BPR) (Davenport, 1993; Hammer and Champy, 1993). BPR's chief characteristics are that it concentrates on business processes, it preaches radical redesign and radical improvement, and it is IT-enabled. Its focus on business processes is highly rational in that it concentrates on how the business transforms organizational inputs into deliverables valued by the customer, eliminating all unnecessary detail. The issue BPR addresses is how to be most effective in the most efficient way. Its radicalism lies both in its proposal to obliterate old, inefficient processes, starting redesign with a clean slate, and in its search for strategic improvements in competitive performance and bottom-line outcomes. BPR's advocates have emphasized the need to achieve returns on investment ranging from 50 percent to 100 percent over a five-year period (Davenport, 1993). BPR casts IT as the principal enabling technology because business processes usually cross functional boundaries and IT is able to facilitate integration across them.

There have been a number of high-profile successes with both SIS and BPR projects. Unfortunately, they have been relatively few. Advocates of BPR cite its high failure rate as though it were a badge of honor—if it is so risky, the return must be worth it. The 70 percent failure rate they quote exceeds even the worst figures for automation projects (Sauer, 1997). The absence of a continuing stream of new success stories indicates that IT-based transformation is difficult to achieve.

Not only is the risk substantial, but the stakes are unusually high. The cost of failure for a project that involves organizational transformation is likely to be much greater than the simple loss of investment. The time lost in undertaking a project that fails may give competitors a lead that cannot be recovered.

The management challenge is to move companies from their current competitive situation to a position where IT defines a new way of doing business. The challenge is acute because at the start the corporation may still have a performance problem and hence a management problem with IT. For transformation to be successful not only do new IT systems have to be devised and constructed, but organizational change has to be undertaken in order for the corporation to fit the business to the new systems.

The evidence to date suggests that most organizations still struggle to manage IT effectively. Chapters Two, Three, and Four analyze many of the shortcomings of strategic planning and alignment. Chapters Seven and Eight do the same for BPR. The failure of the various approaches to managing IT-based organizational transformation is another signal that we need new ideas.

The New Approach to IT

In this book, the contributors address different aspects of IT-based transformation. Consequently, they present a range of new ideas. In order to explain the connections among them and to reveal the common thinking that binds them, we have organized the book into four main parts. Part One explains the deficiencies of traditional approaches to IT management. Part Two describes the prerequisites for successful change. Part Three discusses process change and develops strong recommendations about where management attention should be directed. And Part Four develops new and simplified explanations for some of the puzzling results of IT-enabled organizational transformation.

The comparison below of the assumptions of the new mind-set with those of more traditional thinking shows clearly that the new approach is truly new and that it avoids the errors of the past.

New Ideas

The new ideas described in this book are distinctive in two respects. First, they are the result of critiques of the traditional ways of thinking about IT; these critiques led the authors to ask new and different questions and openly confront paradoxical ideas and data. Two examples illustrate the value of this approach in leading us to new conclusions. In Chapter Eleven, Claudio Ciborra poses a new and different question that leads us away from familiar territory. Asking what is fundamental in all the different change programs managers undertake, he concludes that it is the importance given to and the pervasiveness of experimentation, an organizational practice that has received little explicit attention. M. Lynne Markus and Robert Benjamin in Chapter Five confront an apparent paradox: Why do IT professionals, who see themselves as agents of change, know so little about organizational change? They conclude that a proactive change-management role for IT professionals is necessary.

Second, the new ideas presented here have a different emphasis from traditional thinking. Much traditional IT thinking has been devoted to ascertaining how to achieve successful outcomes, which is usually seen as a matter of following the "right" formal processes— the right planning method or the right systems development methodology. The new ideas are more concerned with having "the right stuff"—being able to put in place the right conditions and to deploy the right inputs. The "right stuff" is important because the transformation process has a strong element of experimentation and improvisation that cannot be anticipated in a formal process.

In the remainder of this chapter, we describe the new mind-set and show that it is a coherent and different way of thinking about IT management. In Chapter Twelve, we outline a set of practical rules of thumb for managers grounded in this way of thinking. However, it is important to recognize that techniques alone are no substitute for deep understanding. There are no foolproof recipes. Chapter Twelve is therefore a complement to the rest of the book, not a shortcut.

A Different Way of Thinking

Underpinning the new way of thinking about IT is a set of assumptions, or mind-set. The ideas presented in each chapter of this book are consistent with these assumptions. Together they form a worldview quite distinct from that of the traditional mind-set.

Kling and Scacchi (Kling, 1980; Kling and Scacchi, 1982) have attempted to explain some of the contrasting ways of thinking about IT. What we term the traditional mind-set is similar to Kling's systems-rationalist and discrete-entity models in that it rests on a highly rationalistic view of organizational life. Organizations in these models are typically goal-directed and mechanistic. This view encourages IT professionals to make a number of false assumptions including assuming that IT is necessarily acting in the interests of the business and that all organizational stakeholders pull toward the same goal. These assumptions lead to ignorance both of business priorities and of the full range of interests that may affect IT initiatives. The mechanistic organizational model also encourages the development and adoption of inflexible management and technical processes that have adverse effects on IT performance. By contrast, the new mind-set takes a multiple-constituency perspective. It assumes organizations have many stakeholders with competing interests and objectives. This assumption is in tune with the IT community's actual experience in that it explains the apparently uncooperative behavior of other departments.

The traditional mind-set has typically viewed IT systems as discrete entities. As a result IT professionals have felt justified in drawing a line around their development activities as though they need concern themselves only with producing a system. This result has been unfortunate in two respects. First, it has encouraged structural differentiation, which inevitably breeds special interests and hence entrenches IT's lack of concern with business priorities (Pfeffer, 1981). Second, it fails to acknowledge the inevitability of environmental turbulence and the need for IT and the business organization to be mutually accommodating. The upshot on both scores is that IT fails to deliver what the business wants. By contrast, the new mind-set sees IT as integral to the business and organization. Decisions about the one should be decisions about the other. In this view, all important decisions must respect both the business and IT implications. They are two facets of a single decision.

The traditional mind-set embraces technological determinism. It assumes that there are consistent causal relationships between technology and organizational outcomes. If the right technology is installed, the organization will change accordingly and deliver the desired business outcomes. This view thus reinforces the discrete-entity assumption and further encourages the separation of IT and the business. As several contributors to this book argue, there is no persuasive evidence for technological determinism (Chapters Five, Nine, and Ten). Daniel Robey (Chapter Nine) contends that the evidence of our eyes denies consistent cause-effect relationships. Rather, we encounter countervailing forces, the outcomes of which are unpredictable.

The discrete-entity and cause-effect assumptions of the traditional mind-set encourage a view of knowledge as well-defined, explicit, and articulate. It is well-defined in the sense that there are clear boundaries around systems, organizations, and people such that the relationships among them are definite. There are no ifs, buts, and maybes. Knowledge is explicit in that it is consciously perceived with nothing hidden, and it is articulate in the sense that it is made clear and is accessible to those who need it. This view results in an emphasis on formal knowledge as the basis for technical and management processes. Know-how is understood to mean having access to relevant facts and being able to extrapolate logically from them. Action based on these assumptions founders because our formal knowledge of IT is so limited and because logic alone cannot explain the outcome when countervailing forces are in play. This view of knowledge reinforces the rational view of organizations with all its limitations. It underplays the importance of uncertainty, and it hides from view much important knowledge in the forms of intuition, experience, and the like. Consequently, when IT systems are being developed, there is a gap between what the organization actually knows and what IT professionals recognize as relevant. Indeed, IT professionals often do not possess or do not know where to look for important knowledge and information.

The new mind-set defines knowledge quite differently. It accepts that we have limited formal knowledge. Because the world of business is highly dynamic, knowledge is ephemeral rather than lasting and partial rather than total. The new mind-set sees knowledge as ill-defined, tacit, diffuse, and embedded. If we recognize that we have limited formal knowledge, we cannot expect formal processes alone to generate the desired IT outcomes. At the very least, formal knowledge must be supplemented. Much of the knowledge that distinguishes an organization is not formal but tacit and is often derived from experience and only realized in adaptive, improvised behavior. Such knowledge is also diffuse in that it is spread around the organization and comes together only through coordinated action. This knowledge may be embedded in organizational structures and processes without being explicitly or formally recorded. The new mind-set thus has a broad understanding of knowledge that influences its distinctive understanding of the status quo and organizational change.

The traditional mind-set sees the status quo as a baseline against which improvement can be measured. In this view, the status quo is fundamentally dispensable. Once the baseline is understood, a design can be prepared for a transformed organization that will produce a better set of outcomes. However, the quality of the design is inevitably diminished because the traditional approach makes unrealistic assumptions about organizations and knowledge. It is likely to misunderstand the baseline by overlooking important but hidden knowledge. It therefore fails to recognize, for example, that the common resistance of users and executives to IT-designed systems has its roots in the desire to protect much that is valuable but not explicit in the established order. A further consequence is that new methods replace old ones without much thought being spared for the costs of abandoning the old and learning the new. The traditional mind-set's rationalistic and mechanistic approach encourages the development of designs that do not respect the diversity, hidden richness, and complexity of a business organization.

The new mind-set values the status quo for its embedded knowledge. This view implies that organizations be cautious about change. Effective change emerges from experimentation and improvisation, which allow improvements to be made through the use of individuals' tacit knowledge about the business and without the loss of valuable knowledge that is embedded in existing structures and processes. This process implies quite different IT practices and hence demands a different approach to IT management. IT-based transformation will be an extended, iterative, and improvised process rather than the outcome of a visionary design implemented through a single large program of change.

The new and traditional mind-sets can be thought of as reflecting quite different views of business. The traditional mind-set has much in common with the design school of strategy. According to design-school thinkers (Porter, 1980), firms formulate strategy by identifying a position they would like to occupy in an industry. They then redesign to fit that position. Performance benefits follow from occupying that preferred position. In this school, rational decision making, design, and planning have central roles much as they do in the traditional IT mind-set. To the extent that IT management thinkers have in the past been influenced by the design school, this view of business has not provided a reason to reject the basic principles of IT management. IT therefore has continued to be conceived of as a technical activity separate from the business. Even the newer developments of strategic planning, strategic alignment, and BPR have been dominated by this kind of rational, design-oriented thinking.

The new mind-set is far closer to a new theory of competitive strategy, the Resource Based View (RBV) of the firm (Barney, 1991; Collis and Montgomery, 1995). In this theory, corporations are viewed as collections of resources that are heterogeneously distributed within and across industries. What makes the performance of a firm distinctive is the unique blend of resources it possesses. A firm's resources include not only its physical assets such as plant and location but also its competencies and capabilities. Competencies and capabilities are less readily identified than other resources because they are based in the interaction of individuals, knowledge, structures, processes, and other resources. They are usually developed over relatively long periods of time, not acquired in shrink-wrap packaging. Truly distinctive competencies are deeply rooted in organizational practice. They are acquired through repeated performance of the same or similar tasks as members of the organization come to master a particular area of activity. The knowledge and skill residing initially in individuals become institutionalized through organizational learning over time and eventually become documented organizational procedures and relationships.

RBV is consistent with the new mind-set. Corporate performance is not explained by neat causal laws. Knowledge is hard-won and over time becomes distributed and transformed within the organization; at that point it cannot be apprehended as a discrete entity located exclusively within a person or persons but rather takes the form of a capability or competency. Change then takes considerable time to be assimilated and entrenched because simple possession of new knowledge or the design of a new set of procedures does not provide the depth of understanding necessary for doing things differently. The outer forms of activity may change quickly when a new system is implemented, but it takes much longer for a new way of thinking to take hold within a company. The separatist view of IT is therefore completely out of step with RBV because IT cannot change the organization by the simple application of rational principles of design. IT will be most successful when it infuses the organization and embeds itself alongside other changes. IT will provide sustainable competitive advantage only when the organization as a whole has a distinctive ability to use it (Mata, Fuerst, and Barney, 1995). What counts is not clever designs that can be imported into the organization but the organization's cleverness in working with IT. Transforming an organization means learning to do business differently—that is, dispensing with old competencies and replacing them with new ones. RBV's contribution to the new mind-set helps us see how difficult that is.

In characterizing the traditional mind-set as we have, we do not intend to suggest that all managers and management thinkers consciously and explicitly accept all the assumptions we have attributed to that mind-set. Rather our point, and that of many of our contributors, is that some of the traditional assumptions have pervaded almost all attempts at innovative thinking about IT management. For example, we know both managers and theorists who espouse a multiple-constituencies model of organization but who embrace planning and design because they see power as an attribute of stakeholders who can cause predictable change. Thus explicit rejection of the traditional mind-set in one respect is undermined by the pervasiveness of its other assumptions. Of course, just as we do not claim that all traditionalists accept all of the traditional mind-set, so too our contributors do not all make all the assumptions we have characterized as new—for example, they do not all subscribe to RBV. But just as the assumptions of the traditional mind-set form a consistent whole, so too do the assumptions of the new mind-set. Thus, proponents of the new mind-set will be drawn to assumptions they have not explicitly accepted because they are consistent with assumptions they have already embraced. Table 1.1 compares the two mind-sets.

Summary

The new thinking about IT rejects any idea that organizations are easily understood and hence that it is possible to devise simple routines for managing IT-enabled organizational transformation. Whatever advances may be made over time, in the foreseeable future, we shall continue to lack the relevant knowledge to simplify the management task. In the absence of general-purpose or

Table 1.1. Comparison of Traditional and New Mind-Sets.

	Traditional	New Wave
Organizational model	Mechanistic, goal-oriented	Multiple constituencies
View of IT	Discrete systems	Integrated systems
Causation and outcomes	Consistent causes, technologically determined outcomes	Countervailing forces, unpredictable outcomes
Knowledge	Well-defined, explicit, articulate	Ill-defined, tacit, diffuse, embedded
Status quo and organizational change	Dispensable status quo, change by design	Status quo valued for embedded knowledge, change emergent
View of business and competitive advantage	Design school, design for strategic position	Resource-based view, advantage through learned competencies

even contingently applicable management methods, the new thinking emphasizes the importance of building up competencies that allow organizations successfully to take advantage of IT in their specific contexts even if these competencies are not generalizable and cannot be articulated. The central question is how to build the relevant competencies when we have limited knowledge of what they are. The answer is to build on existing competencies in which much relevant knowledge is already embedded and to develop and transform them through learning by doing. Change initiatives have to be managed so that outcomes are rapidly fed back into the organization to permit learning to take place. Change takes place one step at a time. The new form of the organization is discovered rather than designed. The future emerges from the process of change.

The advantages of the new way of thinking are its acceptance of the magnitude of the task of changing the way an organization does business and the pragmatic way it addresses the task. Despite much uncertainty and risk, by developing areas where the organization already has strengths—its existing competencies—a company increases the probability of getting ahead and staying ahead of its rivals. Starting from scratch simply brings the company back to a position easily accessible to its competitors. It is preferable therefore to develop a competitive edge from a basis of distinctive competencies.

References

Barney, J. B. "Firm Resources and Sustained Competitive Advantage." *Journal of Management*, 1991, 17(1), 99–120.

Collis, D. J., and Montgomery, C. A. "Competing on Resources: Strategy in the 1990s." *Harvard Business Review*, July-Aug. 1995, 118–128.

Copeland, D. G., and McKenney, J. L. "Airline Reservations Systems: Lessons from History." *MIS Quarterly*, 1988, 12(3), 353–370.

Davenport, T. H. *Process Innovation: Reengineering Work Through Information Technology.* Boston: Harvard Business School Press, 1993.

Hammer, M., and Champy, J. *Reengineering the Corporation: A Manifesto for Business Revolution.* New York: HarperCollins, 1993.

Henderson, J. C., and Venkatraman, N. "Strategic Alignment: A Model for Organizational Transformation Through Information Technology." In T. A. Kochan and M. Useem (eds.), *Transforming Organizations*. New York: Oxford University Press, 1992.

Hopper, M. D. "Rattling SABRE—New Ways to Compete on Information." *Harvard Business Review*, May-June 1990, 118–125.

Ives, B., and Learmonth, G. P. "The Information System as a Competitive Weapon." *Communications of the ACM*, 1984, 27(12), 1193–1201.

Kling, R. "Social Analyses of Computing: Theoretical Perspectives in Recent Empirical Research." *Computing Surveys*, 1980, 12(1), 61–110.

Kling, R., and Scacchi, W. "The Web of Computing: Computer Technology as Social Organization." In M. Yovits (ed.), *Advances in Computers*. Vol. 21. Orlando, Fla.: Academic Press, 1982.

Mata, F. J., Fuerst, W. L., and Barney, J. B. "Information Technology and Sustained Competitive Advantage: A Resource-Based Analysis." *MIS Quarterly*, 1995, 19(4), 487–505.

Pfeffer, J. *Power in Organizations*. Marshfield, Mass.: Pitman, 1981.

Porter, M. E. *Competitive Strategy: Techniques for Analyzing Industries and Competitors*. New York: Free Press, 1980.

Porter, M. E., and Millar, V. E. "How Information Gives You Competitive Advantage." *Harvard Business Review*, 1985, 63(4), 149–160.

Sauer, C. "Deciding the Future for IS Failures: Not the Choice You Might Think." In W. Currie and R. D. Galliers (eds.), *Rethinking MIS*. Oxford: Oxford University Press, 1997.

Scott Morton, M. S. (ed.). *The Corporation of the 1990s: Information Technology and Organizational Transformation*. New York: Oxford University Press, 1991.

Strassmann, P. A. *Information Payoff: The Transformation of Work in the Electronic Age*. New York: Free Press, 1985.

Ward, J., Griffiths, P., and Whitmore, P. *Strategic Planning for Information Systems*. New York: Wiley, 1990.

Yetton, P. W., Johnston, K. D., and Craig, J. F. "Computer-Aided Architects: A Case Study of IT and Strategic Change." *Sloan Management Review*, 1994, 35(4), 57–67.

Zmud, R. W., Boynton, A. C., and Jacobs, G. C. "The Information Economy: A New Perspective for Effective Information Systems Management." *Data Base*, fall 1986, 17–23.

Zuboff, S. *In the Age of the Smart Machine: The Future of Work and Power*. New York: Basic Books, 1988.

Part I

The Traditional Solutions

The three chapters in this part explode misconceptions about the viability of the traditional solutions to managing IT. They expand our understanding of strategic alignment, point to some practical lessons about alternative solutions, and, where these may be unavailable, describe how to live with alignment.

Philip Yetton provides an incisive analysis of why IT has been so problematical for general managers and why the conventional solutions inevitably miss the mark (Chapter Two). In looking at IT management from the general manager's perspective, he notes four contrasts that create a divide between business and IT and that prevent a satisfactory and easy-to-manage accommodation between them. As a result, general managers have not been able to take control of IT in the same way that they control other functions such as human resources or marketing.

The popular solution advocated by many managers, consultants, and researchers has been strategic alignment. Yetton argues that in multidivisional structures aligned IT inherits the classic tension between corporate head office and devolved business units, and thus central and local IT units must engage in perpetual negotiation and compromise. This tension can be managed in the long term only through the exercise of advanced interpersonal skills, which are not the qualities for which IT managers are traditionally selected.

Yetton concludes that as a management solution strategic alignment is unstable.

Janice Burn (Chapter Three) approaches alignment differently. In a thorough and detailed study lasting more than six years, she observed hundreds of Hong Kong companies that were practicing alignment. She shows that alignment is not a one-time-only project followed by easy adjustments to keep IT in line with shifts in the business. Rather it is a continual balancing act, with companies cycling between states in which IT drives transformation and states in which IT plays catch-up. Burn's Lead-Lag Model is a powerful revision of traditional thinking about alignment.

A further outcome of Burn's study is that alignment appears to have a serious downside that has generally not been discussed by its proponents. She and Christopher Sauer investigate a number of cases in which different types of pathological outcomes arise in organizational transformation—misalignment, stagnation, and global complications (Chapter Four). Examination of the underlying logic of alignment emphasizes once again that the separation that exists between IT and the business is the source of pathology and is a reason why such adverse outcomes are bound to arise.

All three chapters show that strategic alignment is as much of a problem managerially as it is a solution. A better way forward, Yetton argues, is to think smarter, to think differently. He observes that, at least at the business unit level, organizations that succeed in making IT relatively unproblematical are those that do not try to solve the problem of alignment; they simply do not have it. Either they make IT integral to their business so that it is not managed independently, or they acknowledge that IT is not integral to their business and outsource it.

The weakness of Yetton's solution is that it does not solve the problem of IT management for the multidivisional corporation. The strength of strategic alignment is that it brings IT and business closer at the different levels of the organization. Even if it is not the whole solution, the main elements of alignment may yet prove to be part of a wider set of organizational competencies characteristic of successful users of IT (see Part Two). It is also still the most popular way to organize IT. Lessons in how to manage alignment are therefore useful.

In Chapter Three Burn tells us that alignment is a process and so requires continual management. IT can thrive even through cycles of change if there is full organizational support for it and its goals. Unfortunately, support has traditionally been at the heart of IT's problems, and this chapter confirms that organizational transformation cannot be successfully achieved without it. The value of Burn and Sauer's analysis in Chapter Four is that it alerts managers to the circumstances in which alignment is likely to exhibit pathological characteristics and it describes the costs they are likely to incur. Because the work on which this chapter is based is exploratory, the authors do not specify a set of well-defined management interventions. Rather, they emphasize awareness of potential pathological outcomes on the basis that forewarned is forearmed.

2

False Prophecies, Successful Practice, and Future Directions in IT Management

Philip W. Yetton

The benefits of information technology (IT) continue to be more potential than real for most organizations, which is surprising in light of both the substantial levels of investment in the area and the continued predictions of a substantial payoff from the "IT revolution" (Kalakota and Whinston, 1996; Keen, 1991; Scott Morton, 1991). The management literature on IT is still full of graphs and charts showing an ever brighter future for organizations that are in the forefront in IT developments. But while the promise is clear, the payoff is not (Strassmann, 1990; Brynjolfsson, 1993). Although there are some well-known examples of major strategic gains from innovative IT applications, such as American Hospital Supply/Baxter's ordering system (McKenney, Copeland, and Mason, 1995), one might reasonably expect that the past levels of IT expenditure would have resulted in too many examples to name. Instead, you hardly have to take your shoes off to count the small number of examples in the business press and academic journals. Large-scale failures, such as the London Stock Exchange's Taurus

Note: A previous version of this chapter was presented at the IFIP TC8 Conference, Queensland, May 1994. I would like to thank Jane Craig and Kim Johnston for their help in writing this chapter and Chris Sauer for his comments on a draft.

and the Australian bank Westpac's CS90 projects, are much more common. And the senior managers who consider that their own large investments in IT have not paid off far outnumber those who sing the praises of their IT managers.

How can this apparent failure of IT to deliver on its promise be explained? In the first part of this chapter, I address this question. To do so, I examine four factors that impeded our ability to harness the new phenomenon that was IT. These are all dynamics that we can understand relatively easily with 20/20 hindsight, but obviously they were far from clear as they unfolded. Also, these factors do not begin to represent a complete explanation.

However, even though learning how to manage IT has been slow, some progress has been made. So the second question we face is whether the present can, and the future will, deliver on the promises of the past. The threat to current performance is that existing theory on how to manage IT is at best misleading and at worst damaging, while future performance may depend on the ability of theorists to learn from, and then help to develop, successful practice. These issues are addressed in the second part of the chapter.

So a considerable portion of this chapter is devoted to a reanalysis of efforts by organizations to harness the potential of IT since the mid-1970s and then to an evaluation of current theory. This stream of thinking about IT management seems to be coming to an end, in the sense that it may no longer be productive either for research or for practice. We have begun to examine Australian best practice that is different from current theory and have found that it is helping to clarify future theoretical directions. That is the focus of the third and final part of this chapter.

False Prophecies

Many writers have prophesied and advocated the considerable benefits to be obtained from the application of IT to business (Scott Morton, 1991; McKenney, 1995). Some have even claimed that we have gone beyond the industrial revolution to the information revolution (Cash, Eccles, Nohria, and Nolan, 1994; Nolan and Croson, 1995). So why then do we joke that being appointed CIO means not only that you are "chief information officer" but also that your "career is over"? Here I use four examples to illustrate past barriers to the successful management of IT, which help to explain line management's frustration.

First, there is a common experience of budget blowouts on IT expenditures. IT department budgets grew much bigger and more quickly than was ever anticipated. Second, cost-benefit analyses seem to have failed as a procedure for evaluating IT investments. Even though such analyses were routinely conducted before IT projects were approved, cost blowouts were commonplace, and realized benefits were typically well below expected levels. Third, in spite of these consistent experiences, organizations seem not to learn over time how to improve their management of IT investments, even though in other domains organizations have shown themselves able to adapt quickly. Finally, given these difficulties, why did line management not simply take hands-on control of IT? The time horizons and scope of IT projects provide part of the answer.

Cost Blowouts

The initial assumption was that an investment in IT would be like any other, but it turned out that there was at least one major difference—new systems typically involved high "maintenance" costs that were quite unanticipated. In reality, these costs related more to service enhancements or preventive maintenance than to fixing problems. Once a system was in place, line management would routinely ask for "minor" changes to the specifications, partly as business requirements shifted and partly as managers discovered new functions they wanted the system to perform. Importantly, as the system got better and better in the eyes of the line users, it became more and more difficult to maintain from a systems design point of view. With incremental and ad hoc additions or amendments over time, the system came to do more and more of what line management wanted, but this process resulted in a patchwork configuration that compromised the integrity and stability of the system.

Consequently, systems development, which was the approved expenditure, was only the most visible part of IT. The operating and enhancement costs of the system were ongoing and substantial. As a rule of thumb, for every dollar spent developing software, an additional sixty cents was paid every year for operation and "maintenance" of that program. It is easy to see how, under those circumstances, simply keeping existing programs operating effectively quickly chewed up an IT budget, leaving little capacity to develop new programs. Even keeping the systems development budget constant would mean that the overall IT budget would grow by 15 percent per year. And if the overall IT budget were frozen, systems development would have to be cut by 93 percent over five years (Keen, 1991).

This high maintenance requirement for ongoing expenditure on "new" capital investment is atypical for most investments in plant and equipment. In general, the expectation is that new investments increase reliability of performance and reduce maintenance costs in comparison with the preceding system or equipment. So investment proposals did not routinely require estimates of ongoing "maintenance" expenditures. It was neither anticipated nor understood by senior management, the strategic-planning department, and the IT department that IT investments would be any different. The managerial budgetary-control processes did not have any flags to signal that an investment might incur not only initial development and installation costs but also substantial recurrent expenditures.

Failure of Cost-Benefit Analysis

Clearly, no organization embarks on expenditures of the magnitude involved in the typical IT investment without first conducting a rigorous cost-benefit analysis or its equivalent. Equally clearly, however, firm after firm found that this process at once underestimated the costs that were actually incurred and overestimated the bene-fits that resulted. In effect, the cost-benefit analysis process failed in the case of IT investments.

Above, I explain one reason for cost overruns. Here, I note two issues that appear to contribute to overestimating the realized ben-efits. The first is an issue of ownership—specifically, the costs and the benefits of an IT investment were usually owned by two differ-ent parts of the organization. In general, responsibility for systems design and development (the costs) would lie with the IT group, while responsibility for the delivery of the benefits would rest with line management. Because the IT department spent the money but the savings were to be captured in the business operations where the system was implemented, there was little incentive or rationale for the IT department to pursue these savings rigorously or to insist on accountability for achieving them.

The second issue relates to the imbalance between the ease of identifying the costs and the difficulty of measuring the benefits of many IT projects. The costs were typically visible and managers made a commitment to them. But the benefits rarely had either of these characteristics. Because of the nature of the implemented IT systems, they typically saved small parts of many jobs, rather than freeing one or two specific positions within a particular department. To translate the savings into one or two units of cost in the man-agerial budget would have required that line management restruc-ture or reallocate roles. And such changes often did not take place.

The net effect was that IT was blamed for the fact that benefits were not being visibly realized on the bottom line. The tendency to blame IT was exacerbated by escalating costs in the IT area as well as the move to bottom-line accountability and cost centers; IT expenditure was highly salient for all senior managers and was often resented by profit center managers who were subject to large and, in their eyes, uncontrollable and arbitrary overhead charges.

IT does not receive credit for the many large savings now being made in middle-management ranks, through downsizing and moves toward flat structures, which are made possible by the long-term cumulative effect of system improvements. Arguably, over the years system developments and applications have provided platforms that make a lean organization feasible in a way that would not have been possible without that legacy. Of course, the link to IT is not usually made. The separation of ownership of costs and of benefits was symptomatic of a world in which the separation between IT and the business was substantial and detrimental to performance (Boynton, Jacobs, and Zmud, 1992). That separation also contributed to the failure of organizations to learn how to manage IT investments, which is the third of the factors that help explain current IT-management outcomes.

Failure to Learn

If firms were going to build on their experience as a basis for learning how to manage IT investments better, a continuing, constructive dialogue between the two main groups involved—senior management and the IT specialists—would have been needed. But this rarely happened. The dialogue was difficult because the sender and receiver came from different backgrounds. And the difficulty was heightened because of the complexity of the subject and the necessity of bringing together different bodies of expertise—strategic understanding of the business on the one hand and technical skills in systems design and maintenance on the other. Each of these areas has its own jargon for defining and discussing the problems.

The backgrounds, experience, and languages of senior managers and IT specialists are very different. IT specialists are mainly "cosmopolitans"—hired guns who do not "belong" to the firm and may not even belong to the industry in which the firm operates. Their referent group and the standards by which they are judged and by which they judge their own performance are external to the firm. Consequently, their experience of the firm or even the industry and of what it takes to win in that environment is often limited.

For their part, the senior line managers often have trouble admitting that they do not understand IT. They are busy and do not have time to invest in learning and mastering new ideas. They have typically learned about their business through experience over a long period of time—experience they do not have with IT. And they cannot learn the area quickly because they have not spent time in it. The resulting gulf between a business-illiterate IT group and an IT-illiterate top management made it difficult for each to assimilate and master the essential understanding required to add value to the other and thus made it difficult for firms to learn how to manage IT better.

Time Horizons and Project Scope

With the above history of problems and the failure of the organization and top management to learn how to manage IT, one might have expected line management to roll up its sleeves and take hands-on control. Why did this not happen? Part of the answer, as discussed above, was the lack of ownership by the users. Developing systems was IT's responsibility. But two other factors, the time horizons and the scope of the systems being developed, contributed to this problem.

Many of the systems development projects of the 1970s and 1980s had three-year time horizons. In contrast, most line managers operated with twelve-month budgets. Budgets are major frameworks that support and focus the actions a manager takes (Merchant, 1989). Routinely, perhaps every month or so, managers review their department's or division's performance against budget. It would have made little sense, however, to review the performance of a three-year IT project every month. Not enough progress would have been made in a month, and, in any case, line managers had more pressing priorities.

Not only did the IT projects have long time horizons, they also tended to span a number of organizational boundaries. A user department was likely to be only one of many clients for a large project. Furthermore, because IT departments typically used a single, sophisticated presentation to brief all users, each user was confronted with a global picture of a project in which their subsystems were just a small component. A generalized context and professional presentation tended to reduce the ease with which users could evaluate and contribute to the systems of which they were the nominal owners. By the time they became aware of problems, they were halfway into the project, flexibility was limited, and the cost of change was high. Both sides tended to place blame rather than resolve problems.

Current Solutions

Up to this point we have been looking at some of the problems that occurred in part because IT was a new phenomenon that was not well understood and in part because no one anticipated that managing IT would be quite so different from managing other functions. At the same time, however, these problems occurred within a macrolevel framework that also worked to sustain them. To understand this phenomenon, we need to examine current IT management theory and practice in the context of prevailing strategic-management and organization theory.

Through the 1970s and early 1980s, many firms adopted market segmentation strategies. They moved to divisionalized organization structures, using internal differentiation to get bottom-line accountability for units that were focusing on what were becoming increasingly differentiated marketplaces. In this dominant design, as far as possible, profit centers were established low down in the organization, with individuals carrying bottom-line accountability, even if that required a complex transfer-pricing system (Rumelt, 1974; Merchant, 1989). This fit of strategy and structure was accepted with little question in a whole range of industries, and in many of these it was successful, although in some, such as banking, successful fit proved difficult to achieve.

Not surprisingly, IT management theory adopted this dominant conceptual framework of strategy-structure fit, which in strategic-management theory is followed by the alignment of management processes, roles, and technology. The role of technology in the prevailing models of fit is perhaps best captured by the MIT90s framework (Figure 2.1).

Although all the elements of the model are shown as interdependent, in practice most who use it are wedded to the dominant paradigm, which states that IT must be aligned to the established strategy-structure fit (Scott Morton, 1991). This implicit conventional path to fit is shown in Figure 2.2.

The argument is that a firm follows three steps: first it develops its strategy; then it designs the structure to support the strategy; and, finally, to implement the complete design it builds new management processes, aligns IT, and ensures that appropriate roles are

Figure 2.1. Model of Strategic Change and Fit.

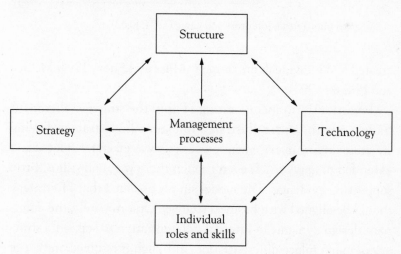

Adapted from Scott Morton (1991, p. 20).

Figure 2.2. Conventional Model of Strategic Dynamics.

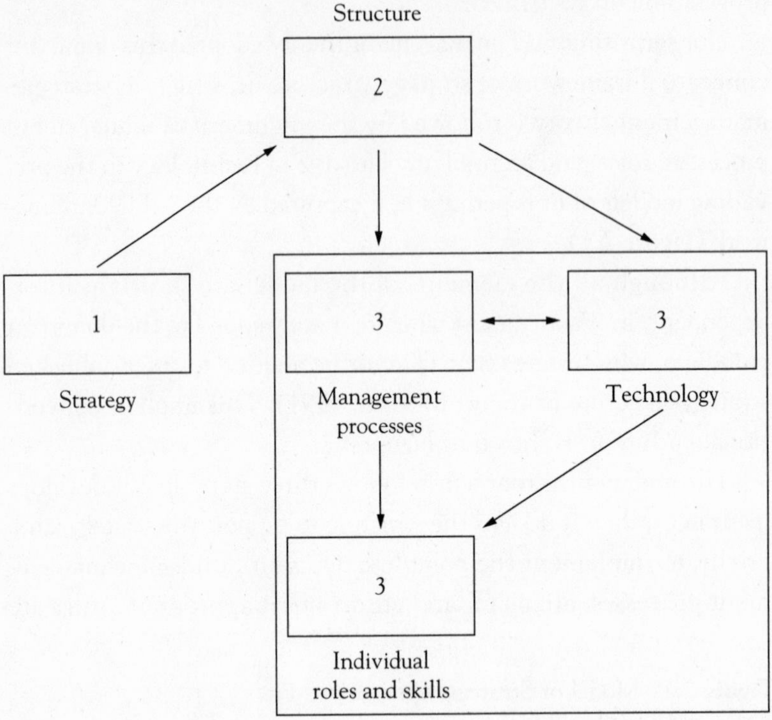

Adapted from Yetton, Johnston, and Craig (1994, p. 62).

created and individuals are trained (Miles and Snow, 1994; McGee and Prusak, 1993).

Importantly, in incorporating IT into the strategic-alignment framework, the order illustrated in Figure 2.2—strategy driving structure driving management processes—was taken for granted and extended to apply to IT, even though there was, and still is, little supporting evidence. The model simply assumed that IT strategy should be aligned with business strategy. Unfortunately, the dominant design dynamic of internal differentiation to support a strategy of marketplace differentiation, although it resolved one set of organizational issues, was not a solution to managing IT.

IT did not fit easily into that world for a number of reasons. We begin with two. First, IT did not lend itself to being split up across divisions. The big mainframe platforms and other systems investments were typically so large and the potential economies of scale around large data-processing operations were so great that individual business units were not going to be given full ownership of their own computer systems. It definitely paid to centralize the investment in hardware and operating systems.

Second, a number of the IT services and projects spanned more than one division. They performed some of the integration that made it possible to run the business. Even with the move to divisionalization, there still remained a considerable body of information that might be used by more than one business unit, including information on customers, and a whole range of information that the head office required. So IT was one of the few functional areas that had the potential to integrate across the business. Of course, to the business unit manager this "benefit" was simply one more unwarranted overhead, and any corporate intervention meant a reduction in autonomy. Not surprisingly, such interventions were resented and resisted.

These two issues imposed significant limitations on the degree to which IT could be integrated into the dominant design and resulted in the second best strategy of aligning IT to that design. Even at this weaker level of fit, however, there were problems. By the end of the 1980s, consistent with the trend in all other areas of business, the emphasis was on trying to get low-cost, high-quality IT systems. But this attempt generated a natural tension because low cost tended to be associated with standardization and centralization, and high quality tended to be associated with decentralization and business unit control.

These apparently conflicting demands were at least intellectually resolved in large, complex organizations by adopting a federal IT-management structure (see Figure 2.3). This is one of the most

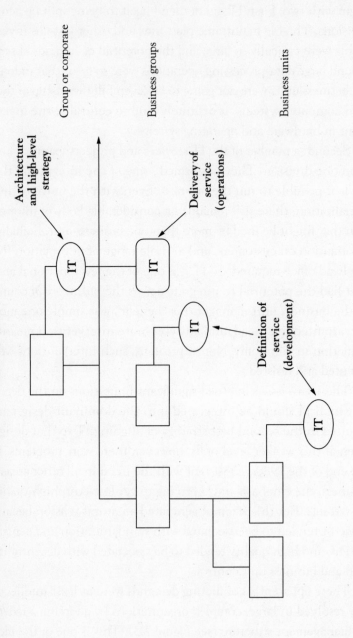

Figure 2.3. Current IT Management: The Federal Solution.

Group or corporate

Business groups

Business units

Architecture
and high-level
strategy

Delivery of
service
(operations)

Definition of
service
(development)

IT

IT

IT

IT

elegant and complete designs for IT management and is advocated by many consultants and academics (Davenport, Eccles, and Prusak, 1992; von Simson, 1990).

The federal design involves creating a "division of powers" in IT management between the corporate, business group, and business unit components of the typically divisional organization structure. The IT management structure is essentially folded around the divisional design. Architecture and standards are controlled at the corporate level, and user-driven development is located at the business group or business unit level. IT services such as data operations, maintenance, and telecommunications (service delivery) are managed separately from business systems development and corporate IT management. They are treated as a "shared resource" and managed as a quasi-business with complex transfer-pricing systems. In effect, then, the current solution to the problem is to seek a balance between centralization and devolution—to ask which activities and functions should be centralized and which devolved. Unfortunately, however, this theoretically elegant solution does not work well in practice.

On the surface, this "strategic alignment" seems to provide a solution to the tug of war between IT strategies that focus on cost efficiencies and corporate standards and those that are value-added and business-driven. However, the IT structure it creates depends on IT managers' ensuring that the activities of the different work groups, which can all have strongly competing interests, are integrated across the whole organization. This integration requires that the IT groups in business units continue altruistically serving overall corporate goals and that the IT group at the center remains entrepreneurial and focused on meeting business unit needs. The reality is that IT people at the business unit level tend to be "captured" by the goals of the business units (or "go feral," as one corporate IT manager put it), while IT people at the center tend to become divorced from the business and to be seen as bureaucratically "policing" a particular technology architecture and set of standards.

A structure that requires behaviors that are in such conflict with job pressures is usually under considerable stress. To make it work, you need IT managers with high interpersonal skills, particularly conflict-management and negotiating skills, married to a good grasp of the business. But these skills are in very short supply. So this structure is likely to be inherently unstable. It is likely to revert to one of the two more stable alternatives: a centralized, cost-driven structure or a decentralized, business-unit-driven one. Alternatively, the organization could find itself on an expensive reorganization merry-go-round as it oscillates between one strategy and the other.

Furthermore, the dominant design also does not stay sufficiently stable for long enough to permit alignment of IT. The business target typically changes more quickly than IT lead times can accommodate. Consequently, IT gets caught up in the white water in the wake of the business rather than riding the crest of the wave.

For these reasons then, the federal system does not work well. Because the nature of the technology and of organizations' information systems means that IT cannot be broken up and allocated separately to divisions, it is difficult for IT to become fully integrated into the dominant divisionalized design. So, if anything, it has been pushed further away from the core of business and wrapped around it as an outer layer. This can be no more than a second best solution because IT will tend to be passive and reactive to the business rather than proactive and integral to it.

Successful Practice and Future Directions

What is the problem people should have been addressing? At the Fujitsu Centre in the Australian Graduate School of Management, we have studied a number of instances where Australian companies have successfully managed IT. These cases suggest alternative approaches that either integrate IT into the business and make it the core of operations or manage IT like a car fleet—as a high-quality service that is contracted out. These cases do not so much resolve the problems described above as simply not have them. Understanding what was critical in the success of these businesses may, therefore, suggest alternative and more fruitful areas for organizations to focus on than those that currently preoccupy them.

Elsewhere we describe and analyze some of these cases in detail (Yetton, Johnston, and Craig, 1994; Yetton, Craig, and Johnston, 1995). Here, I will briefly describe a few of these instances to see how different they are. In two cases, the organization has moved from a relatively low level of technology to a situation where IT is integral to its success. One of these cases is the Australian Stock Exchange (ASX), where IT has been at the core of its strategic transformation. Another is an architectural firm that gradually shifted to a position where its mastery of IT systems became the basis of its strategic competency. These two cases illustrate how IT can become an integral, even central, part of the organizational design and effectively shape the strategic fit of the firm. The third case involves the first large-scale outsourcing of computer operations by a department of the Australian federal government. It illustrates how to achieve fit via outsourcing when mastering the technology is not central to the strategic agenda of the organization. So instead of IT's being aligned with the strategy-structure fit, in two cases it is integral to the firm's operations, and in the other it is outsourced.

In contrast to the now accepted practice of aligning the IT strategy to the business strategy, in all three cases here the process by which the service is delivered to the customer has been changed, in the sense of becoming more integrated and simplified (Yetton, Craig, and Johnston, 1995). The current term for this change is Business Process Reengineering (BPR) (Hammer and Champy, 1993). Whereas the driver for the dominant design referred to earlier was internal differentiation to match market complexity, the pressure is now for internal integration to better meet customer needs. Thus, these three cases suggest a different approach to the management of IT.

To show the ways in which these cases differ from current theory, I will begin with the case of the architectural firm (see Yetton, Johnston, and Craig, 1994). In 1987, Flower and Samios was a small architectural practice in Sydney, with an annual project portfolio worth $A20–30 million. No computers were used in the business. Within five years, the entire practice had been transformed. By 1992, the company employed fewer staff but had an annual project portfolio of over $A100 million. Drawing boards and pencils were no longer used. Instead, all design work was undertaken on networked Apple Macintosh computers, using a range of integrated computer-aided design (CAD) and multimedia software packages. I briefly describe here how the transformation was initiated, how it evolved, and how it has changed the business both internally in terms of management structure, roles, and processes, and externally in terms of relations with clients, suppliers, and competitors.

Over the years, the senior partner, John Flower, had periodically examined the computer systems available to assist with architectural design. However, on each occasion, he had been concerned about the expense, size, and complexity of the systems. The trigger for his move to computers came in 1987, when he lost a design competition to a rival. Inquiring as to why his "terrific" design had not won, he was shown his rival's winning entry—a computerized 3-D "walk-through" of the building design. The contrast in presentation was dramatic. In response, Flower and Samios initiated their use of IT by leasing two Apple Macintosh computers so that they could compete in presentations. From this hesitant beginning, and as they gained mastery of the range of design functions and capabilities, they gradually expanded their involvement with computers until their IT investment reached over $A20 thousand per employee. Within a few years, the firm's technology platform had become integral to its professional and business success.

As Flower and Samios's IT strategy evolved over five years, it had three main elements. First, the principal partners agreed that they would learn the new systems. This was essentially a tactical decision. John was determined not to repeat the mistake of a col-league elsewhere who was "held to ransom" by a CAD operator who had become indispensable because of his specialized knowledge.

Second, with experience and increasing mastery over the new technology, John soon realized that cost and productivity benefits could be gained from the investment in IT. To achieve these sav-ings, the technology had to become integral to many aspects of the business rather than being marginalized and used primarily for pre-sentations. This strategy required continuing mastery of the systems by the senior partners and dissemination of the technology within the practice. This mastery was achieved on a project-by-project basis. A staff member would be given a computer at the beginning of a job and would learn to use the system along with relevant soft-ware packages with help from other staff members who had already mastered them and were using them all the time. Through this pro-cedure and the insistence that staff "put down their pencils" in favor of CAD, knowledge of the system was disseminated quite rapidly throughout the firm. Proceeding gradually, with IT investment costs spread across projects, meant that the investment did not involve high risks for the small firm, costs could be absorbed within the overheads for each project, and management and supervision demands were low.

The third important component of Flower and Samios's IT strat-egy was their decision to use only proven, "off-the-shelf" hardware and software systems that were relatively easy to learn and easy to use without reliance on technical specialists. This component of the strategy was, in fact, critical to the achievement of the first two elements mentioned above. The firm could leverage its business, allowing this technology to become central to core business pro-cesses, without the firm's becoming dependent on a technology it could not understand or operate. In this way, first professional needs and then business needs predominated in decisions about technol-ogy. In a sense, the technology became the engine of the business, but the business professionals remained firmly in the driver's seat.

As John Flower noted, "We are computer-aided architects, not CAD operators." As experience with the software and hardware accumulated, staff began increasingly to utilize the capabilities of the technology. They developed skills in moving between packages and integrating particular software components when working on designs and design presentations.

The Macintosh system simplified design tasks and allowed them to be performed faster, more flexibly, and more reliably. The draftsperson, for example, became redundant because drafting capabilities are built into the system. It is faster because it contains much automated, specialized knowledge. It is more flexible because it allows a number of alternative design ideas to be tested quickly, to be easily amended, and then to be stored and reused. It is more reliable because it automatically ensures that the geometrical and other calculations are accurate. Materials quantities and costs can also be estimated from the design itself by the software program and are automatically updated as designs are amended.

The change process we observe in Flower and Samios's progression to a new organizational fit is not one of strategic alignment. Their dynamic path is represented by Figure 2.4. Here, the initial intervention was a limited tactical one at the level of technology in response to a perceived threat; this intervention was followed by a transformation of individual skills and roles, then by changes in structure, and finally by adjustments to the management processes. The clarification of strategic intent and insights into the strategic drivers of this new configuration occurred only after the initial organizational "gestalt" was in place. The strategic vision grew out of the implementation.

Awareness of the strategic importance of the firm's experience and skills with the technology platform developed out of the initial application and integration of technology into the organization rather than preceding it. In effect, once the new organizational gestalt was in place, the implicit strategic drivers could be assessed, and decisions could be made about which of those drivers should be

Figure 2.4. Strategic Dynamics at Flower and Samios.

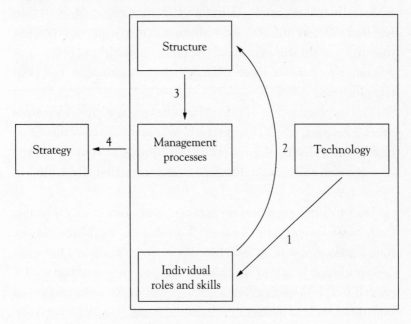

Adapted from Yetton, Johnston, and Craig (1994, p. 63).

the focus of future developments. Looking backward, it is clear that time-based competition and customer-driven business-process redesign are important strategic elements of the new configuration: the technology enabled not only lower-cost operations but, more important, the creation of competitive advantage through the provision of high-quality, timely, and unique customer service. Flower and Samios is only now becoming aware of how these value-added services differentiate them from their competitors and form the basis of their distinctive competency.

Originally then, the computers were adopted in order to do three-dimensional presentations, but the partners discovered a whole range of other ways they could be used and that they could substantially reduce costs and increase efficiencies. Importantly, the computers were not just doing tasks faster but were able to operate differently. For example, once technical drawings could be routinely created, amended, and printed by the architects, the draftsperson essentially disappeared. Although this new mode of operation required different information systems and management processes, the organization still performed the same set of tasks as before, but in a different manner. Essentially, the whole organization had been reengineered.

The application of IT also transformed how the Australian Stock Exchange (ASX) competes, how it serves its customers, and how it performs its core functions. In coming to that point, the organization followed a different route from that illustrated in Figure 2.4.

Prior to 1987, there was no national Australian stock exchange. Each of six states had its own stock exchange, established under state legislation, with its own board, and each conducted independent trading operations. In this old system, the same shares were often listed on more than one exchange within Australia and would sometimes trade at different prices at the same time. A broker wishing to buy shares in other states had to transact via a broker in that state and pay an additional fee. Settlement was exceedingly slow by world standards, and the liquidity and volume of trading in many shares were low.

Now the six trading floors are closed, all equities are traded on computer screens in a single national market (SEATS), with integrated support functions and an electronic settlement system (CHESS) under development. The high quality and reliability of these new systems has given ASX a worldwide reputation as a leader in the design and management of electronic markets, as is illustrated by the sale of its system software to the Swiss and New Zealand stock exchanges. IT is now at the core of ASX's business processes. Almost 70 percent of the fixed assets of ASX and one-third of its operational expenditures are attributable to computer and communications systems.

In addition to improved quality and reliability, the new IT systems have increased the efficiency and flexibility of ASX. For example, SEATS created significant staff savings for both ASX and brokers, with ASX staff being reduced by 17 percent (from 688 to 572) in 1991 alone. Greater operating flexibility is also possible, with twenty-four-hour trading now an option. Although it is estimated that CHESS will cost $A35 million to develop, it has the potential to eliminate $A20 million per year in costs imposed by the existing manual system of clearance and settlement. It will also significantly improve effectiveness, reducing the delay and uncertainty associated with finalizing transactions.

When the six stock exchanges merged their operations in 1987, the need for immediate change was apparent to all. The new organization had inherited a complex web of IT systems, mostly obsolete or incompatible or both. Four major hardware platforms with complex interdependencies made systems development, operations, and maintenance a cumbersome and expensive process. A simplified and integrated systems architecture was adopted, and the structure of the IT platform formed the basis for developing ASX's new organizational design. What began as a threat to the survival of the organization—the tangle of obsolete and increasingly unreliable systems inherited from the amalgamation of the state stock exchanges—initiated a process of IT-driven BPR that resulted in cost and scale efficiencies in the medium term and created an advanced electronic market that places the ASX as a strategic leader internationally.

Once again, this was not a case of alignment of IT to the business strategy of ASX. The IT strategy, developed prior to the appointment of the CEO of the new organization, was effectively the blueprint for the business strategy and structure of ASX. In the absence of a business strategy, the architecture of the IT strategic plan essentially became the architecture for the business. In effect, the business strategy and structure of ASX emerged from the technology changes. Technology is not aligned with the business; it is inseparable from the core business processes of the organization.

In the third case, involving the Department of Veterans Affairs (DVA), the dynamics were more like the conventional model, with a strategic decision affecting the other elements of the model in turn. But in this case IT was contracted out rather than being more closely aligned to the structure. The decision occurred in the context of an overall downsizing of a department that went from being the fourth largest federal department in terms of budget to a relatively small unit. Two major functions were moved outside in anticipation of a substantial drop in client numbers as the war-veteran population ages and decreases. The Defence Service Homes Mortgages operation was privatized, and the specialized veterans' hospitals were integrated into state government health systems, cutting ten thousand jobs. That left DVA a continuing target for restructuring. The most obvious option would have been to fold it into Social Security, which had similar data management and pension- and service-delivery operations, but such a move would have been strongly resisted in a number of quarters, particularly by the powerful veterans' interest groups.

Against this background, DVA decided to explore the outsourcing option when its IT planning group revealed, in 1989, that the department would require a major computer upgrade in the following year or risk running out of mainframe processing capacity. The usual decision would have been to ask the Department of Finance for the required $A8–10 million to purchase a new computer system.

Outsourcing looked attractive to DVA for a number of reasons. First, it would preempt possible moves to have DVA's IT operations integrated into those of Social Security—a move that would reduce the opportunity to resist later pressure to incorporate all of DVA into that department. Second, outsourcing was in line with the downsizing strategy of DVA and would permit greater flexibility in meeting future fluctuations in IT needs. The uncertainty surrounding the types of services required by a declining but increasingly dependent client group would make capacity-demand management problematical over the medium term.

The outsourcing decision effectively reduced complexity for the DVA by removing a problematical link from the internal value chain and improving its coherence and focus. It reduced IT costs and secured DVA's services to its clients over the medium term. Thus, through an innovative outsourcing strategy, the DVA not only increased its survival prospects but achieved considerable cost efficiencies in the medium term with a simplified internal value chain. At the same time, through achieving closer integration with elements of the external value chain, the DVA gained long-term flexibility in IT capacity management and staffing/industrial relations and facilitated a strategic focus on its customers.

These cases suggest a different approach to the management of IT. The three organizations did not solve the problem of strategic alignment—they did not have such a problem. In two of the cases gaining thorough mastery of the technology as part of the business led to the transformation of the business. Out of that transformation emerged a set of strategic options that then needed to be explored and developed. Such options are grounded in the mastery of "what we can do with this technology," and therefore, in choosing between them, the firm chooses activities that it can actually perform. So neither implementation nor alignment is the problem. Instead of having to be solved, they no longer exist as central problems for the organization. The organization uses the technology, which is integral to its operations, in the same way that it uses any other part of the organizational design. The architectural practice and ASX happen to use the technology well, and IT is therefore a powerful force for generating strategic options.

On the other side, DVA perceived that mastering the technology was not going to add value; at the same time the department recognized that it could negotiate with firms that had mastered IT to provide them with a high-quality service. And the quality of that service depended as much on a sound joint venture with the outside supplier as it did on writing a detailed contract. Outsourcing in this sense is not a process of working out what you want to outsource and then writing the contract, with the purchaser of the service focusing on keeping the costs down as far as possible and the supplier trying to keep the price up. That win-lose game is difficult to manage. Instead, the organization looking for the service ideally will negotiate with potential suppliers about how they can add value to each other, so that both sides win.

Traditionally, strategic alignment as described in the first part of this chapter has meant the alignment of IT to the prevailing organizational form. The dominant divisional design, to which IT is aligned, reflects a preoccupation with internal differentiation and neglects the need for organizational integration. The experience of these three successful users of IT suggests an alternative, in which IT is used to achieve simplification and integration across functions, enabling a horizontal focus on core business processes. IT has the unique capacity to manage diverse activities so that value is added as work flows across the organization rather than up and down within functional units. According to this perspective, IT can play a central role in the creation or evolution of strategic fit. Indeed, in some organizations, IT is the primary driver of strategic change, reshaping management processes, roles, structures, and strategies. It is embedded in core business processes and proactively involved in organizational transformation.

Unfortunately, these cases do not suggest alternatives to the federal structure, which I argued earlier is unstable. The cases are examples of how to manage the dynamics of fit for a business unit rather than for the total corporate system. The resolution to this problem of corporate fit lies elsewhere. Recall that this issue arises because the IT factory and, particularly, strategic investments in both hardware and application platforms cannot be disaggregated and their responsibilities assigned to each business unit. Instead, they are treated as shared resources across the business units and charged out to those units by centrally mandated and complex transfer prices. Naturally, the business units are tempted both to resist the overhead charges and to become free riders on a corporate asset.

The development of open-systems architectures and powerful distributed systems with client servers may abolish the problem for some organizations. With this new technology, the business units can be held responsible for and manage their investment to meet their own IT needs relatively unconstrained by the economies of scale of a shared IT factory, corporate requirements for a coherent and limited technology set, corporate standards for connectivity, and corporate needs for aggregate performance and financial data.

The new technology makes possible the devolution of both capital budgeting and IT operations to the business units, at least on a service contract, without blowing out costs or compromising standards. Some units will internalize IT, as has Flower and Samios and ASX. Others will outsource their IT functions, as has DVA. In both cases the goal will be increased service efficiency and an enhanced fit between the business unit and its customers. Again, this proposal is not another solution to the current problem, in the sense that the federal structure is a solution, but a means for some organizations to abolish the problem by advances in technology.

Reintegration of functions within the business unit and devolution of IT responsibility together have the potential to help solve the problem of gaining the benefits of BPR. In BPR, IT is a major enabler (Davenport, 1993) because much of reengineering revolves around issues of reintegration. Activities are reorganized to make the links between suppliers and customers (internal or external) simpler and more coherent than they have been in the past. And this reintegration, usually across the functional structure of the business, is now providing major opportunities for gains, particularly in areas such as the process that starts at order entry and concludes in delivery (Hammer and Champy, 1993). What is not understood as yet is how to manage the process of BPR change, in particular the relationship between BPR and existing organizational structures, and the role of multifunctional teams and how they operate. Much of the prescriptive literature on BPR refers to the management of IT as a kind of alignment process. IT still seems to lie outside the core business (Craig and Yetton, 1994). However, the joint outcome within a distributed IT system of reintegration within the business unit and devolution of IT responsibility to the business unit may eliminate this kind of thinking and the problems that result from it.

Summary

In this chapter, I have examined the ways IT has been managed since the mid-1970s and current state-of-the-art theory from a different perspective. This analysis suggests that simply bringing more effort, energy, and talent to bear on the current problems will not necessarily resolve them. Indeed, considerable energy, effort, and talent have already been expended in that direction, with few convincing results. So, in the first part of the chapter, I explored why the prophecies about IT appear to have been false. At one level, even when all the managers involved are rational, talented, and motivated, the dynamics of some situations generate problems that are by their very nature difficult to solve. At another, the overall direction of managerial evolution has made managing IT difficult structurally because it has been driven by other agendas. Therefore, I conclude that the current state-of-the-art models, such as the federal one, are the end of a series of developments that are not moving in the right direction; they are focused on yesterday's problems and opportunities.

   In the second part of the chapter I described some successes and showed them to be the potential source of new ways of approaching the management of IT. These cases all share the characteristic that IT is managed as an integral part of the business, rather than being made to align with or fit into existing arrangements. That discussion briefly covered a wide and complex range of issues in the management of IT. It has led us to some surprisingly simple and straightforward conclusions.

Because existing directions have not yielded the anticipated gains, we should look elsewhere. For future research, then, the powerful conclusion is that we need to stop building sophisticated models on questionable foundations and, instead, study and understand the few successful exemplars from business. Frequently, these will not be the market leaders in fashionable industries, which have probably been partly captured by the existing dominant but flawed theory. Instead they will often be the "deviant" cases, which for one reason or another had to manage IT differently—they did it their way. Identifying and analyzing such successes as the basis for building new conceptual and theoretical understanding is the research strategy of the Fujitsu Centre. This understanding is a substantial change from current received theory. The aim is to develop new theory, grounded in Australian best practice.

For management, the conclusion is just as powerful. IT needs to become part of the business rather than be treated as something "out there" that needs to be passively aligned with the business. Success will come to those who make IT managers an integral part of defining business opportunities and not simply the builders of other managers' solutions. The strategic shift is from a focus on organizational structure, which separates activities, to a focus on processes that integrate IT into the central business activity of fulfilling customer needs.

References

Boynton, A. C., Jacobs, G., and Zmud, R. "Whose Responsibility Is IT Management?" *Sloan Management Review*, summer 1992, 32–38.

Brynjolfsson, E. "The Productivity Paradox of Information Technology." *Communications of the ACM*, 1993, 36(12), 66–67.

Cash, J., Eccles, R., Nohria, N., and Nolan, R. *Building the Information-Age Organization*. Burr Ridge, Ill.: Irwin, 1994.

Craig, J., and Yetton, P. W. "Top-Down and Bottom-Up Management of Business Process Redesign." In B. Glasson and others (eds.), *Business Process Reengineering: IFIP TC8 Proceedings, Gold Coast, Queensland*. New York: Elsevier, 1994.

Davenport, T. H. *Process Innovation: Reengineering Work Through Information Technology*. Boston: Harvard Business School Press, 1993.

Davenport, T. H., Eccles, R., and Prusak, L. "Information Politics." *Sloan Management Review*, fall 1992, 53–65.

Hammer, M., and Champy, J. *Reengineering the Corporation: A Manifesto for Business Revolution*. New York: HarperCollins, 1993.

Kalakota, R., and Whinston, A. *Frontiers of Electronic Commerce*. Reading, Mass.: Addison-Wesley, 1996.

Keen, P. *Shaping the Future: Business Design Through Information Technology*. Boston: Harvard Business School Press, 1991.

McGee, J., and Prusak, L. *Managing Information Strategically*. New York: Wiley, 1993.

McKenney, J. L., Copeland, D., and Mason, R. O. *Waves of Change: Business Evolution Through Information Technology*. Boston: Harvard Business School Press, 1995.

Merchant, K. *Rewarding Results: Motivating Profit Center Managers*. Boston: Harvard Business School Press, 1989.

Miles, R. E., and Snow, C. C. *Fit, Failure and the Hall of Fame*. New York: Free Press, 1994.

Nolan, R. L., and Croson, D. C. *Creative Destruction: A Six-Stage Process for Transforming the Organization*. Boston: Harvard Business School Press, 1995.

Rumelt, R. *Strategy, Structure and Economic Performance*. Boston: Graduate School of Business Administration, Harvard University, 1974.

Scott Morton, M. S. (ed.). *The Corporation of the 1990s: Information Technology and Organizational Transformation*. New York: Oxford University Press, 1991.

Strassmann, P. A. *The Business Value of Computers: An Executive's Guide*. New Canaan, Conn.: Information Economics Press, 1990.

von Simson, E. "The Centrally Decentralized IS Organization." *Harvard Business Review*, July-Aug. 1990, 158–162.

Yetton, P. W., Craig, J. F., and Johnston, K. D. "Fit, Simplicity and Risk: Multiple Paths to IT Strategic Change." In *Proceedings of the Sixteenth International Conference on Information Systems*. December 10–13. Amsterdam, 1995.

Yetton, P. W., Johnston, K. D., and Craig, J. F. "Computer-Aided Architects: A Case Study of IT and Strategic Change." *Sloan Management Review*, 1994, 35(4), 57–67.

3

A Professional Balancing Act

Walking the Tightrope
of Strategic Alignment

Janice M. Burn

Information technology (IT) has for some time been recognized as an enabler of business transformation through redesign of business processes and business relationships, to achieve redefinition of business scope (Venkatraman, 1991). This role in business transformation has underlined the need to ensure that IT is strategically aligned with the business mission and the business infrastructure. Alignment is now the most common single approach to IT management. But alignment alone is not sufficient to effect a transformation because IT is sometimes aligned with a conservative business strategy and so does not enable change.

Alignment describes a desirable state for the organization, but it does not tell managers how to achieve transformation with and through IT. If an organization is undergoing transformation, its strategy, structure, processes, and skills are likely also to be changing. How does IT enable transformation while retaining alignment? What are the dynamics of IT alignment? Might not IT sometimes be an integral part of an organizational strategy of change? Might it not, on occasion, play the driving role in change? The study described in this chapter has approached these questions by examining alignment as a process in the context of organizational transformation.

This chapter develops a dynamic model of alignment. This model is cyclical, at least for highly competitive industries characterized by rapid technological innovation. It is called the Lead-Lag Model because organizations may over time alternate between IT leading change and IT catching up on change. The model indicates that to activate change it will often be necessary to drive the organization out of alignment; this is not a case of misalignment (see Chapter Four) but part of a deliberate process of change. The model also implies that the management of alignment is a balancing act. Too long a lead or lag may be damaging to the firm. The more realistic dynamics presented in the model are the basis for a new, improved approach to IT planning. This chapter starts by reviewing current alignment models and some of their inherent weaknesses. It then describes a study undertaken over six years to examine alignment in practice, and it highlights some of the salient results. IT develops the Lead-Lag Model from the different states of alignment identified in the study. The chapter then examines in detail three types of dynamic paths: *IT-lead*, *IT-lag*, and *cyclical*. Finally some conclusions are drawn about the effective management of alignment, specifically:

- Alignment is not a one-time activity but a constant balancing act between a lead or lag strategy.

- Alignment through lead-lag is typified by cycles of change, and these cycles tend to be specific to particular organizational types and particular industries.

- Knowing these cycles of change and your organizational position in relation to them will facilitate management of the alignment process.

The Practice of Alignment

Alignment is a much misconstrued concept. It is typically characterized as a fit between the business and IT, but the processes involved in achieving and sustaining that fit are not included in the characterization. Consequently, it is too readily assumed that alignment implies a relatively permanent relationship that should remain in equilibrium. Stated this way, of course, the concept can easily be ridiculed because in a changing world maintaining equilibrium requires immediate compensating change to balance external perturbation. In reality, alignment is a balancing act in which perturbation creates swings that subsequently have to be corrected. Managing the swings helps to achieve alignment.

A further common misunderstanding of alignment is to suppose that it is asymmetric in practice. Normally alignment means support, specifically IT supporting the business, and so it is assumed that IT makes adjustments to fit the business, not the reverse. Yet, in today's world the reverse—business adjusting to fit IT—is exactly what may be required and is, in fact, the theme for many strategic success stories (Davenport, 1994; Hammer, 1990).

An important consequence of the work described in this chapter is the recognition that being in a state that is not aligned is not necessarily undesirable if that state is viewed as part of the continuing balancing act of the process of alignment. Knowing how to drive your organizational strategies out of alignment may be far more important than striving to maintain a stable balance. Furthermore, it may be that IT has driven the organization out of alignment and the business is adjusting to fit. In order for organizations to live and work with these consequences the concept of alignment must be clearly understood, and, more important, the processes by which alignment can be achieved must be well documented and part of every manager's tool kit.

Strategic-Alignment Models

A major focus of the Management in the 1990s (MIT90s) program developed at the Sloan School of Management at the Massachusetts Institute of Technology was investigating the link between business strategy and IT (Scott Morton, 1991; Allen and Scott

Morton, 1994). Four of the conclusions were particularly relevant to the development of a sophisticated model of alignment (Henderson and Venkatraman, 1992). These conclusions were:

- IT does not provide sustainable competitive advantage by itself.

- IT requires integration with the organization's processes and structure to achieve lasting advantage.

- IT capability is now sufficiently influential that it can drive change in the organization, its processes, its products, and even its market.

- Although IT is an agent of transformation, significant technical problems still exist and constrain effective deployment of IT in the business domain.

The specific model of alignment suggested by Henderson and Venkatraman identified four alignment components: business strategy, organizational infrastructure and processes, IT strategy, and IT infrastructure and processes (Figure 3.1). Instead of consisting solely of a fit between IT strategy and business strategy, alignment involves fits between business strategy and organizational infrastructure, IT strategy and IT infrastructure, organizational infrastructure and IT infrastructure, and then cross-alignments between business strategy and IT infrastructure, and IT strategy and organizational infrastructure. A major contribution of this model has been the recognition that at any one time any of its four components may be the major focus for change in the strategic-alignment process and may have an impact on the other components and their cross-alignment. IT is no longer seen only as a support to business strategy and can itself be a driver. Furthermore, both the external strategies and the internal infrastructures are seen to be part of the overall balancing act.

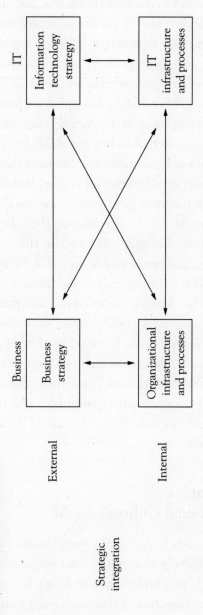

Figure 3.1. Alignment Model.

Adapted from Henderson and Venkatraman (1992, p. 99).

The model implies that it is necessary to follow a single pattern of behaviors to achieve effective alignment, but Henderson and Venkatraman indicate that the pattern will vary according to circumstances. The message to managers is "Know thyself and to thine own self be true"; acknowledge your dependence on IT and identify your overall business perspective, and you will then be able to define the route to follow to align these philosophies.

Although the complexity of this model endows it with a degree of sophistication, it nonetheless has certain shortcomings. First, it assumes a more rational and stable environment than real life normally offers. It makes no allowance for the fact that the component of the model that is the focus for change at any one time may have a moving target with which to align because the other components too may be changing. Second, it is based on the assumption that alignment is a state, and hence its description of the dynamics of the model is limited. It is a contingency model but says little about the actual contingencies defining preferred paths or patterns of alignment behavior. From a managerial perspective, it does not describe or explain the change processes involved in strategic alignment nor does it provide any guidelines as to how change can be effected. Notwithstanding these criticisms, Henderson and Venkatraman's model (Figure 3.1) is a good starting point from which to develop an empirically grounded model. This is the task of the remaining sections of this chapter.

Hong Kong Study: The Organizational Cultural Audit

Few alignment models have actually been tested to see whether or how they work. To help understand the complexities involved, a longitudinal study was undertaken in Hong Kong (Burn, 1993, 1996). One major objective of this work was to identify the processes that influence the alignment of IT and business. A survey instrument (the Organizational Cultural Audit, described below) was developed and administered to senior and middle managers in 250 Hong Kong organizations over a period of six years. The managers were asked to complete audits as a prerequisite to their evaluation of their current organizational strategy for business and IT or, in some cases, their development of an IT strategy. None of the managers was an IT professional, but all were concerned with policymaking within their organization. A wide range of both public and private organizations was covered. Alignment processes cannot be studied through a single snapshot but need to be regularly reviewed as part of an ongoing organizational audit. A number of the organizations were therefore reviewed each year by different internal managers to provide a picture of ongoing change.

In developing a framework within which to study alignment, I started with the model shown in Figure 3.1 and added a number of dimensions to create the audit model shown in Figure 3.2.

The starting point in collecting data about the organizations (the audit) was the alignment framework, which consisted of three dimensions, each with a matching pair of business and IT components: external-strategy models for business and IT, internal-infrastructure models for business and IT, and planning models for cross-alignment of external and internal alignment. All six relationships were examined by applying recognized models of process change to each and then matching the results obtained to see whether they provided a change model of alignment processes. Each of these process models is briefly reviewed here before the study results are introduced.

The first dimension of the audit relates to the external strategy of the organization in relation to both business and IT. This dimension reflects the positioning of the organization in its market and the organization's dependence on IT to maintain this position. Figure 3.3 outlines the external business-strategy component of the model, classified by type of strategy and linked to the strategic processes organizations adopt.

Figure 3.2. Organizational Cultural Audit Framework.

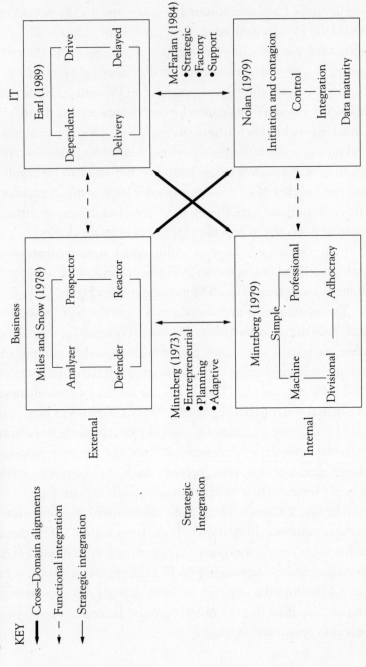

Figure 3.3. External Business Strategy Model.

Organizational Cultural Audit

Q: What strategic processes does my organization adopt?

Strategic Typology	Defender	Prospector	Analyzer	Reactor
Focus	Today	Tomorrow	Today and tomorrow	Yesterday
Environment	Stable	Dynamic	Balanced	Unstable
Entrepreneurial problem	Niche positioning	Innovation	Dual focus	Survival
Product/market	Narrow segment	New product and markets	Market penetration, product and market development	Inconsistent
Engineering problem	Efficient production/ distribution of services	Flexibility	Flexibility and stability	Cost minimization
Technology	Single core Centralized	Multiple/prototype Decentralized	Dual Distributed/linked	Mixed Ad hoc
Administrative problem	Strict control	Facilitate	Differentiate structure and process	Weak links
Emphasis	Mechanistic	Organic	Matrix organization	None
Orientation for top management	Production and control	Marketing and R&D	Key functional areas and product lines	Semiautonomous groups
Planning	Formal/hierarchical	Low formalization	Intensive planning	Loose

Implied planning styles	Bottom-up	Inside-out	Top-down/bottom-up	None

Compiled from material in Miles and Snow (1978).

Miles and Snow (1978) suggest that this external position will fall into one of four classifications—Analyzer, Prospector, Defender, Reactor—and this position will change over time, reflecting different external circumstances and their influence on internal behavior. Analyzers are organizations that operate in two types of product-market domain, one relatively stable and the other changing. To be efficient in both domains they need to adopt a dual approach to strategic planning that provides for a top-down focus to identify the mission in the external market and a bottom-up focus to align internal operations with the overall vision. Prospectors are organizations that almost continually search for market opportunities and are often the creators of change to which competitors respond. This search for opportunities is frequently supported by an inside-out approach to strategy, where the planner, often a consultant, scans the market-place for innovative developments that can act as a vehicle for change. Defenders are organizations with narrow product domains and a narrow management focus. Attention is devoted to improving the efficiency of existing operations, and a bottom-up style of planning for both business and IT strategy is preferred. Finally, Reactors are organizations that lack a consistent strategy-structure relationship; they are able neither to adjust nor to respond. There is no alignment of IT and business strategy because strategy is nonexistent or ad hoc. Only when the organization moves out of this mode into one of the other three can an appropriate strategy link be developed. As shown in Figure 3.3, managers were asked to classify their organizations by exploring a number of dimensions related to focus and market; entrepreneurial, engineering, and administrative problems; and technology and environment. Organizations could be in a process of change and so could reflect one classification predominantly with emerging characteristics of another.

Figure 3.4 illustrates the IT strategy component of the model as it relates to the dependence of the industry on IT for survival; this dependence is classified by Earl (1989) as Delivery, Dependent, Drive, and Delayed.

Figure 3.4. External IT Strategy Model.

Organizational Cultural Audit

Q: How dependent are we on the use of IT?

Sector	Delivery	Dependent	Drive	Delayed
Context	IT is the means of delivering goods and services	Business strategies increasingly depend on IT	IT potentially provides new strategic opportunities	IT has no strategic impact
Characteristics	Computer-based transaction systems underpin business	Business and functional strategies are automated	Specific applications are exploited	Opportunities not yet apparent
Information management style Planning Organization Control Technology	Integral Corporate Tight-loose Architectural	Derived Business unit Loose-tight Pragmatic	IT-push Line Loose Enabling	Default IT Tight Ad hoc
Implied planning styles	Bottom-up	Top-down	Inside-out	None

Adapted from Earl (1989, p. 195).

In the Delivery sector IT has become the means of delivering goods or services, as in banking. The infrastructure is often IT itself, and so the planning of goods and services and of product-market strategy is inextricably linked to IT. Earl suggests that this configuration favors a bottom-up approach to strategic planning, where the strategy is infrastructure-led and the organization uses IT to defend its business position. The Dependent sector includes those industries such as manufacturing where the implementation of business and functional strategies is becoming increasingly dependent on IT. Critical success or even survival is often directly related to IT, and so strategic planning is effected top-down to analyze business positioning. In the Drive sector, the requirements and imperatives for IT are by no means clear, and there has to be a continual push to identify the greatest benefits. As in the Prospector business model, this configuration requires an inside-out approach to IT strategy. In the last sector, Delayed, the strategic use of IT is not yet apparent, has a minimal effect on company performance, or supports a reactive business strategy.

The business strategy and IT strategy elements of the model were used to evaluate the tightness of fit between the external strategies at any point in time and, more important, to analyze how changes in these strategies over a period of time influenced the alignment process.

The second dimension of the audit related to the internal alignment of the organization. The matching pair of components on this dimension can be viewed as the organizational structure, roles, and processes adopted by the business, and the stage of IT growth. For the organizational component Mintzberg's (1991) five-part classification of organizational configurations was applied: Simple Structures, Machine Bureaucracies, Professional Bureaucracies, Divisionalized Forms, and Adhocracies. The Simple Structure configuration corresponds to owner-operated and controlled firms, where authority is vested at the top. Machine Bureaucracies are typified by government departments or allied subvented organizations, where authority is rigidly distributed through a chain of command. Professional Bureaucracies include the professional partnerships and collegial arrangements of architects, lawyers, accountants, and educators, where authority rests with the individuals. Divisionalized Forms, including multinational corporations, are those where authority is distributed to lower levels defined by distinctive geographical regions, markets, or production technologies. Adhocracies are organizations with project teams, where the structure is fluid and related to specific projects rather than to functional groupings. Each of these configurations displays distinctive patterns of behavior that help define the organizational infrastructure, as shown in Figure 3.5. A Machine Bureaucracy, for example, is typified by formal rules and processes with a hierarchical management structure that is heavily dependent on standard procedures for control and hence favors a top-down approach to strategic planning with bottom-up implementation.

The IT infrastructure is characterized by stages in the use of IT systems as identified by Nolan (1979). This model suggests that the growth in IT usage is evolutionary and is directly related to the growth in IT expenditure. The model has been modified by a number of researchers; the four-stage growth model (as adapted by Earl, 1989, and shown in Figure 3.6) was used in the audit.

Stage 1 of the model is the initiation stage, in which organizational use of IT is directed toward operational control, and applications are developed using a bottom-up approach to strategy. At Stage 2 of growth the focus is on new functions and increasing the use of IT for management control. A top-down approach is necessary to prioritize applications and allocate costs. In Stage 3 effort is devoted to organizational change through IT and involves a restructure or retrofit of existing applications. This stage needs both a top-down and a bottom-up approach to planning. In the final stage an organization reaches a mature level of IT development, and IT is seen as a strategic weapon for business development. At this stage multiple approaches to strategic planning are needed, and long-range strategy is supported by multilevel plans.

Figure 3.5. Organizational Infrastructure Model.

Organizational Cultural Audit
Q: What is the shape of my organization?

Configuration	Simple Structure	Machine Bureaucracy	Professional Bureaucracy	Divisionalized Form	Adhocracy
Key coordinating mechanism	Direct supervision	Standardization of work	Standardization of skills	Standardization of outputs	Mutual adjustments
Key part of organization	Strategic apex	Technostructure	Operating core	Middle line	Support staff
Design parameters					
Specialization of jobs	Little specialization	Much horizontal and vertical specialization	Much horizontal specialization	Some horizontal and vertical specialization (between divisions and headquarters)	Much horizontal specialization
Training	Little	Little	Much	Little	Much
Indoctrination	Little	Little	Little	Some of divisional managers	Some
Formalization of behavior, bureaucratic/organic	Little formalization, organic	Much formalization, bureaucratic	Little formalization, bureaucratic	Much formalization (within divisions), bureaucratic	Little formalization, organic
Grouping	Usually functional	Usually functional	Functional and market	Market	Functional and market
Unit size	Wide	Wide at bottom, narrow elsewhere	Wide at bottom, narrow elsewhere	Wide (at top)	Narrow throughout
Planning and control systems	Little planning and control	Action planning	Little planning and control	Much preferential control	Limited action planning

Liaison devices	Few liaison devices	Few liaison devices	Liaison devices in administration	Few liaison devices	Many liaison devices throughout
Decentralization	Centralization	Limited horizontal decentralization	Horizontal decentralization	Limited vertical decentralization	Selective decentralization
Situational factors					
Age and size	Typically young and small (first stage)	Typically old and large (second stage)	Varies	Typically old and very large (third stage)	Often young
Technical system	Simple, not regulating	Regulating but not automated, not very sophisticated	Not regulating or sophisticated	Divisible, otherwise typically like Machine Bureaucracy	Very sophisticated, often automated, or else not regulating or sophisticated
Environment	Simple and dynamic, sometimes hostile	Simple and stable	Complex and stable	Relatively simple and stable, diversified markets (especially products and services)	Complex and dynamic, sometimes disparate
Power	Chief executive control, often owner-managed, not fashionable	Technocratic and external control, fashionable	Professional operator control, fashionable	Middle-line control, fashionable (especially in industry)	Expert control, very fashionable
Implied planning styles	Bottom-up	Top-down/bottom-up	Bottom-up/top-down	Multiple	Multiple

Adapted from Mintzberg (1983, pp. 280–281).

Figure 3.6. IT Infrastructure Model.

Organizational Cultural Audit
Q: To what extent are we using information systems?

Stages of Growth	Stage 1	Stage 2	Stage 3	Stage 4
Applications portfolio	Operational control	Operational control and some management control	Operational control/ management control	Operational control/ management control and some strategic planning
Focus	Cost reduction	New functions	Restructure or retrofit existing application	Database and on-line inquiry systems
Development (maintenance ratio)	1 : 0	0.75 : 0.25	0.5 : 0.5	0.8 : 0.2
Management planning	Technology focus/computing plan	Loose budget/ applications plan	Budgetary planning steering committee	Low-range planning Multilevel planning
Control	Lax	Encouraging	Standardization	Organizational prioritizing
Costs	No charge-out	Costs allocated	Full charge-out	Selective charge-out
Growth focus	Technological Applications testing	Applications User learning	User advice Management learning	Management advice

| Implied planning styles | Bottom-up | Top-down | Top down/bottom-up | Multiple |

Adapted from Earl (1989, p. 29).

To continue the example of the Machine Bureaucracy, such an organization, with its emphasis on control, would need to reach Stage 3 of IT development. The focus here is on management reporting for control; IT costs are controlled by a steering committee to achieve a suitable alignment. Both infrastructure models operate most effectively with a top-down and bottom-up approach to strategic planning.

The final dimension of the audit characterizes the way components are cross-aligned. This cross-alignment reflects the planning models in place and the revealed IT strategy of the organization. Mintzberg (1973) suggests three planning styles—Entrepreneurial, Planning, Adaptive—each having specific conditions for use and a set of typical decision-making characteristics, as shown in Figure 3.7.

In the Entrepreneurial mode a bold strong leader takes risky actions on behalf of the organization. Strategy making is characterized by dramatic leaps forward in the face of uncertainty and typically reflects an inside-out approach. In the Planning mode formal analysis is used to devise explicit, integrated strategies for the future; this mode encompasses anticipatory decision making, a system of decisions, and a clear direction. These elements are most commonly effected through a dual focus on top-down and bottom-up planning. Finally, in the Adaptive mode the strategist consciously seeks to avoid uncertainty, solving pressing problems rather than developing long-term plans. This approach favors a bottom-up style.

The IT systems portfolio will reflect the IT applications in place and identify their organizational role as Strategic, Factory, Turnaround, or Support (McFarlan, 1984). These four classifications all have different characteristics, which support different management and planning styles, as shown in Figure 3.8.

The particular emphasis here is on change management. A Strategic portfolio implies that IT is critical now and in the future; because it dominates the capital budget and all levels of planning, multiple styles of planning are required. Factory portfolios are prevalent in organizations where IT underpins the operations but is not

Figure 3.7. Business Planning Model.

Organizational Cultural Audit
Q: What mode do we adopt to formulate our strategy?

Characteristics	Entrepreneurial Mode	Adaptive Mode	Planning Mode
Motive for decisions	Proactive	Reactive	Proactive and reactive
Goals of organization	Growth	Indeterminate	Efficiency and growth
Evaluation of proposals	Judgmental	Judgmental	Analytical
Choices made by	Entrepreneur	Bargaining	Management
Decision horizon	Long term	Short term	Long term
Preferred environment	Uncertainty	Certainty	Risk
Decision links	Loosely coupled	Disjointed	Integrated
Flexibility of mode	Flexible	Adaptive	Constrained
Size of moves	Bold decisions	Incremental steps	Global strategies
Vision of direction	General	None	Specific
Condition for Use			
Source of power	Entrepreneur	Divided	Management
Objectives of organization	Operational	Nonoperational	Operational
Organizational environment	Yielding	Complex, dynamic	Predictable, stable
Status of organization	Young, small, or strong leadership	Established	Large
Implied planning styles	Top-down	Bottom-up	Top-down/bottom-up

Adapted from Mintzberg (1973, p. 49). Copyright 1973 by The Regents of the University of California. Reprinted from the *California Management Review*, vol. 16, no. 2. By permission of The Regents.

Figure 3.8. IT Planning Model.

Organizational Cultural Audit

Q: What is our strategic approach to the use of IT?

Strategic Typology	Support	Factory	Turnaround	Strategic
Characteristics	IT little impact	IT crucial to operations and management but not for strategic control	IT becomes strategic	IT crucial now and in the future
Applications type	Operational support	Operations and planning	Emphasis on strategic applications	All levels of planning
Investment	Low	Average	Incremental leaps	Dominates capital budget

Implied planning styles	Ad hoc	Bottom-up	Top-down	Multiple

Compiled from material in McFarlan (1984).

viewed as essential for strategic planning. The emphasis on operations suggests that a bottom-up approach to planning will be most appropriate. The Turnaround portfolio implies change: IT is increasingly viewed as a strategic necessity, and incremental leaps in investment are supported by both a top-down and an inside-out approach to planning. A Support classification implies that IT has little impact and that investment levels are low; consequently there is little emphasis on IT planning.

Both the strategic and functional pairs of organizational and IT components (Figure 3.2) imply a certain alignment that would normally achieve maximum equilibrium. In addition, the cross-alignment between each set of dimensions shows whether the positioning is in line with the pattern and perspective and the planning style adopted. In a Machine Bureaucracy that adopted an Analyzer mode for external strategy and a Planning mode to integrate the external and internal focus, the model would be consistent, and top-down and bottom-up strategic-planning styles would be appropriate. Many government-based Machine Bureaucracies, however, tend to favor Defender strategies and an Adaptive style of planning, which pull much more toward bottom-up planning styles and a short-term rather than a long-term focus. Even where consistent organizational and IT models are found, they may be highly inconsistent with each other and hence provide no possibility of alignment.

Study Results

The 250 organizations in the Hong Kong study were classified into five categories related to Mintzberg's configuration model (1979): Simple, Professional, Machine, Divisional, Adhocracy. The total numbers per category were: simple, 40; adhocracy, 12 (half of them subsidiaries or divisions); professional, 51; machine, 101; divisional, 46. I briefly summarize here some of the general results of the study.

First, most of the organizations studied follow a highly conservative and traditional approach to the alignment process; they consider IT a support to business strategy rather than an integral part of that strategy. In this respect they confirm the assumption of earlier alignment models that the relationship between business and IT is asymmetrical.

Second, many organizations found great difficulty in sustaining alignment, and frequently periods of innovation and change were followed by periods of retrenchment in which the organizations were unable to cope with further change processes and gradually lost their competitive advantage (see Chapter Four).

Third, not all organizations can follow the same path for organizational transformation through IT. The study found a number of different paths reflecting the dynamics of change in relation to different organizational cultures and their associated infrastructures. The study suggests that the different paths relate to: the organization's degree of dependence on IT, the organization's need for change, and the organization's strategy.

In regard to organizational strategies, a review of the study results supports the following conclusions about the development of planning relating to alignment:

Organizations change IT planning styles as they progress through stages in their use of IT. The pattern supported by the study is shown in Table 3.1; it indicates that the style for planning changes from a bottom-up, or functional, approach through a top-down approach to a combined approach that leads finally to the use of multiple styles in a mature environment. Organizations frequently find the need to adopt an inside-out approach at significant transition points.

Table 3.1. IT Planning Style.

Stage	Style of Planning
1	Bottom-up
2	Bottom-up/top-down
3	Top-down/bottom-up
4	Multiple

Table 3.2. Organizational Planning Styles.

Configuration	Style of Planning
Simple/Adhocracy	Bottom-up
Professional	Bottom-up/top-down
Machine	Top-down/bottom-up
Divisional	Multiple

Different organizational configurations lead to a preference for different approaches to planning. This pattern of preferences, shown in Table 3.2, closely resembles the model of IT planning shown in Table 3.1.

Different organizational configurations show different IT growth patterns, which suggests that these patterns relate directly to the type of organizational configuration.

The results show that Machine Bureaucracies were at the greatest level of maturity; 70 percent of these organizations were at Stage 3 or above. Only 44 percent of Professional Bureaucracies were at this stage or at the transition level from Stage 2; and only 20 percent of Simple configurations had developed IT usage beyond Stage 2. Divisional configurations varied. All multinational corporations were at Stage 3 or 4, but within a number of locally owned public corporations each subsidiary was run independently of the parent and therefore many different levels of IT maturity could coexist.

Lead-Lag Model of IT and Organizational Alignment

The pattern of growth and change can be identified as a Lead-Lag Model of IT and organizational alignment. Figure 3.9 shows the match of organizational configuration (the business infrastructure) and the stage of growth in IT (the IT infrastructure). It suggests a specific "fit" of the majority of organizations operating within these structures and the appropriate IT support level. More important, it

Figure 3.9. Strategic-Alignment Model.

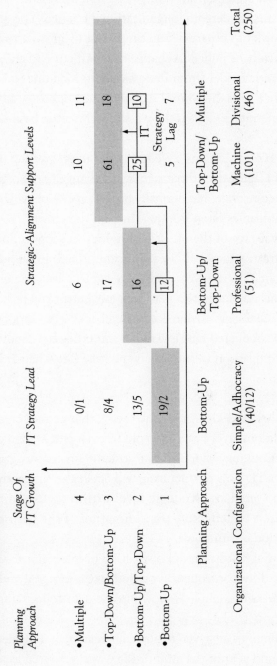

shows that organizations rarely experience dramatic growth in IT without first undergoing organizational change. The arrows show that in order to progress from Stage 1 of IT growth, organizations will typically be pulled to change their structure to an increasingly bureaucratic model (from Professional to Machine to Divisional), which then suits the control requirements implied by a higher level of IT penetration. This is the classic, asymmetric business-lead, IT-lag path.

When organizations have succeeded in progressing through the stages of IT growth without significant change to the organizational infrastructure, there has normally been a process of dynamic change. Such companies often leapfrog through the growth process and so take advantage of the latest technology to support and enhance their infrastructure without significant growth in resources (other than profits). In these cases, there may be IT lead and business lag.

It is also significant to note that movement can be both up and down. Technology has outpaced a number of organizations for which we have conducted multiple audits, and they have moved down a step in comparison with their competitors (see Chapter Four).

Challenges of Change

The study found support for the theory that certain organizational configurations favor faster rates of IT development than others, and organizations may be forced to restructure in order to facilitate the growth of IT. This restructuring will affect the ease with which IT can be adopted at a strategic level within the organization and hence limit the effective transformation of the business into an information organization.

External factors tend, however, to play a major role and have unplanned-for consequences on both organizational and IT strategies. One such example is shown in the data collected from a public authority (PHA) over four years (for reasons of confidentiality all organizations are given fictional abbreviations as names). In 1992 (the second year of the study), PHA was analyzed as a Machine

Bureaucracy adopting an Analyzer strategy with a Planning mode. It was at Stage 3 of IT growth and about to enter a transition from Dependence on IT to Strategic use.

In the following year, PHA underwent considerable change as the government granted it autonomy under its own board of directors. Employees, who had previously enjoyed government privileges, had to choose whether to remain in government service or join PHA with new conditions of service.

The next audit, in the fourth year of the study, showed a remarkable transformation, with PHA now operating as a Professional Bureaucracy but with a Defender and Adaptive approach to strategy. IT was found to be at only the first stage of growth, providing Support services in a Delayed environment. This change reflected the sudden culture shock within PHA. The new Professional organization found that existing information systems, which had previously provided support for planning at the strategic level for a Machine Bureaucracy, were inappropriate for its new mode of operation. However, the amount of change had also forced the organization to become defensive about its position and unable to clearly pursue a change strategy. This was a matter of grave concern because PHA believed that maximum IT support was needed to attract top-quality professionals.

By the fifth year, a new mission statement and IT policy were paying off. The organization retained its Professional configuration but had adopted an Analyzer approach to strategy with a Planning mode of operation. Several new systems, developed over two years, had been implemented, and PHA had reached Dependence on IT at Stage 3 of growth and in Turnaround mode, which was driving the organization into Stage 4.

In its last review, in the sixth year, the organization retained its overall profile but was still at Stage 3 of IT growth and in Drive mode. This position reflected recent developments in Smartcard for client records; PHA saw these developments as offering the core input to all existing systems, but they would necessitate considerable development and resources. In this case an external intervention by government caused a major disruption in the alignment strategy. Subsequently a further external change in the form of technology caused a minor perturbation with a reappraisal of strategic IT direction.

Neither of these events could have been foreseen or planned for. These are typical of the challenges of change. The organizations that can cope successfully when out of alignment will survive. The balancing act can take many forms; the three cases that follow describe some typical change paths.

IT-Lead Change

In the first year in which it was studied (1991) a large government division (FINAC) with more than one thousand employees was analyzed overall as were its three separate subdivisions. All were at Stage 1 of IT growth with one subdivision operating as a Simple Structure and the other two as Professional Bureaucracies. Overall, through an analysis of business strategy and planning, FINAC was shown to be at a transition stage; it was moving from Defender to Analyzer mode and from Adapter to Planning style. In the third year of the study, FINAC was analyzed as a Machine Bureaucracy in Stage 2 of IT growth with Factory support. The Planning style was still used, but a Defender strategy was reestablished. The organization had moved rapidly into the stage where it had to use IT for delivery of services and had a need for even faster transition into Stage 3 of IT growth. In the fourth year of the study all subdivisions were identified as Machine Bureaucracies at Stage 2 of IT growth with a Factory portfolio of systems and at the Dependence level of IT usage rather than Delivery. The organizational strategy remained as Defender mode, and planning had returned to an Adapter model. In the sixth year FINAC was analyzed as a Professional Bureaucracy adopting an Analyzer strategy and a Planning style. The IT strategy remained at Dependence level but had reached Stage 3 of IT growth and was operating at Factory level.

Explanations from the study for this growth pattern are as follows:

- Change was needed, but "quantum" change takes time to stabilize and normally forces defensive, adaptive strategies in the period immediately following the change.

- The IT strategy played a "leading" role in the transition stage and had to wait for organizational strategy to realign itself. (This process can be seen particularly in government organizations, where change is often viewed with suspicion.)

- The move to an IT Dependence mode required a significant "culture" change, which takes time to develop from both an IT and a business perspective.

An examination of the alignment of strategic planning during this period shows an initial alignment of bottom-up planning for both the organization and IT, an organizational shift to bottom-up and top-down leading the IT strategy of bottom-up, a top-down and bottom-up IT strategy leading the organizational strategy, and most recently an organizational transition to top-down and bottom-up planning with a return to the Professional Bureaucracy model.

IT-Lag Change

In the private sector one of the large multigroup holdings (HWS)was analyzed as a Machine Bureaucracy, adopting a Reactor strategy, with Adaptive planning, a Delayed use of IT at Stage 2 of the IT infrastructure model, and a Support portfolio. HWS operated as many different companies with bottom-up planning as a business focus and ad hoc planning for IT. In the first year of the study serious problems were diagnosed with regard to the lack of IT support, and the organization needed to become more proactive than it had been in the use of IT. After two years, the organization remained at Stage 2 but had moved into the Dependent sector and

Turnaround mode. The overall business strategy had become that of Analyzer and Planning/Entrepreneur. HWS had moved from a number of discrete Machine Bureaucracies to adopt the structure of a Divisional Bureaucracy, and planning in all areas was clearly top-down. The organization intended to use this focus to direct the transition into Stages 3 and 4 of IT growth.

One year later HWS still provided the same profile with no advancement of IT stage growth. This lack of movement was ascribed to the large number of new business ventures the holding group had undertaken, which had diverted capital resources away from infrastructural growth.

This organization, despite its size, was the creation of one entrepreneur, and in such cases support for IT expenditure will be found only if such expenditure is directly aligned with the organizational (Entrepreneur's) mission. In these circumstances, HWS is always likely to follow an IT-lag path.

Cyclical Change

The third case described here, a large multinational bank (SBC), was one of the few organizations in the study found to have already achieved Strategic use of IT in the first year. SBC was a clear Divisional configuration acting as an Analyzer and Planner. It relied on IT as a Delivery of services with Strategic use of IT at Stage 4. Planning within the organization was top-down and bottom-up with "multiple" planning styles for IT and a declared need within the bank to move the organizational configuration toward an Adhocracy and to adopt multiple styles of business planning.

Two years later, SBC no longer found itself comfortable with its strategic use of IT because technological changes had overtaken its IT development; the organization rated itself only at Stage 3 with a Dependence reliance on IT. SBC indicated itself as being at Turnaround mode, and all planning had reverted to top-down and bottom-up in a formal, controlled drive to regain a competitive edge through IT. SBC remained firmly a Divisional Bureaucracy with a tendency to Machine Bureaucracy at control level. The 1996 audit showed the same organizational configuration, but a move back to a Delivery level at Stage 4 of IT growth. The organization was still in Turnaround mode, which was driving the bank toward a Strategic portfolio through advanced, technology-based systems. This drive had required the bank to adopt multiple approaches to strategy to reflect the different system objectives and user profiles.

In the six years of the study, data were collected from twenty banks. This particular group seems especially vulnerable to changes in technology; these changes cause the group to continually perform a balancing act between defending its positions and driving to regain strategic advantage. The Lead-Lag Model is most noticeable here and can be seen over short periods. However, the model applies to all IT alignment with business strategy and encompasses a number of factors related to the strategic approach of the organization—specifically, organizational structure, strategy, and planning approaches, and IT reliance, strategy, and stage of experience.

Balancing Act

An innovation model proposed by Slevin and Covin (1990) suggests that a cyclical model applies within entrepreneurial and highly enterprising organizations, as shown in Figure 3.10.

Figure 3.10. Organicity and Entrepreneurship.

Management style	Mechanistic	Organic
Entrepreneurial	2 Pseudoentrepreneurial firms	1 Effective entrepreneurial firms
Conservative	3 Efficient bureaucratic firms	4 Unstructured, unadventurous firms

Organizational structure

Adapted from Slevin and Covin (1990, p. 45).

An entrepreneurial firm may adopt any of the four cell positions in Figure 3.10 as environmental forces change. Effective Entrepreneurial Firms (Cell 1) have the desired combination of entrepreneurial behavior as well as an organic structure to support and nurture that behavior. Their structures work because they enhance communication and minimize bureaucracy. These firms thrive in a highly competitive, often hostile environment. Pseudoentrepreneurial Firms (Cell 2) take risks and act in an entrepreneurial manner but are stymied by a mechanistic, bureaucratic, rigid organizational structure. The emergence of this type of firm is often a response to an inherently uncertain environment, where managers believe that tight controls and centralized decision making will increase predictability. Efficient Bureaucratic Firms (Cell 3) adopt a mechanistic structure; their emphasis is on the accomplishment of routine or repetitive tasks with maximum efficiency. This type of firm is likely to be found in a stable, predictable environment. Unstructured, Unadventurous Firms (Cell 4) are organic, adaptable, and conservative. They can respond quickly but do not, and they are likely to be inefficient at performing even routine operational tasks. They are most often found in a benign, or nonhostile, environment.

The successful firm will cycle between Cell 1 and Cell 3. This model can be adapted for organizations that wish to maximize their utilization of IT throughout the change cycle. Figure 3.11 shows a revised model that can be applied to IT innovation.

Cell 1 represents the external-strategy-lead model when organizations are risk taking and innovative in their application of IS and emphasize effectiveness. Cell 3 represents the internal-infrastructure model, in which the organization pursues functional alignment of IT within the organization and emphasizes efficiency. Of the change models examined previously FINAC is an example of an organization cycling from Cell 2 through Cell 1 to Cell 3. The danger with this cycle is that the organization will return again to Cell 2 and stifle innovation. HWS is representative of an organization cycling from Cell 4 through Cell 1 to Cell 3 and on to Cell 2 with the similar inherent danger that it will recycle into Cell 4 and

Figure 3.11. Model for IT Innovation and Entrepreneurship.

	Mechanistic	Organic
Innovative *IT planning* *management style*	**2** Pseudoinnovative IT Strategies Cycling	**1** Effective IT innovators
Conservative	**3** Effective IT users	Cycling **4** Unstructured, unadventurous IT usage

Mechanistic   Organic

Organizational structure

Adapted from Slevin and Covin (1990, p. 45).

be unable to provide direction for technical innovation. SBC appears to understand the need to cycle between Cell 1 and Cell 3 and has implemented this process with some success.

The IT Lead-Lag Model cannot be a basis for an effective alignment process without full organizational support. Organizations that are not prepared to adopt the cyclical-change model are likely to fall into Cells 2 and 4, where organizational overstructuring or lack of structure inhibits further advancement through IT development. Failure to continually balance organizational and IT change will inhibit innovative use of IT.

Implications

Identifying the existing alignment practices of organizations does not provide a blueprint for achieving alignment, but it does clarify the nature of alignment and the decisions managers must make if they wish to align their IT strategies with the business strategy or if they wish to use IT as a driver for organizational change.

First, the cyclical model (Figure 3.11) demonstrates that alignment is not a one-time activity but a constant balancing act between a lead or lag strategy. Second, alignment through lead-lag is typified by cycles of change, and these cycles tend to be specific to particular organizational configurations at particular stages of IT development, as shown in the Lead-Lag Model (see Figure 3.9). They also seem to be particular to industries. Unfortunately, it is impossible to specify those industries completely although the examples show that banking in Hong Kong and, I would suggest, worldwide is characterized by the changes that lead to lead-lag cycles. By contrast, the entrepreneur-dominated example of HWS appears to be a classic case of IT lag. Not being able to predict which organizations in which industries will be characterized by IT lead, IT lag, or lead-lag cycles, managers need to discover these for themselves if they are to take a realistic approach to planning and managing the alignment process.

These patterns of change suggest that managers must first be aware of the problems associated with the exploitation of IT in their particular operating environments and then plan to manage the change processes by balancing IT innovations and business transformations simultaneously. Because this process is highly complex, the solution can sometimes be found by forcing an existing alignment out of balance in order to drive one change to effect the other. This is like deliberately disturbing the balance of a tightrope walker when there is no safety net, except that in this case overbalancing will cause permanent misalignment.

Summary

This chapter has reviewed the results of a six-year study into the alignment of IT strategies with organizational strategies. A strategic-alignment model has been shown to exist at the functional level (internal alignment) and a dynamic model of change at the strategic level (external alignment). Both these models support the need to understand and manage a Lead-Lag Model of IT development. A cyclical model of IT innovation has been proposed; it can assist the innovative organization to adapt effectively and efficiently to the impact of IT on organizational change. Managing this change model is more akin to a professional balancing act than stage management of a sequential growth process. This model is proposed as a revolutionary concept for IT planning.

Achieving alignment is not the end of the process. The balancing act must go on. Minimizing the swings requires an understanding of the organizational dependence on IT, the organizational need for change, and the strategy that the organization wants to pursue and that best defines its pattern of behavior. Even with a well-developed audit of organizational and IT strategy, managers still have to contend with real life and its many vagaries. These can knock the organization completely off balance unless the dynamics of change are fully understood and the organization can take advantage of the business and IT opportunities that realignment can offer.

References

Allen, T. J., and Scott Morton, M. S. (eds.). *Information Technology and the Corporation of the 1990s: Research Studies*. New York: Oxford University Press, 1994.

Burn, J. M. "Information Systems Strategies and the Management of Organisational Change." *Journal of Information Technology*, 1993, 8(4), 205–216.

Burn, J. M. "IS Innovation and Organizational Alignment—A Professional Juggling Act." *Journal of Information Technology*, 1996, 11(1), 3–12.

Davenport, T. H. "Saving IT's Soul: Human Centered Information Management." *Harvard Business Review*, 1994, 72(2), 119–131.

Earl, M. J. *Management Strategies for Information Technology*. Englewood Cliffs, N.J.: Prentice-Hall, 1989.

Hammer, M. "Reengineering Work: Don't Automate, Obliterate." *Harvard Business Review*, 1990, 68(4), 104–112.

Henderson, J. C., and Venkatraman, N. "Strategic Alignment: A Model for Organizational Transformation Through Information Technology." In T. A. Kochan and M. Useem (eds.), *Transforming Organizations*. New York: Oxford University Press, 1992, pp. 97–117.

McFarlan, F. W. "Information Technology Changes the Way You Compete." *Harvard Business Review*, 1984, 62(3), 98–103.

Miles, R. E., and Snow, C. C. *Organizational Strategy, Structure, and Process*. New York: McGraw-Hill, 1978.

Mintzberg, H. "Strategy Making in Three Modes." *California Management Review*, 1973, 16(2), 44–53.

Mintzberg, H. *The Structuring of Organizations: A Synthesis of the Research*. Englewood Cliffs, N.J.: Prentice-Hall, 1979.

Mintzberg, H. *Structure in Fives: Designing Effective Organizations*. Englewood Cliffs, N.J.: Prentice-Hall, 1983.

Mintzberg, H. "The Effective Organization: Forces and Forms." *Sloan Management Review*, 1991, 54, 54–69.

Nolan, R. L. "Managing the Crises in Data Processing." *Harvard Business Review*, 1979, 57(2), 115–126.

Scott Morton, M. S. (ed.). *The Corporation of the 1990s: Information Technology and Organizational Transformation*. New York: Oxford University Press, 1991.

Slevin, D. P., and Covin, D. P. "Juggling Entrepreneurial Style and Organizational Structure: How to Get Your Act Together." *Sloan Management Review*, 1990, 31(2), 43–55.

Venkatraman, N. "IT-Enabled Business Reconfiguration." In M. S. Scott Morton (ed.), *The Corporation of the 1990s: Information Technology and Organizational Transformation*. New York: Oxford University Press, 1991.

4

The Pathology of
Strategic Alignment

Christopher Sauer and Janice M. Burn

The central tenet of strategic alignment is that information technology (IT) should be aligned with the business (see Chapter One). This tenet makes such obvious sense that its value has rarely been questioned. Its efficacy has been taken on trust rather than having been convincingly demonstrated.

In Chapter Two, Philip Yetton argued that it is best either to integrate IT into the business so that a single set of decisions covers business and IT issues alike or to accept that IT is a service and outsource it. Strategic alignment can be thought of as a compromise between these two options: it values IT more than as a service to be outsourced but stops short of total integration. There are usually good reasons for compromise. IT may be considered too valuable to outsource, but the current business strategy may be too important to undertake the massive organizational transformation involved in integrating IT. Compromise aside, integration has been shown to work only at the business unit level, so for multidivisional organizations alignment may be the best available solution. Many corporations will therefore continue to manage by strategic alignment of IT in the foreseeable future.

In Chapter Three, Janice Burn took a cold, hard look at alignment practice. She found that in competitive environments alignment is a dynamic concept. Corporations cannot implement an aligned organizational design and expect IT to cease to be a problem. Alignment must be managed dynamically as the business changes. As Yetton suggested (Chapter Two), alignment is as much a problem to be managed as a solution.

Here we explore further the statics and dynamics of alignment to reveal the previously hidden downside of alignment. We examine a number of cases we have encountered where alignment is not merely exhausting to manage but results in seriously adverse outcomes for the organization. We want to stress that this work is very much exploratory, and hence we make no claim to completeness in our discussion. We refer to this investigation as the *pathology of strategic alignment*.

In talking of the pathology of strategic alignment we are making a statement. We want to emphasize that strategic alignment inherently causes managerial headaches and worse. Our purpose in this chapter is to draw attention to some of the different types of problems companies experience in practicing alignment. Our analysis reinforces Burn's view of alignment as a balancing act. It goes further and shows the importance of maintaining momentum in cycles of change. We are led to conclude that the pathologies we have observed are inherent in alignment rather than the result of some contingent shortcoming. The root of these pathologies is the deep assumption that the business and IT should be kept separate.

The examples we present should bring to the attention of both general managers and IT managers the potential downside of alignment. Those contemplating pursuing an alignment policy can be more fully informed by understanding the downside, while those already aligned can be alerted to the pitfalls. The contrast between the pathological outcomes of alignment and the ease of managing IT when it is integrated with the business should encourage general managers to review their commitment to alignment.

We start by briefly explaining the fundamental relationship between alignment and organizational fit. We then describe and analyze examples we have encountered of three types of pathological outcomes from strategic alignment: misalignment, which occurs when a company tries to align IT with the business but the business is not in a state of tight fit; IT stagnation, which occurs as part of a common, almost natural, cycle of innovation; and globalization, which presents special difficulties for alignment. We then examine the fundamental theoretical principle of strategic alignment to demonstrate that the potential for pathological outcomes is firmly embedded in that principle. We conclude by drawing implications for managers.

Strategic Alignment and Organizational Fit

Organizational fit consists of external fit and internal fit (Miller, 1992). External fit is between an organization's strategy and its market environment. Internal fit is fit between strategy and other organizational elements including structure, technology, management processes, and roles and skills. Theory predicts, and study results confirm, that organizations that are in fit perform better than those that are not (Doty, Glick, and Huber, 1993).

The principal characteristic of the strategic-alignment approach is that IT fits or is aligned with the business (Chapter One). Thus, the IT strategy should serve the business strategy; the IT structure should mirror the business structure; and the portfolio of IT applications should deliver systems and processes that contribute to the realization of the strategy, fit with existing company systems and processes, and are compatible with staff roles and skills. The presumption is that if the business is in fit, then aligning IT will ensure that IT is easy to manage and that it will contribute significantly to company performance (Henderson and Venkatraman, 1992).

Burn (Chapter Three) has made two contributions to our understanding of alignment. First, she has shown that alignment is a dynamic concept because in practice corporations are all the time taking new initiatives whose effect may be to disrupt any state of alignment. If either business or IT changes, the other will probably have to adapt. Second, Burn has demonstrated that the dynamics of alignment are asynchronous. Either IT or business takes a lead, and the other has to catch up. The important implication of this insight is that under conditions of significant, transformational change there is no mechanism built into aligned organizational states to automatically maintain alignment. In making these two contributions, Burn has shown the complexity and hence difficulty of successfully managing alignment. Substantial management effort on a number of dimensions including strategy, structure, and planning is both necessary and normal. Normal difficulties with managing alignment are not pathologies. Pathology occurs when aspects of alignment result in seriously adverse outcomes for the corporation. Burn's contributions help us analyze examples of alignment pathology to show why they occur and enable us to warn managers of dangers that are not otherwise mentioned.

Misalignment

Strategic alignment typically assumes that the organization is in fit—that is to say that both external strategy and internal configuration of organizational elements are consistent and mutually supportive. To our knowledge, no one has ever suggested that IT can be made easier to manage by aligning it to an organization that does not have such a fit. Such situations do arise, however, and we refer to these as cases of *misalignment*. Misalignment is essentially a static pathology. It may occur because the organization is not in fit when alignment is first attempted or because the organization loses its fit after IT has been aligned.

ResourceCo

One example of an organization that lost its fit is a mid-sized, Australian primary resource firm called ResourceCo (all corporate names in this chapter are assumed names for real organizations that have been studied by the authors). In the 1980s and early 1990s ResourceCo expanded rapidly, increasing its IT investment substantially. The company's strategic emphasis was on technical excellence. Its structure was dominantly functional. Because it had never invested in a large, shared computing facility, the company's IT acquisition, use, and management were largely internal to its functional units. Its human resource policy was to hire highly professional staff for its core business activities and give them autonomy. It encouraged them to acquire the most up-to-date IT systems so that their performance would continue to be technically excellent. A small corporate group provided network services and company-wide support for office technology systems and also had a limited role in devising and maintaining corporate standards. The company was able to manage its IT growth easily because IT was so tightly aligned to the business.

In 1993, the stock market began to question whether ResourceCo was creating sufficient value from its projects, with the result that its share price dropped. Initially the company behaved as if it thought the market was making an ill-founded evaluation. By its own subsequent admission it was slow to respond.

During the time the company was trying to ride out its market difficulties, the accounting and finance department decided that ResourceCo should adopt a more disciplined and integrated approach to its commercial information processing because it was concerned that rapid growth had caused administrative systems to multiply in an unplanned and undisciplined fashion. It purchased a package solution from a software supplier for $A5 million. This package provided a range of accounting and commercial functions including a project management module that was supposed to control the company's major resource-development projects.

ResourceCo slowly came to recognize that it would have to act decisively to stop the damaging slide in its share price. In mid-1994, it made a strategic decision to reduce its risk exposure by using a joint-venture company to develop its primary asset rather than doing so itself. It modified its structure by disbanding its projects department. Because this excision did not halt the slide in the share price, in 1995 it refocused its strategy and redesigned its structure.

The period from mid-1993 on proved difficult for IT management within ResourceCo. The new commercial information system was implemented across the company but was not well received. One year after implementing the system, the company had to write down the book value of the system by half because of the problems encountered and because, with the projects department disbanded, the project management capability was now redundant. At the same time, although ResourceCo's corporate IT unit recognized the need to undertake an IT strategy exercise for the first time, this exercise did not get off the ground. While the company was deciding how to refocus and restructure, IT received no sustained management attention.

Analysis

Misalignment occurred at ResourceCo because the organization lost its fit. Internally, the organization remained in fit with its strategy, but externally this fit was no longer consonant with market expectations. Its strategy of providing technical excellence failed to deliver the returns on assets and equity expected by investors. For at least two years the company was struggling to come to terms with this problem. During that time IT experienced some serious difficulties; we regard these difficulties as pathologies arising from misalignment.

The write-down of the commercial-system investment resulted from misalignment. The commercial system was purchased with the expectation that the company's internal configuration would remain the same for the foreseeable future. But, in trying to rectify its external fit by forming a strategic alliance to develop its major asset, it made internal organizational changes that resulted in the project management part of this particular investment being rendered redundant. Misalignment therefore resulted in wasted investment.

The difficulties the company encountered with implementation may also be regarded as partly a result of misalignment. Once the company lost its original fit, it entered a period of uncertainty, turbulence, and change. This situation was not ideal for implementing a system that management expected to introduce new discipline. It is not surprising therefore that the company encountered more problems in implementation than were anticipated.

Misalignment also resulted in a lull in IT activity in the company. Senior management was far too absorbed with managing its external fit and then redesigning the organization in line with the new strategy to give time and attention to IT. The fact that management attention was distracted from IT was a clear indication that at ResourceCo IT had only been aligned to the business, not integral to it. When organizational fit weakened, IT was not considered integral to the business response.

Misalignment is important because it has damaging effects and because it is a common occurrence. It can be expensive and make management of IT difficult. Misalignment can be expected to occur because, contrary to common assumptions, alignment is not a one-time project; in fact once alignment has been achieved companies continue to move in and out of fit. This fragility of fit makes misalignment a likely prospect. Although in our example external fit changed, in other cases internal fit may change as the organization seeks to improve its performance. The link between the occurrence of misalignment and adverse outcomes is the lag between the occurrence of misfit and corrective organizational change. It is to be expected that during the relatively long periods involved in transformation, pathological outcomes will occur as a result of misalignment.

Stagnation

Stagnation occurs when IT is out of phase with the business. Stagnation is a pathological outcome of the dynamic nature of alignment. It occurs when IT finds itself unable to develop in a way that serves the business, and the business loses competitive position as a result. Stagnation is different from misalignment in that it can occur even when companies are in a relatively tight fit. We describe three different ways in which stagnation can occur: through cyclical effects, through deliberate policy, and as an unintended by-product of business decisions.

Banking in Hong Kong

In her studies of Hong Kong firms (described in Chapter Three) Burn observed a number of examples of cyclical stagnation in the banking industry. In that industry, IT is recognized as the driver for competitive advantage, but the role the technology now plays is such that new developments offer both threats and opportunities. Automatic teller machines (ATMs) changed the focus of the industry from branch-based transaction processing to centralized management of electronic transfers. Smartcards threaten even more far-reaching change because the user can perform accounting and auditing functions without recourse to traditional banking operations (Burn, 1996). Other innovations, such as electronic banking systems, allow home banking and office-based treasury management, while the Internet offers transactionless banking. New information technologies are thus a competitive necessity for today's banks.

But, while banks may aim to sustain their IT alignment to the business, the expense of introducing a new IT-based development often means that there is a delay after a major upgrade before reinvesting. A period of stabilization is appropriate while the organization settles down and the new technology becomes completely integrated. This period is essential because each cycle of innovation requires deep changes to the organization. However, this period is normally followed by competitive stagnation. This is part of the cycle of innovation and is typical of a highly competitive environment: IT drives a major change; IT throttles back on innovation to initiate a stabilizing period for the business; the business reinitiates change and finds IT stagnant, not prepared for a return to innovation. The stagnation period is normally short-lived. However, we have observed a number of cases in Hong Kong where it has become overextended and has damaged the bank's competitive position, in particular leaving it exposed to a takeover by more technologically sophisticated players.

USINC

Stagnation can be a deliberate part of a policy of alignment, as often occurs when IT is viewed as a necessary support or service provider. For example, one large and profitable international insurance company headquartered in the United States (USINC) had been an early developer of information systems. As these systems underpinned its worldwide operations, USINC maintained a large IT support group but found it difficult to retain IT staff. An expensive review by a consultant revealed that the technology and software used were so outdated that staff were not enthusiastic about working on IT support even though salaries were much higher than the industry standard.

USINC was afraid to upgrade its systems for two reasons. First, the cost would represent a large percentage of its operating budget for several years and so could seriously affect profits without guaranteed returns. Second, the existing systems did work, and it was not clear that new systems would. Thus, the corporation consciously endorsed a stagnation policy for IT despite its high level of dependence on the technology. The other downside risk was that the company was unprepared for major technologically driven changes in the market. If such changes developed, USINC would suffer severe damage to its market position because from a standing start it would take it so long to respond to the new competitive challenge.

TRADEP

A third type of stagnation occurs when IT's capability exceeds that of the business and yet IT is unable to lead the business into a better position. A large government trade department (TRADEP) is a case in point. TRADEP was run on traditional lines prior to 1991, and at best the IT systems could be described as simple, stand-alone support. Then TRADEP was entrusted with the implementation of electronic data interchange (EDI) throughout the trading community. The department made major efforts to transform itself for this task. After three years it had successfully implemented the EDI trading network. Unfortunately, TRADEP found that in its new form it could not operate effectively in the traditional government environment so it chose to revert to its previous organizational form structured on traditional functional lines. TRADEP was therefore left with excess IT capability. In effect IT was stagnant. A year later EDI was transferred to a newly created joint private and publicly funded consortium. TRADEP has now returned to the model of IT as a support tool and has a deliberate strategy of IT stagnation because after its prior traumas it has sought to protect itself from further power erosion through the risks associated with innovative IT initiatives.

Analysis

We can look at stagnation in terms of life cycles at either the industry or firm level. Figure 4.1 presents a typical industry life cycle with a number of transition points—standardization, maturity, and rejuvenation—that can each offer the opportunity for growth but also for a slide into stagnation. As we have seen in the banking and insurance examples, if firms are shooting for a particular goal, say a given competitive position, they may permit IT to stagnate once they have achieved their goal. However, if firms view themselves as simply moving to the next point in a life cycle, they are more likely to be aware of the need to retain IT capability.

An alternative perspective that we have found helpful for understanding stagnation at the level of the individual firm is illustrated in Figure 4.2. Business and IT dynamics are represented as independent axes. Alignment can be thought of statically as positions where business orientation and IT management are consistent. In this figure cells 1 and 3 represent aligned states of innovation and consolidation respectively, whereas cells 2 and 4 represent a lack of

Figure 4.1. Industry Life Cycle.

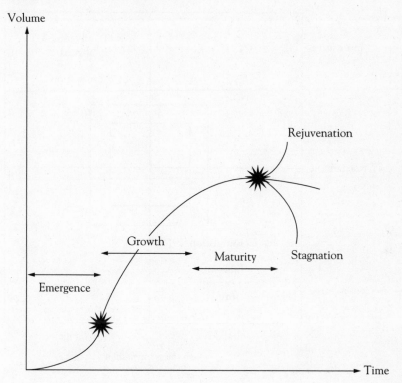

alignment between business and IT. However, in today's increasingly competitive environments alignment is dynamic and hence requires more than achieving a particular goal state. In practice achieving alignment is a matter of lead-lag (Chapter Three). Where IT leads, the dynamic will follow the clockwise direction in Figure 4.2, and where the business leads the direction will be counterclockwise. In other words, from an existing position of fit (cells 1 and 3), a first move by the business will be horizontal (counterclockwise), whereas a first move by IT will be vertical (clockwise). Both are naturally occurring cycles of innovation and consolidation. Stagnation can occur as firms cycle through stages of innovation and consolidation.

Figure 4.2. Cycles of IT-Business Alignment.

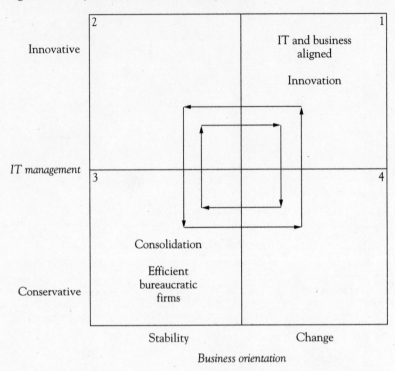

Business orientation

Our observations suggest that stagnation can occur in any of the cells except innovation (box 1). The three cases we have described illustrate stagnation in these cycles of IT-business alignment (Figure 4.3). Cell 1 does not risk stagnation because both IT and business are in an innovative, change-oriented phase in which the firm either is a market leader or is playing catch-up. IT is aligned with the business and delivers what the business needs. Unfortunately, within the dynamic conception of alignment, cell 1 cannot be a permanent state for most firms, not least because of the high cost involved (although see Chapter Eleven for Claudio Ciborra's account of what it might be like for a corporation to remain permanently in a state of IT and organizational innovation).

Figure 4.3. Stagnation in Cycles of IT-Business Alignment.

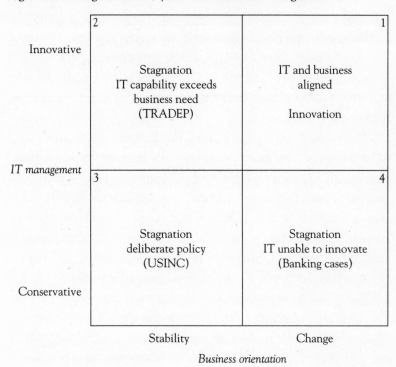

TRADEP illustrates stagnation in cell 2. In that case the organization, in taking on its EDI role, followed an IT-led strategy from cell 3 to 2 to 1. However, it rapidly found that it could not remain in cell 1 because its changed organizational form meant that it had now lost external fit and consequently could not satisfactorily conduct its traditional, mainstream business. It therefore made a business-led, organizational shift that took it back to cell 2, reflecting its desire to consolidate while IT was still in innovation mode. While TRADEP retained its EDI responsibility and capability and remained in cell 2, IT simply stagnated because its traditional organizational configuration did not allow it to make full use of its advanced IT capabilities.

USINC illustrates stagnation in cell 3. Normally, in this cell, IT and business are aligned, with both united in trying to consolidate. In moderately competitive industries we would expect competitive drivers to reassert themselves before too long and cause the business to move back toward change. USINC made a strategic decision to stay in cell 3, but it stayed too long and started to experience pathological consequences.

The Hong Kong banking examples illustrate stagnation in cell 4. In these cases the banks were typically moving from consolidation in cell 3 toward a fresh round of competitive innovations. If a firm moves swiftly through this cell, stagnation may be little more than a transitory state in a "natural" life cycle. If, however, the firm stays too long in cell 3, when it chooses to move ahead, it may struggle to move IT into a more innovative mode, and it may become trapped in cell 4 with adverse competitive effects.

The dynamics of alignment mean that organizations have no stable equilibrium state that they can aim for. Cells 1 and 3 have significant benefits, but it is not appropriate to stay too long in either. In cell 1 IT is employed effectively for competitive purposes but usually at a high cost. In cell 3 IT is employed efficiently, but over time fails to adapt to new competitive challenges. Cells 2 and 4 lack alignment, and as a result in them IT will fail to serve business purposes. In cell 2 bad technology decisions are likely as IT remains bullish compared with the business bears. In cell 4, poor business decisions may be made in ignorance of the difficulties of mobilizing IT. Firms would do better to avoid cells 2 and 4 altogether, but they cannot because of the lead-lag dynamics of alignment.

Global Complications

Globalization is both a product of IT capabilities and a driver for IT exploitation. This interrelationship suggests that IT management will be an important issue at the global level. The applicability of alignment to global organizations has not been much discussed. On the face of it globalization appears only to add another level to the corporation so that in principle alignment is feasible. However, initial indications are that new and different problems arise because of complications in the form of alignment conflict or alignment confusion, their most significant effect being to make alignment much harder to manage than in a nonglobal corporation.

Alignment conflict occurs most often when international growth has been achieved through a process of acquisition. Although individual subsidiaries may have had an effective alignment strategy, that strategy may be out of alignment with the overall global strategy. *Alignment confusion* is typically the result of expansion into less-developed markets; if the corporation's subsidiaries are at many different stages of IT growth, it is difficult if not impossible to standardize IT strategies.

Alignment Conflict

An example from banking illustrates global alignment conflicts. One of the top ten banks in the world (WBC) has identified globalization as its primary strategy for the future. Its business strategy document reveals it to be a multidomestic firm. In its own words it is "an international collection of domestic franchises. Our business is global—but for us, the local identity of the individual company member comes first." By contrast, the global IT strategy has a "philosophy to avoid complexity and random development, and to use common systems and operating processes." This combination of local business autonomy and global IT conformity implies a conflict in strategic alignment.

WBC has Asian, British, and American holdings. In Asia the focus has been on the development of global electronic-banking systems for access through personal computers. In the United Kingdom the fastest growing part of the business is personal telephone banking. In the United States, WBC has not yet entered either market. Some subsidiaries are focusing on ATM network expansion, whereas others are building up their branch networks. The development of

Smartcard is an additional complication, especially in conjunction with cyberbanking. Standard IT systems cannot support such diverse strategies, yet global standardization is WBC's IT strategy.

Alignment Confusion

Alignment confusion arises when there are different stages of growth within the same corporation. For some industries, such as the worldwide courier industry, the operating environment includes all parts of the globe. Corporations in these industries are obliged to accommodate different stages of IT maturity throughout the organization despite, as in the case of courier companies, being completely dependent on common standards because they cannot risk breakdown of communication at any point in the value chain. When a substantial part of the corporation's value addition derives from its global reach, global considerations will be critical regardless of local variation. It is therefore difficult to achieve alignment at the global level and hence to manage IT.

One solution may be that adopted by Acer Computer in its Vision 21/21: to have twenty-one of its subsidiaries or joint ventures publicly listed in the markets they serve by the twenty-first century. Vision 21/21 is part of the "global vision, local touch" philosophy of Acer's founder, who wants Acer to have businesses all over the world but to remain in the hands of local managers who share ownership with other domestic investors. These subsidiaries have full autonomy for developing IT in line with local requirements.

Analysis

In a study, Cheung and Burn (1994, 1995) found that global organizations align on structural issues for internal consistency rather than strategic issues for external consistency. Confusion occurs when there is low internal consistency in a global corporation with respect to the extent of data sharing, the extent of data standardization, and the stages of IT growth throughout the corporation. Two points are particularly worth mention. First, Cheung and Burn found internal consistency and hence the degree of alignment confusion to be contingent on the process by which expansion is conducted, whether by acquisition, which might introduce an incongruent IT organization, or by joint venture, in which the global corporation is able to exert more control over IT developments. Second, they found alignment affected by factors specific to individual nation-states, such as the stability of the countries in which the multinational corporation operated and the extent of government impositions on foreign ownerships. Companies operating in the People's Republic of China, for example, must be prepared to enter joint-venture partnerships in which China retains overall control. Given variable stages of IT development in China, this requirement is likely to complicate the alignment issues. The economic infrastructure, social and cultural values, organizational cultures, and personal readiness to accept IT all influence the efficacy of technology transfer and make global alignment a multicultural issue with many dimensions rather than the single dimension of business alignment. All the more reason then to expect alignment confusion in the global corporation.

Our purpose in this section has been to show that although in principle alignment at the global level might seem like alignment at the level of the firm, in reality major complications make managing IT through global alignment especially difficult. It must be said that issues related to global organizations are not well understood by researchers or practitioners, and it may be that much of the confusion arises because we are trying to apply outdated concepts in a radically different operating environment. Because the field is still very much at a learning stage in relation to global management, we have restricted ourselves to identifying some of the circumstances that make for global complications.

Source of Alignment Pathology

The pathologies we have described are a natural consequence of strategic alignment as a management policy and practice. Alignment is predicated on the assumption that IT should remain a separate function distinct from the business (Chapter One). Alignment describes a static design in which IT mirrors the strategies, structures, and processes of business. In theory, these arrangements ensure coordination of IT and business operations in stable environments. However, in most of today's highly competitive environments there is little business stability and much change. Unfortunately, alignment does not embody mechanisms to maintain business-IT coordination during change. Such coordination occurs only when IT is fully integrated with the business, as in the case of Flower and Samios, the architects described in Chapter Two. Where there is integration, business and IT move together (Figure 4.4). Where there is alignment, business and IT remain independent. As Chapter Three shows, during periods of change, organizations pursuing alignment try to maintain that alignment through the asynchronous dynamics of lead-lag. The independence of the two dynamics is compounded by the fact that IT often cannot reconfigure itself at the speed at which organizations change, so to some extent it must proceed alone, sometimes blazing a path ahead of the organization and at other times trailing behind. The types of pathology we have described have their origin deep in the very DNA of alignment, in its acceptance of a separation between IT and the business. Misalignment is a static consequence of this separation, whereas stagnation is a dynamic consequence, and global complications are a mixture.

Considered purely statically, alignment's major weakness is that it presumes that the business organization is in a tight fit and will remain that way. Once IT is aligned with an organization that is struggling to achieve or retain external and internal fit, it will be extremely difficult for IT managers to deliver value-adding service because the logic of how the business should be conducted will be confused and unclear to them. ResourceCo demonstrates how easy it is in such circumstances to make inappropriate decisions. WBC's experience of alignment conflict also exemplifies the static weak-

Figure 4.4. Innovation-Consolidation Cycle for an Integrated Firm.

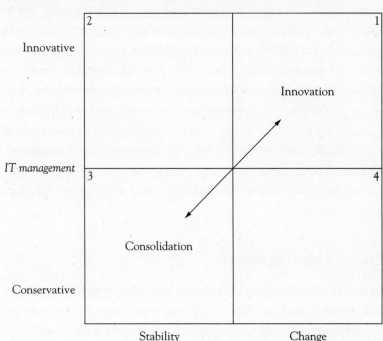

nesses of alignment. At the level of local divisions and business units it is almost impossible to achieve alignment because of the global IT strategy.

Considered dynamically, alignment's weakness is the independence in decision making of business and IT. In the banking cases, business controlled the cycle of innovation and consolidation but failed to appreciate that while it was consolidating, IT was losing more momentum than could easily be regained. USINC had a similar problem except that it chose for business reasons not to innovate. This decision created a spiral of stagnation for IT that not only resulted in loss of IT capability for innovation but also made it a struggle to service the consolidated business. At TRADEP, the business retreated from an IT-led innovation, leaving IT with a capability it could not use to benefit the organization. When it divested itself of its innovative IT capability, it returned to an aligned state, but its loss of momentum in the innovation cycle suggests that it will encounter USINC's problems. In all these cases, decisions were made independently of IT, leaving it partially stranded, unable to develop in ways that would advance its ability to provide business value. In the case of alignment confusion once again independent business decisions following from a growth by acquisition strategy result in the near impossibility of achieving a global alignment. There can be no guarantee that the next business acquisition, made for reasons independent of IT, will not throw an existing alignment into disarray.

Living with Alignment

In this chapter we have described some of the pitfalls or pathologies corporations face when they pursue a strategic-alignment policy for managing IT, and we have shown that these pathologies are a natural consequence of alignment as a management approach. In other words, strategic alignment cannot be cleverly rejigged to avoid the pitfalls, rather they are part of the bargain when you buy into strategic alignment. This is not to say that alignment should be avoided, but it does have a downside and it is better to be aware of the downside in advance than ignorant of it.

Alignment is a compromise. It hedges the different strategic bets represented by full business-IT integration and IT outsourcing (Chapter Two). We therefore confidently expect alignment to continue to be popular among many managers who do not wish to take the risk of implementing either of the more extreme options. For those corporations that choose to live with strategic alignment, our analysis of its pathologies permits us to make suggestions for minimizing the risks of misalignment and stagnation. (We do not make any suggestions about globalization other than to be awake to the dangers of alignment conflict and confusion.)

At present successful avoidance of pathologies depends on recognition of their possibility and understanding of their source. It is easy to see alignment as a relatively permanent state preceded by a process of coming into alignment. This view encourages us to think that once alignment has been achieved, the process is complete. In consequence we may not watch out for those changes that take organizations out of alignment. A lack of vigilance in this respect will prolong periods of misalignment and stagnation, and compound their pathological outcomes. Also, in order to remain ready for further changes, we should keep in mind that each shift within a company is only part of a larger cycle and that sooner or later it will be necessary to move on.

The separation between business and IT means that it will not be possible for IT to prevent misalignment. But both business and IT management need to recognize when misalignment occurs and seek to avoid the worst consequences for IT. The complexity of the situation militates against simple solutions. In the case of ResourceCo, had it been aware of the implications of misalignment, it might have chosen to hold off undertaking IT investments such as its commercial-system implementation; it would thereby have saved itself money and implementation problems. However, by acting cautiously, it would have risked causing IT stagnation. Either way there is a downside while the organization is in a poor fit. The priority therefore is to return it to a good fit as swiftly as possible.

The problem of stagnation occurs when a corporation stays too long in cells 2, 3, or 4 of Figure 4.3. Because corporations do not remain in cell 1 forever for business reasons, the task of managing the dynamics of alignment involves keeping both business and IT in a state of readiness to move forward so that when one leads, the other will not lag too far. Thus, even though in cell 3 the corporation is aligned and concentrating on consolidation, it will need to retain a degree of IT vitality or risk being stranded when organizational change is called for. The greater the lag between change and response, the greater the likelihood of adverse outcomes. Such lags are likely to be most pronounced when, despite alignment, IT and business managers remain relatively uninformed about the other's plans.

In the final analysis, alignment's weakness is that it does not guarantee effective interaction between business and IT management. Both groups of managers must exert a lot of effort to make alignment work. If IT is to be kept responsive and ready either to lead or to lag closely, it may be that running a larger number of smaller IT projects will be more appropriate than undertaking a single, grand-scale, strategic IT project that leaves the whole corporation so out of breath it is unable to make another move for a long time.

Summary

The main purpose of this chapter is to sound a warning that alignment by its very nature gives rise to pathologies that may not always be avoidable and that therefore require careful management if undesired business and IT costs are to be avoided. To summarize the major implications for managers:

- Aligning the business and IT strategies is not a guaranteed cure-all; it may cause as many problems as those it seeks to address.

- Misalignment and stagnation are the direct consequences of alignment strategies and are damaging to both business and IT development.

- Being aware that alignment is a dynamic process minimizes the possibility of incurring alignment pathologies.

- Loss of momentum in the innovation cycle should be avoided.

- Incipient pathologies need to be watched, and communication links between IT and the business need to be maintained.

- Instituting large numbers of small IT projects will maintain adaptiveness better than implementing large, one-time strategic projects.

- It may be impossible and completely undesirable to pursue alignment strategies in global corporations.

References

Burn, J. M. "Out'smart'ing the Competition with Information Technology— A Review of Smartcards in Asia." *International Journal of Information Management*, 1996, 16(4), 277–288.

Cheung, H. K., and Burn, J. M. "Distributing Global IS Resources in Multinational Companies—A Contingency Model." *Journal of Global Information Management*, 1994, 2(3), 14–27.

Cheung, H. K., and Burn, J. M. "Managing Distributed Information Systems Resources in a Globalised Environment." In *Proceedings of the Sixteenth International Conference on Information Systems*. Amsterdam, 1995, pp. 255–275.

Doty, D. H., Glick, W. H., and Huber, G. P. "Fit, Equifinality, and Organizational Effectiveness: A Test of Two Configurational Theories." *Academy of Management Journal*, 1993, 36(6), 1196–1250.

Henderson, J. C., and Venkatraman, N. "Strategic Alignment: A Model for Organizational Transformation Through Information Technology." In T. A. Kochan and M. Useem (eds.), *Transforming Organizations*. New York: Oxford University Press, 1992, pp. 97–117.

Miller, D. "Environmental Fit Versus Internal Fit." *Organization Science*, 1992, 3(2), 159–178.

Part II

Competencies for IT-Enabled Organizational Change

The two chapters in Part Two focus on competencies for managing IT-enabled organizational change. Chapter Five concentrates on the roles and skills necessary for IT professionals involved in organizational change. Chapter Six identifies organizationwide competencies.

Lynne Markus and Robert Benjamin (Chapter Five) primarily address IT professionals in advocating the adoption of change-management skills as a way of reducing the tensions between IT and line managers. Their analysis of the IT worldview and the possible ways in which IT professionals can make themselves increasingly relevant will be a revelation for many readers. Successful IT projects, they argue, usually involve the application of change-management skills, but IT professionals have been reluctant to acquire these skills. The reason, they suggest, is that IT professionals already see themselves as change agents because their worldview embraces a misplaced technological determinism.

The remedy, Markus and Benjamin suggest, is the acquisition of change-management competency through adoption of organizational-development skills and techniques. By adopting these skills IT professionals will make information systems more successful than they have been, they will reduce business clients' resentment by promoting reduced dependence on IT practitioners, and they will help clients make use of packaged and commodity technologies such as videoconferencing and the World Wide Web. The authors issue a call for the IT profession to change itself and for IT managers to lead the way. The new role for the IT profession should be to help the clients do what the clients need to do.

V. Sambamurthy and Robert Zmud start from a resource-based view of the firm (Chapter Six). This is a new economic and organizational paradigm that defines businesses by the collection of resources they comprise. In this paradigm resources are broadly interpreted to include sets of skills and competencies as well as tangible assets. The authors ask which firmwide IT-management competencies permit some companies to consistently take advantage of IT. In their extensive, two-stage study of U.S. companies they found twenty-nine distinct IT-management competencies, which they group into seven broad clusters. Only two of the clusters are specific to the IT function. The other five pertain to the general management of IT. Sambamurthy and Zmud show that the possession of these competencies is closely related to a firm's ability to take advantage of IT successfully. They have not stopped at identifying IT-management competencies but have also developed a self-assessment tool that enables firms to identify areas in which their IT-management competencies have been deficient and to undertake remedial initiatives.

Two themes emerge powerfully from Part Two. First, both chapters challenge the traditional view of IT as a discrete organizational element. Second, both attend to what it takes to transform organizations through IT rather than to specific, formal processes. Neither tries to spell out how to carry out successful change but rather concentrates on the necessary competencies.

5

IT-Enabled Organizational Change

New Developments for IT Specialists

M. Lynne Markus and Robert Benjamin

Change management is a perennial issue where information technology (IT) is concerned. Every few years, a new label appears to describe how IT is going to bring untold benefits to the organizations that deploy it: business systems planning, information resource management, Business Process Reengineering (BPR), and most recently organizational transformation have been the buzzwords of choice. The names change, we think, because the failure rates are so high. To sell the promises of IT people have to create a new fad in order to avoid being tarred with the old brush of failure. But, whatever one calls these promises, organizations now need, and will continue to need, to make significant changes in their processes and in their people's behavior in order to remain competitive in a rapidly changing world.

The pressures for continual organizational change involving IT are many. One source of pressure is of course the emergence of the world economy and the intense competition that started with the Japanese approach to lean production (Womack, Jones, and Roos, 1990), and that continues even today with an emerging "confrontation" style (Cooper, 1995). Another source of pressure is the cost-performance dynamics of IT itself, which extend the uses to which computing can profitably be put (Yates and Benjamin, 1991). Yet another is companies' increasing recognition of the benefits of being wired through the World Wide Web. Although we expect that the cost per unit of computing will continue to decrease sharply, we believe that organizations will face ever-increasing expenditures for IT-enabled change projects in all facets of their internal and external operations as they review and revise them to meet competitive pressures.

Collective experience with IT-enabled change under whatever faddish name tells us that although such change is becoming ever more common, it is not getting any easier. Much has been made of the high failure rates of BPR (Bashein, Markus, and Riley, 1994), but these rates are no higher than for any other type of technological innovation (Majchrzak, 1991). We expect the failure rates for future IT-enabled changes to remain equally high unless we can begin to learn as systematically about the process of making IT-enabled organizational change as we have about IT itself.

Consider BPR. There are many suggestions for how to make it succeed. Hammer and Stanton (1995) advise following the reengineering methodology carefully, anticipating resistance and dealing with it as it arises. Martinez (1995) tells us, as Rockart (1992) has done before, that although line managers should take a leadership role, they should do so in partnership with the IT function in their organization. Yet others tell us to go back to the basics of management development, participation, and creative tactics for changing entrenched mind-sets (Cooper and Markus, 1995).

It may be that BPR and newer IT-enabled fads contain some unique elements that warrant change management innovation. But, in our experience, the change management basics are neglected even in pedestrian IT projects (Benjamin and Levinson, 1993; Markus and Keil, 1994). Even when the IT part of the change is well understood, change often founders on the human aspects, such as:

- radical change in skills, jobs, and organizational control, requiring great attention to training and to the need for commitment by the key organizational stakeholders

- change reaching across functional and even organizational boundaries with consequent threats to culture, resources, authority, and power

- shifts in knowledge and power as people's roles and skills become embedded in data and knowledge bases

There is a mountain of research and prescription on the effective management of change in the general management, human resource (HR), and organizational-development (OD) literature. Little of this knowledge has worked its way into IT education and practice. At the same time, HR and OD practitioners are becoming increasingly inclined to insert themselves, sometimes aggressively, into what has been until now an all-IT preserve (see for example, Mumford and Weir, 1979; Gash and Kossek, 1990; Bancroft, 1992). Perhaps IT specialists should welcome this development. But it carries the threat that if IT specialists fail to acquire change management skills they face the same fate as was suffered by the organization and method experts who did industrial engineering for white-collar work but did not acquire computer systems analysis and programming skills in the 1960s and 1970s. With the development of ever more powerful and customizable packages and computer systems development environments, one can easily foresee a day when in-house IT analysts and programmers will not be needed to the extent they are currently, while the need for IT specialists with change management skills coupled with knowledge of technology and its capabilities will continue to increase.

We need to understand why IT specialists have not moved more quickly than they have to acquire change management competency and what can and should be done about this problem. Is this just a case of simple and temporary resistance to change? Is the solution just a matter of training? Or are there more fundamental conflicts of skills, values, and beliefs? To answer these questions we decided to compare the worldview of IT specialists with that of OD practitioners. Our findings surprised us.

We searched the literature on IT, OD, and organizational change, conducted interviews with IT specialists and OD practitioners, and compiled some new case studies of IT-enabled change. We found striking differences in what these professionals did and how they thought about being agents of organizational change. Below, we describe these two different perspectives. For each, we provide a summary of the worldview, discuss the organizational factors that might promote or inhibit behavior consistent with the worldview, and draw the implications for IT specialists. See Table 5.1 for a summary comparison. Finally, we discuss ways in which the IT discipline must change itself.

IT Worldview: Change Agent by Virtue of the Technological Imperative

We have often been struck by the number of times we have heard IT specialists refer to themselves as "change agents." "I've always thought of myself as an agent of change" is a fairly typical sentiment. But when we probed the meanings of these statements in in-depth interviews, we found that many IT specialists consider themselves change agents by virtue of their identification with the technology they create. In other words, many IT specialists believe in the technological imperative: technology creates change (Markus and Robey, 1988). Because IT specialists create change-producing technology, they believe they have no other responsibility for organizational change.

Despite widespread academic debates on technological determinism—the ability of technology (rather than people) to cause change—the belief that technology itself can make a big difference is widely held, both in academic and in practical circles. Silver (1990), for example, refers to "a computer-based system whose introduction into a decision-making environment *causes* change by intervening in the processes through which decisions are made" (emphasis added). The notion that technology is powerful underlies IT specialists' conviction that they do not have to do anything once the system is built (McWhinney, 1992); the system itself can be counted on to bring about change.

The IT worldview implies that the specific goals of technical change should be set by others, usually managers, not by the specialists themselves. In Block's useful characterization of the roles that consultants can play (1981), IT specialists act as "pairs of hands" for managers who decide what the technology should accomplish and as technical experts with respect to how these objectives should be realized with IT. (Block's third role for consultants, "collaborators," is more consistent with the OD role described below.)

An IT specialist might summarize the IT worldview as follows: "IT changes people and organizations by enabling them to do things they couldn't previously do and by constraining them to work in different ways than they worked in the past. I am an agent of *change* because I design and build the systems that enable and constrain people and organizations. My role is to design and build systems that will produce desirable change when they are used by people and organizations. I am also an *agent* of change because I do not set the goals. I do not determine what is a desirable organizational outcome. I act as an agent for the managers of the organization by building systems that, when used, will achieve their objectives. I am not responsible for setting the objectives or for achieving them, but only for providing the technological means by which managers and system users can achieve their objectives. I am an expert in technological matters, not in business matters or in the behavioral issues involved in the use of systems."

Table 5.1. Comparison of Two Worldviews on Change.

	IT View: *Technological Imperative*	OD View: *Facilitator of Others' Changes*
Summary	• Technology causes change • IT specialist has no change responsibilities beyond building technology • Specialist works as an agent of change by building technology that causes change; specialist is a technical expert • Specialist works as an agent of change by serving the objectives of others; specialist is the manager's pair of hands • Specialist does not hold self responsible for achieving change or improvements in organizational performance	• Clients make change using technology; technology alone does not • Facilitator promotes change by helping increase clients' capacity for change • Facilitator avoids exerting expert or other power over clients • Facilitator serves interests of all clients, not just funders and direct participants • Facilitator values clients' informed choice about conditions of facilitator's work; works to reduce client dependence on facilitator • Facilitator does not hold self responsible for change or improvements in organizational performance
Promoting factors	• IT is sole provider of services • Clients have limited technical and sourcing options • Low IT budget pressure exists • IT is centralized, responsible for many clients • IT is "staff" function, responsible and rewarded for expert/functional performance, not business performance • IT holds "control" role with delegated authority over certain processes, decisions, behaviors • IT builds systems	• Facilitator is not a member of client group • Facilitator's function lies outside the hierarchical chain of command • Facilitator is not formally responsible for business results, although some functional responsibility is inevitable

Inhibiting factors	• Decentralized IT • Outsourced IT • Purchased systems • Diversity of client technology and sourcing options • Strong IT budget pressure • New technologies demand different "implementation" activities	• Valuable expertise in technical or business matters • Formal responsibility for business or technical results • Staff control over clients' processes, decisions, behaviors • Concerns about locus of employment
Implications for IT work	• Widespread system failures for social reasons • Key systems success factors defined as outside IT role and influence • Technical organizational change blocked by IT • Low IT credibility • IT resistance to role change	• Increased attention to building user capacity might increase project success and IT credibility • Emphasis on client self-sufficiency would reduce client resentment and increase IT credibility • Many new ITs offer more scope to IT specialists who act as facilitators than to those who act as experts/builders

Promoting and Inhibiting Factors

The IT worldview is highly consistent with the ways in which IT work has historically been structured and managed in organizations. Internal IT shops have traditionally been sole providers of computing services, and clients have generally had a relatively limited range of options available to them (Friedman, 1989). Furthermore, IT specialists frequently worked in central IT departments. Because IT specialists were required to support many different organizational groups, they could not be expected to know all their clients well enough to help determine the goals of change. Consequently, they were limited to acting as pairs of hands (literally, agents) for their clients. This role, in turn, led the rest of the organization to perceive IT departments as "staff" units. As such, IT departments did not have line responsibility for key organizational results (for example, profitability). Instead, these groups were measured and rewarded on how well they achieved "functional-unit" goals, such as delivering usable systems on time and on budget. Over time, this reward system led to goal displacement—the cultivation of technical expertise and the substitution of functional goals for the organization's goals of improvement and performance.

Nevertheless, these structural arrangements have led to many technical successes: systems development and operations are now accomplished much more reliably than they were in the past. But these very successes have established a culture that makes the IT role hard to change. Furthermore, many systems specialists still continue to work under the structural conditions that promoted the traditional IT role.

However, the factors that underlie the traditional worldview are changing. Organizations are radically decentralizing or outsourcing their internal IT services. Many new information technologies—from groupware to the World Wide Web—are acquired more or less as packages, without in-house development other than user-supplied content. Users increasingly have considerable knowledge of IT and what it can do for their businesses. Where these factors have changed, the old IT worldview seems distinctly dated. By contrast, we studied a company that had recently decentralized its IT department, sending personnel to the business units. Both the CEO and the IT manager told us in no uncertain terms and in almost exactly the same words that "there are no systems projects here, only business projects." Similarly, we find that the most successful external IT consultants measure their success on their clients' success factors rather against traditional indicators such as system cost and schedule. Furthermore, their behavior on the job differs quite substantially from that of traditional IT specialists.

Implications

Although the traditional IT worldview has led to many technical successes, business systems failures abound. Decades of implementation research have provided substantial confirmation of a variety of social factors for the success of systems (compare Walton, 1989), but most of them have been defined as outside the traditional IT role (Markus and Keil, 1994). For instance, despite the large and growing IT academic literature on end-user training and learning (Gattiker and Larwood, 1990; Compeau, Olfman, Sein, and Webster, 1995), we have observed that most IT organizations consider training to be a relatively minor part of their mission (in terms of resources allocated to it). Some IT departments even outsource all systems training to human resource specialists and external vendors. Whatever the economic and practical rationales for these decisions, we believe they reflect deeply held beliefs about what constitutes IT work. By and large, the IT view is that building systems is IT work, while training users is not.

An excellent example of the crucial business factors that are defined as being outside the IT job can be seen in a research study of groupware implementation. Organizational culture and reward mechanisms inhibited consultants from sharing information on Lotus Notes databases, but IT implementors maintained a deliberate hands-off policy except for technical matters: "We're [the IT group is] a common carrier—we make no guarantees about data quality. As for the problem of obsolescence, if they [the users] don't know it by now it is not my job to tell them" (Orlikowski and Gash, 1994).

Another consequence of the traditional IT view of the role of change agents is that it can ironically inhibit desirable organizational change rather than promote it (Markus and Robey, 1995; Nance, 1995). This is perhaps one of our most surprising conclusions. We found, for example, that IT specialists occasionally try to block organizational changes desired by their clients and users in order to preserve their self-esteem as experts and to minimize disruptions in their own work routines. As technical experts, IT specialists are often stereotyped as being in love with technical change for its own sake. And many of the IT specialists we spoke to described their understandable pleasure in learning new technologies. But this interest in learning more about technology did not always mean that new technologies were made available to clients and users, even when they desired technological change. The reason appears to be that IT specialists feared that the new technology would damage their credibility and self-esteem. In part, this fear may stem from recognition that the critical factor for IT department success is maintaining reliable operations despite constant technological advances and user demands for change. A former chief information officer (CIO) at Du Pont recounted how he spent the first five years of his tenure achieving a highly reliable operation and the next five unsuccessfully trying to unleash an entrepreneurial, "help the business," culture.

The IT specialists we interviewed described feelings of vulnerability about new technology. They thought that unless they knew everything about the new technology, they would look bad when the users inevitably experienced problems. Furthermore, even when the problems with the new technologies were known and remediable, they often increased the workload and working hours of IT specialists. Some of those we talked to described a variety of tactics, ranging from persuasion through manipulation to enforcement of standards and controls, as ways of preventing their clients from undertaking technological change.

Perhaps the major consequence of the traditional IT approach to organizational change management is its contribution to eroding the credibility and self-confidence of internal IT specialists. Block (1981) has described how both the expert and the pair-of-hands roles can lead to damaged credibility and the failure of change projects. Little progress seems likely until a truly collaborative relationship develops between IT and the rest of the organization. But although many IT specialists call for such a relationship, they often expect it to occur without effort on their part. They want to be valued for what they do now, without recognizing that what they do now is contributing to the need for *them* to change. "It was easy for [IT professionals] to understand that the business had to change. . . . It was harder for them to understand that they had to change" (Moad, 1993, p. 28).

In short, the traditional IT worldview assumes that technology does all the work of change and allows IT specialists to focus narrowly on building technology in the service of business goals rather than more broadly on influencing social and technical success factors through the use of technology. The climate promoting this worldview is rapidly changing. It does not fit today's world of decentralization and outsourcing, changes like reengineering that cut across organizational functions, and new packaged information technologies that require different approaches to IT implementation. The worldview can be traced to a variety of negative circumstances, such as the failure of information systems to be used and to deliver organizational performance improvements, systems specialists who block rather than promote change, and the reduced credibility of IT specialists, which in turn reduces still further their ability to promote organizational change. In the next section, we describe an alternative view of the change agent that comes out of the literature and practice of OD.

OD Worldview: Change Agent as the Facilitator of Others' Efforts

The OD literature depicts the practitioner's perspective on organizational change something like this: "Organizational change is brought about by people (not technology). In order to make real and lasting change, people in organizations need to be able to make informed choices on the basis of valid information (about others' views, not just about the business issues), and they need to accept responsibility for their own behavior, including the success of the actions they take to create change. I am an agent of change because I help people create the conditions of informed choice, valid information, and personal responsibility. I have an obligation to increase people's capacity to create these conditions so that they do not become or remain dependent on my helping them to do so. I have expertise in various areas (such as group dynamics and the effects of rewards on human motivation), but my primary role is facilitating the process by which people work on content (the particular business issues facing a group, such as the need for an information system). When I act as a process facilitator, I must avoid acting as a content expert and should not express my views about the specific business issues at hand. In performing my role, I am aware that often, maybe always, different parties have different goals, objectives, and interests in change. Therefore, I must always serve the interests of the total client system (for example, the organization and its external stakeholders), even when these interests conflict with the interests of the particular managers who hired me as a consultant or with my own personal and professional interests."

The OD worldview is different in several important ways from the traditional IT worldview. First, it has a different perspective about the origin of change. OD practitioners believe that people (clients) create change, not themselves as change agents or their change "technology" (OD interventions, for example). Therefore, OD practitioners aim to increase the capacity and skills of people (other than themselves) to bring about change. Furthermore, OD practitioners believe that this increased capacity should extend to the domain of OD work, so that the professional services of OD specialists are not permanently required. (Analogously, an IT department might define its role as teaching clients and users how to select and build systems for themselves rather than doing system building and selection for them.) OD practitioners do, however, agree with traditional IT specialists in not accepting personal responsibility for whether change actually happens or performance actually improves. "So long as they act effectively, facilitators are not responsible for the group's ineffective behavior or its consequences" (Schwarz, 1994, p. 11). The client group or organization itself is believed to be responsible for results (Argyris, 1990).

Second, the OD worldview differs from that of IT specialists in its assessment of the value of expertise. OD practitioners view themselves as process experts (behavioral and group process, as distinguished from business process) not content experts (knowledgeable about the particular business or technical matters affected by a change). They are repeatedly warned to stay away from content expertise and recommendations (Schwarz, 1994):

> The facilitator should display no preference for any of the solutions the group considers—and should not have decision-making authority [p. 5].
>
> One risk [of the facilitator's providing content expertise] is that the group will begin to see the facilitator as a substantively non-neutral third party, which reduces the facilitator's credibility and, ultimately, effectiveness. A second risk is that the group will become more dependent on the facilitator. Group members may become sensitive to whether the facilitator approves of their decisions, which affects the decisions they make [p. 17].
>
> The facilitator as content expert or information resource is an acceptable role only when the facilitator and

group have explicitly contracted for it. Even when this
is the case, . . . the facilitator should act as information
resource or expert only when asked by the group, . . .
[and], before doing so, the facilitators always should
announce to the group that they are temporarily leaving
the role of facilitator to serve as an information resource
or expert. . . . When the information has been provided,
facilitators should announce that they are resuming the
role of facilitator. . . . Facilitators should limit their
expert role to factual information and should not indulge
in opinion [p. 17].

Third, OD specialists have an explicit awareness of power and
the dangers of using it. OD specialists' beliefs about the importance
of remaining substantively neutral and their highly developed tactics for "staying out of the content" reflect their belief that they have
power over their clients (compare Markus and Bjørn-Andersen,
1987), that they have personal and group interests that do not
always coincide with the interests of a particular client or the
"whole client system" (Schwarz, 1994), and that exercising even
legitimate expert power can be a disadvantage to some clients and
can undermine clients' abilities to be informed and responsible.

Promoting and Inhibiting Factors

OD specialists recognize that certain factors are necessary or at least
useful in maintaining their change-facilitation role. They believe
that to be effective they cannot be members, either as managers or
as ordinary members, of the groups for which they consult. Of
course, managers and members can successfully practice many OD
facilitation techniques, but formal membership in the client system
prevents a practitioner from acting as a neutral third party. In the
OD field, much attention is paid to the advantages of being an
external consultant and the difficulties of being an internal one.
Internal OD practitioners strive to deal with these difficulties by

removing themselves as far as possible from the formal chain of command, ideally divorced from the rest of the human resource function and reporting directly to the CEO or chair.

OD practitioners' aspirations to remove themselves from membership in the client system have interesting implications for sociotechnical change projects such as systems development and reengineering initiatives. These projects are widely recognized to require skilled facilitation in the OD sense. But, by definition, IT experts are members of these project teams and so cannot fill the formal role of facilitator. According to this view, non-IT people are required to serve in the facilitator role. (Thus, despite some obvious similarities, this view differs from IT-initiated approaches to "user-led design," which usually designate an IT specialist as a leader of the project team.) In addition, the project methodologies devised in the OD tradition differ considerably from those found in the traditional systems development life cycles or reengineering bibles.

The factors that support the OD worldview—outsider status and avoidance of power and authority, including expert status—conflict with the conditions under which most internal IT specialists operate. Thus, it would probably be quite difficult for IT specialists to change their role in the OD practitioner's direction. The key obstacles to changing the IT worldview appear to be the following:

Technical expertise. IT specialists have valuable technical expertise. The classic OD role does not give them a way to use it.

Responsibility for technical outcomes. IT specialists today are generally rewarded and punished for meeting IT departmental or project budgets, project schedules, and operations schedules. According to the OD worldview, these responsibilities can prevent the practitioner from acting in the best interests of the clients and thus may inhibit desired change. For instance, IT specialists may occasionally make or manipulate decisions that reduce IT departmental expenses while increasing the costs borne by users.

Authority for organizational control. Many IT departments have some organizationally delegated or mandated ability to control the behavior of their clients or to influence or override clients' decisions on technology issues, such as standards. As setters and enforcers of these rules and policies, IT specialists would be sending mixed messages if they tried, as OD practitioners try, to increase their clients' ability to make their own informed decisions.

Concerns about employment opportunities. The OD approach places a high value on increasing client self-sufficiency, reducing client dependence, and practitioners' working themselves out of a job. If diligently practiced, this approach would promote downsizing or outsourcing of IT departments. These potential outcomes conflict with the personal interests many internal IT specialists have in their continuing employment with a particular company.

Implications

Why might IT specialists benefit from moving in the direction of the OD worldview, despite the different conditions under which each type of professional typically works? The OD approach to change management directly accommodates several documented success factors that are currently considered outside the IT specialists' role (for example, user knowledge about and skill in using IT). Therefore, it seems likely that a change in the IT role would increase the chances of project success (Markus and Soh, 1993; Markus and Keil, 1994). Improved project success is, in turn, likely to increase the credibility of the internal IT function.

The OD worldview also places a high value on making clients self-sufficient or independent of practitioner interventions. Dependence breeds resentment, and resentment destroys working relationships and professional credibility. We believe that client dependence on IT specialists (whether it reflects a real lack of client skill or is an artifact of organizational policies) is a major factor in the poor credibility of many IT organizations and CIOs today. Steps toward improving client self-sufficiency might help turn this negative situation around.

A final advantage in movement toward the OD worldview is that many new information technologies provide greater opportunities for IT specialists who act as facilitators than for IT specialists who act as systems builders and technical experts. Interviews with IT specialists suggest that many new information technologies are not viewed as part of IT, including digital telephony and voice mail, videoconferencing, and the World Wide Web. Probing revealed that these technologies are often not seen as part of IT because they are "boxes"—that is, they provide minimal opportunities for building and development. Yet many of these "preprogrammed" new technologies, such as group support systems, require considerable facilitation skills for effective set-up and use. IT specialists who learn how to facilitate their clients' use of technology and their decisions about how best to use technologies such as automated call direction or mobile communications can provide a valuable service, even if this service does not employ traditional technical expertise. An improvisational model of IT-enabled change in this new technological world (Orlikowski and Hofman, 1995; see also Chapter Eleven) would benefit considerably from including IT specialists with strong facilitation skills.

In short, the OD worldview has some definite advantages. Therefore, it is worthwhile considering how to move toward it despite the many factors that inhibit change.

Changing the Role of IT Specialists

IT-enabled organizational change requires excellent change management skills. Without them, failure is nearly certain. Even with them, success will be hard-won. The question is Who needs these skills and how can they be acquired? Depending on whom you talk to, you get different answers. Most academic specialists in the management of organizational change argue that change cannot succeed unless line managers have change management skills. Schein (1988) points out that process consulting skills are as important for managerial jobs as for the consulting profession. We agree. But we also think that IT specialists often use this argument as a cop-out to avoid acquiring these skills themselves.

OD specialists know that line managers and workers make change happen, and OD specialists are there to help. Increasingly, they are facing up to the challenge of IT-enabled change, and they are re-skilling themselves and developing new methodologies for information systems development, reengineering, and IT-enabled organizational transformation. (We believe that these new approaches by OD practitioners will probably remain useful in large IT projects, where IT specialists work in teams with OD practitioners and line managers. But we also believe that in many small-scale IT projects, especially those involving emerging technologies, such as the Web and new communication tools, IT specialists will be severely handicapped if they themselves do not acquire OD skills and methods.)

By and large, the IT specialists we know already think they have all the change management skills they need to do their job. (After all, they build technology.) They do not see collaborative facilitation, in the OD sense, as their job. If their credibility is low, their first instincts for improving it are to focus on their technical expertise and performance, even though these parts of their job are not what their clients value most (Bashein, 1995). Failing that, they tend to blame their clients and users for not understanding them or appreciating their technical contributions.

This, we conclude, is a losing game plan. If reengineering has taught us anything, it is that functional specialization leads to problems in end-to-end process performance. This lesson applies to operational work and equally to "staff" work, such as the work of IT specialists and OD specialists, among others. Both these groups are involved in the business process that might be called "organizational improvement" or "organizational innovation" (Markus and Keil,

1994). A winning approach for professionals who now focus narrowly on only part of this process (and who in doing so may actually hurt total process performance) is to become partners with other specialists—for example, by cross-training. We see OD practitioners starting to make this effort, but we do not see comparable efforts on the part of IT.

Corporate executives are starting to realize that organizational improvement is a cross-specialist process. In several companies the IT function has been deliberately mingled with other formerly separate functions like HR or Quality and ordered to coordinate their efforts. It may take powerful, external interventions like this to make many IT units see the light, but we hope this is not the case everywhere. If current trends continue, in-house IT as we have known it since the 1960s may be a thing of the past. More and more organizations will rely on outside firms for packages and services in lieu of in-house specialists. Even if all of what is currently done under the label of in-house information services were to go away, much work related to IT-enabled change would inevitably remain within the organization. If IT specialists do not acquire change management skills, they are putting their careers at great risk because the technology competency of users, line managers, and OD specialists with change management skills continues to increase.

We hope that IT specialists will be motivated to acquire the change management skills we see as essential to future in-house IT-related work. To that end, we now review the options available to promote change in IT practice.

Applying Change Principles to Facilitate IT Change

The sort of change we are advocating is deep cultural change. It will itself require good change management to be successful. We believe that corporate and line executives can play a helpful role. But cultural change in the in-house IT function will be fastest and most thorough if IT executives (1) embrace the need for change, (2) formulate and communicate a clear vision of the needed change, and (3) assume all the responsibilities that line managers (as opposed to staff professionals) are supposed to assume in change efforts (compare Kotter, 1995) because IT executives *are* the line managers of IT specialists.

In other words, IT managers must become effective advocates for change in IT specialists' attitudes and behaviors. Effective change advocates, often referred to as change champions (Benjamin and Levinson, 1993), must understand where they want to take their organizations, must possess sufficient personal authority (through influence over appointments and resource allocations) to manage conflict, and must be willing to exercise the power at their disposal, whether through compensation, recognition, or other rewards.

Culture evolves from successful experiences (Schein, 1992). When external realities change dramatically, as we believe is happening in IT, culture must change too, however painfully, because future performance and survival are at stake. IT executives and the specialists they manage must move away from the technological imperative; they must see their job as facilitating clients' acquisition of IT knowledge and skill, not just their acquisition of technology. They need to recognize that an IT system is successful only if it improves organizational performance. Because such improvement in turn requires clients who are committed to change, have the skills to use IT in ways consistent with the desired change, and have technology that is well aligned with their goals (Walton, 1989), IT specialists must help their clients acquire IT skills, become committed to change, and align technology to their goals. We cannot emphasize enough how great is the needed cultural change among IT specialists—from providing technology to helping clients make the technology useful and value-producing. The first step in this cultural change is for IT executives to recognize the existing IT worldview for what it is and the negative consequences of taking this old mind-set into the new IT world.

Acquiring New Behavioral Skills

The next step is to communicate the need and to develop new behavioral skills among rank-and-file IT specialists. This step will be a major challenge because academic institutions have been remiss in developing "soft skills" courses and other training materials for IT specialists. (For an idea of what is needed, see Buchanan and Boddy, 1992, and Boddy and Buchanan, 1992.) A hopeful sign is a new master's program in management information systems at the Wetherhead School at Case Western Reserve University, which specifically focuses on the change issues discussed in this chapter.

But even without training materials it is possible to create good learning environments without major investments. Recently, one of us had the opportunity to conduct a workshop on professional credibility for a group of high-level staff executives from a variety of disciplines (accounting, HR, IT) in different firms. The participants had many common concerns. They welcomed the opportunity to discuss productively (not just to gripe about!) the credibility crunches they faced on their jobs and to role-play effective strategies for dealing with them. This experience led us to believe that the same approach would be useful for training programs for in-house IT specialists (either with or without the participation of related staff from HR and OD). An example of the difficult credibility crunches IT specialists run into is how to convince autonomous clients to collaborate on issues of IT infrastructure, which, because it is a common good, no one division or unit has an interest in supporting or paying for. (More examples are shown in Table 5.2.) Training of this sort would provide immediately relevant job skills as well as socializing participants into the OD worldview and skill set.

Rethinking Advocacy Strategies

The example of the IT infrastructure brings us back to the topic of advocacy. Change advocacy is a distinct approach to change management.

Table 5.2. Credibility Crunches in IT Work and When They Occur.

Occurring When . . .	Credibility Crunches
Generally	• How to deal with stakeholders having different needs and wants for the same solution, particularly when there are power differences among them • How to explain to clients that their projects are going to be late or reduced in scope • How to convince clients to try a new approach when there is technical risk • How to explain repeated changes or instability in operations • How to deal with clients who have had bad experiences with the IT group in the past • How to deal with clients who have strong, and wrong, opinions about technical matters or the resources required to do the job • How to deal with clients who are angry about poor technical performance or poor customer service from internal providers
Services are *centralized*—that is, the same internal specialist serves several different clients	• How to explain to clients why their work does not receive the requested schedule or budget priority • How to deal with clients who are angry about project schedules or scope
Services are *decentralized* and/or clients have broad discretion in choosing providers and solutions	• How to convince autonomous clients to collaborate on IT infrastructure and other matters of "public good" • How to fix a project that has gone bad with a different provider • How to deal with clients who are angry that internal providers did not prevent them from making a bad decision about an external provider

Providers' services are *charged back to* clients	• How to deal with clients who are angry about the size of their bill • How to convince clients to spend more to get a better solution
The internal specialist group is the *sole source* of services by company policy—that is, IT controls external sourcing	• How to deal with clients who disagree with providers about the preferred solution • How to deal with clients who are resentful because of their lack of choice
The internal specialist group exerts organizational *control*—for example, approves or denies requests for services, prioritizes requests for services, maintains and enforces standards of compatibility and integration	• How to deal with clients who disagree with providers about the nature of the preferred solution • How to deal with clients who may be severely disadvantaged by implementation of the providers' preferred solution but do not know it • How to deal with clients who resent provider checks on their autonomy • How to deal with clients who are politicking to limit providers' control role

The topic deserves more attention than we can give here. IT specialists, and especially IT executives, often view the advocacy or promotion of technology and technological solutions to organizational problems as an important part of their role. Ironically, this role often gets IT executives into trouble. Advocates are generally tolerated as long as they do not venture outside their sphere of influence. But the boundaries of influence are often breached in major change efforts. Senior line executives discover this to their sorrow when the changes they advocate involve business partners with different motivations or cultural outlooks. IT specialists see technology as their domain, but many line managers see technology as inseparable from the units they lead (or at least from their units' budgets). Thus, technology advocacy is shaky ground for the in-house IT function in general.

Technology advocacy is particularly difficult for IT specialists in the area of IT infrastructure and common business process infrastructure, such as worldwide logistics. When there is no strong line advocate for corporate infrastructure enhancement, IT executives often step into the breach because they do not know what else to do. But we find the results of this strategy are almost always bad (for the IT executive). Often, these CIOs are dismissed even before their proposed development programs are funded or run into financial and scheduling problems. These results lead to the following conclusion. The lack of a good corporate IT infrastructure often reflects entrenched problems that organizational members do not want to solve. Line managers in many organizations do not want to collaborate in improving the business; they want to continue to do business without interference from other functions and staff groups just as they are now. Consequently, the proposed IT infrastructure is a solution to the wrong problem. The problem is not lack of the means of collaboration but the lack of will to collaborate. (Even when people say they cannot work together because they lack an infrastructure, this is just an excuse. They know that the infrastructure project involves delay and is likely to fail, so it is a safe change to approve. If the infrastructure should actually be built some years down the road, these people will find another excuse to delay making difficult personal and organizational changes.)

At heart, many line executives know that lack of will is the problem. Thus, rather than exposing themselves to the possibility of failure down the road, they do not take the journey today. In this context, CIOs are expendable. And as long as CIOs continue to advocate technological solutions to organizational problems, they will be expended, unless they find CEOs who also want to believe in the technological imperative.

The OD perspective and strategies offer a potential way out of this box. From the OD perspective, the task of the CIO with respect to IT infrastructure is to convince line managers that they have organizational problems that they need to solve. Technology is one piece of the solution, but technology alone is useless without the commitment of line managers to do what the technology makes possible. Thus, the CIO's focus becomes helping line managers to recognize organizational problems, to seek and obtain valid information about the problem and its solutions, and to take responsibility for solving the problem. The savvy CIO stays away from technological advocacy.

We believe that IT executives are well positioned (if not currently well skilled) to adopt this alternative advocacy role. In many organizations, as Drucker (1995) notes, the IT function, like finance, has a unique view of organizational performance. By identifying and communicating opportunities for performance improvements, clarifying the technological and nontechnological methods for performance improvement (Markus and Keil, 1994), and making clear the benefits and risks of these methods, IT specialists can move toward the OD ideal of enabling their clients to take full responsibility for making informed choices with valid information. To the extent that IT specialists do so, their clients are likely to make good IT-related decisions and to acknowledge that they themselves have done so, rather than placing the blame on the IT experts who did it to them once again.

Summary

In conclusion, we are recommending significant change in the ways IT specialists approach organizational change. We believe that the change we advocate has numerous potential benefits (that far outweigh the risks) both to the community of IT specialists and to the organizations they serve. First, change in the IT approach to creating organizational change will reduce tensions between the IT function and clients and users. Second, such change will facilitate the willingness of IT specialists to acquire new technical (as well as behavioral) skills in areas not now regarded as mainstream IT (for example, the Web and group support) where traditional systems development methodologies are not needed or useful. Third, the IT function will come to be seen as a credible and valuable organizational player because of its contributions to organizational performance, not simply to the development or acquisition of IT.

References

Argyris, C. *Overcoming Organizational Defenses: Facilitating Organizational Learning*. Englewood Cliffs, N.J.: Prentice-Hall, 1990.

Bancroft, N. H. *New Partnerships for Managing Technological Change*. New York: Wiley, 1992.

Bashein, B. J. "Reengineering the Credibility of Information Systems Specialists." Unpublished doctoral dissertation, Claremont Graduate School, 1995.

Bashein, B. J., Markus, M. L., and Riley, P. "Business Reengineering: Preconditions for BPR Success, and How to Prevent Failure." *Information Systems Management*, 1994, 11(2), 7–13.

Benjamin, R. I., and Levinson, E. "A Framework for Managing IT-Enabled Change." *Sloan Management Review*, summer 1993, 23–33.

Block, P. *Flawless Consulting: A Guide to Getting Your Expertise Used*. San Francisco: Pfeiffer, 1981.

Boddy, D., and Buchanan, D. *Take the Lead: Interpersonal Skills for Project Managers*. Englewood Cliffs, N.J.: Prentice-Hall, 1992.

Buchanan, D., and Boddy, D. *The Expertise of the Change Agent: Public Performance and Backstage Activity*. Englewood Cliffs, N.J.: Prentice-Hall, 1992.

Compeau, D., Olfman, L., Sein, M., and Webster, J. "End-User Training and Learning." *Communications of the ACM*, 1995, 38(7), 24–26.

Cooper, R. *When Lean Enterprises Collide*. Boston: Harvard Business School Press, 1995.

Cooper, R., and Markus, M. L. "Human Reengineering." *Sloan Management Review*, summer 1995, 39–50.

Drucker, P. F. *Managing in a Time of Great Change*. New York: Truman Talley Books, 1995.

Friedman, A. L. *Computer Systems Development: History, Organization and Implementation*. Chichester, U.K.: Wiley, 1989.

Gash, D. C., and Kossek, E. E. "Understanding End-User Training as a Lever in Organizational Strategy and Change." In U. E. Gattiker and L. Larwood (eds.), *End-User Training*. Berlin: Walter de Gruyter, 1990, pp. 227–254.

Gattiker, U. E., and Larwood, L. (eds.). *End-User Training*. Berlin: Walter de Gruyter, 1990.

Hammer, M., and Stanton, S. A. *The Reengineering Revolution: A Handbook*. New York: Harper Business, 1995.

Kotter, J. P. "Leading Change: Why Transformation Efforts Fail." *Harvard Business Review*, March-April 1995, pp. 59–67.

Majchrzak, A. "Management of Technological and Organizational Change." In G. Salvendy (ed.), *Handbook of Industrial Engineering*. (2nd ed.) New York: Wiley, 1991.

Markus, M. L., and Bjørn-Andersen, N. "Power over Users: Its Exercise by System Professionals." *Communications of the ACM*, 1987, 30(6), 498–504.

Markus, M. L., and Keil, M. "If We Build It They Will Come: Designing Information Systems That Users Want to Use." *Sloan Management Review*, summer 1994, 11–25.

Markus, M. L., and Robey, D. "Information Technology and Organizational Change: Causal Structure in Theory and Research." *Management Science*, 1988, 34(5), 583–598.

Markus, M. L., and Robey, D. "Business Process Reengineering and the Role of the Information Systems Professional." In V. Grover and W. Kettinger (eds.), *Business Process Reengineering: A Strategic Approach*. Middletown, Pa.: Idea Group Publishing, 1995.

Markus, M. L., and Soh, C. "Banking on Information Technology: Converting IT Spending into Firm Performance." In R. D. Banker, R. J. Kauffman, and M. A. Mahmood (eds.), *Perspectives on the Strategic and Economic Value of Information Technology Investment*. Middletown, Pa.: Idea Group Publishing, 1993.

Martinez, E. V. "Successful Reengineering Demands IS/Business Partnerships." *Sloan Management Review*, 1995, 36(4), 51–60.

McWhinney, W. *Paths of Change: Strategic Choices for Organizations and Society.* Thousand Oaks, Calif.: Sage, 1992.

Moad, J. "Does Reengineering Really Work?" *Datamation*, August 1, 1993, 22–28.

Mumford, E., and Weir, M. *Computer Systems in Work Design—The ETHICS Method.* New York: Wiley, 1979.

Nance, W. D. "The Roles of Information Technology and the Information Systems Group in Organizational Change." Working paper, San Jose State University of California, 1995.

Orlikowski, W. J., and Gash, D. C. "Technological Frames: Making Sense of Information Technology in Organizations." ACM *Transactions on Information Systems*, 1994, 12(2), 174–207.

Orlikowski, W. J., and Hofman, J. D. "Realizing the Potential of Groupware Technologies: An Improvisational Strategy for Change Management." Working Paper 287, Center for Information Systems Research (MIT), Cambridge, Mass., 1995.

Rockart, J. F. "The Line Takes the Leadership—IS Management in a Wired Society." *Sloan Management Review*, 1992, 33(4), 47–54.

Schein, E. H. *Process Consultation: Its Role in Organizational Development.* (2nd ed.) Reading, Mass.: Addison-Wesley, 1988.

Schein, E. H. *Organizational Culture and Leadership.* (2nd ed.) San Francisco: Jossey-Bass, 1992.

Schwarz, R. M. *The Skilled Facilitator: Practical Wisdom for Developing Effective Groups.* San Francisco: Jossey-Bass, 1994.

Silver, M. S. "Decision Support Systems: Directed and Nondirected Change." *Information Systems Research*, 1990, 1(1), 47–70.

Walton, R. E. *Up and Running: Integrating Information Technology and the Organization.* Boston: Harvard Business School Press, 1989.

Womack, J. P., Jones, D. T., and Roos, D. *The Machine That Changed the World: The Story of Lean Production.* New York: Harper Perennial, 1990.

Yates, J., and Benjamin, R. I. "The Past and Present as a Window on the Future." In M. S. Scott Morton (ed.), *The Corporation of the 1990's: Information Technology and Organizational Transformation.* New York: Oxford University Press, 1991.

6

At the Heart of Success

Organizationwide Management Competencies

V. Sambamurthy and Robert W. Zmud

The potential of information technologies (IT) to provide business value, sustain competitive advantage, and enable novel and adaptive organizational forms has been well recognized by practitioners and academicians (Venkatraman, 1991; Rockart and Short, 1989, 1991). However, not all firms succeed equally in exploiting new, or even mature, IT within their business strategies and managerial and operational work processes. This observation is particularly apt with respect to transformational IT applications: "Surprisingly, few firms have broken the mold of history and transformed their industries with a new dominant design for information processing. . . . The difficulty of truly innovating with information technology accounts for the small number of vivid successes. Most firms simply automate, eliminating clerical tasks but requiring only modest process adjustments. To innovate with IT involves changing an organization's information processing infrastructure" (McKenney, Copeland, and Mason, 1995, p. 1).

Why do relatively few firms exhibit consistent success in infusing IT into their work processes and business strategies? Mata, Fuerst, and Barney (1995) argue that a firm's sole IT-related, sustainable, competitive advantage lies with the development of IT management skills—that is, internal-to-the-firm capabilities for conceiving, developing, and exploiting IT in support and enhancement of business strategies and work processes. Similarly, Sambamurthy and Zmud (1992, p. 1) concluded that a "key factor distinguishing those firms able to profit continuously from their IT investments is their managers' ability to direct the many and varied activities involved with the successful application of IT." In our experience the most valued IT management skills tend to require lengthy development periods as they are heavily dependent on local—for example, organization-specific—knowledge. We have also found that not all firms are equally endowed with the most valued IT management skills. Furthermore, in order to be effectively applied, a firm's IT management skills must be intricately woven into the complex milieu of an organization's structures, roles, processes, culture, and the many relationships among a firm's business and IT managers.

If one accepts the importance of IT management skills to a firm's capability of applying IT in an effective, efficient, and timely manner, then firms must focus their attention to a considerable extent on ensuring that appropriate IT management skills exist and are continually enhanced. But what exactly are these critical skills?

Since the early 1980s, a stream of research on the management of information systems has attempted to identify key skills (Martin, 1982; Rockart, 1982; Guimaraes, 1984; Henderson, 1990; Saunders and Jones, 1992). Skills that have surfaced in these research efforts include: development of reliable, timely, and cost-effective applications; management of reliable and responsive data-processing operations; appropriate management of human resources in IT; integration of long-range and tactical business and IT planning processes; ability of senior management to value IT activities and initiatives; and harmonious and trustful relationships among business and IT managers. This important research has, among other outcomes, sensitized IT professionals (both practitioners and academics) to the broad range of technical, managerial, and political skills required in order to plan, acquire, develop, implement, operate, and control IT business applications.

All too often, however, these studies have been conducted with an organizational view that accords the corporate IT group a monopoly position with regard to IT management. Today, however, most organizations reflect a different view of IT management: the networked organization paradigm (Tapscott and Caston, 1993), where the authority and responsibilities for IT management are no longer concentrated within the corporate IT group. Rather, this authority and these responsibilities have been dispersed among a wide variety of stakeholders, including corporate IT, divisional IT, business line management, senior management, and even external partners, such as vendors, consultants, systems integrators, and third-party developers. Variations in industry, business, and organizational factors may influence the extent to which these individual actors are influential in the IT decisions of firms (Brown and Magill, 1994; Sambamurthy and Zmud, 1996a). In such a dispersed managerial context, there is a great need for understanding the IT management skills that contribute to sustained IT-based innovation.

This chapter identifies a set of IT management competencies for this networked mode. IT management is viewed as an enterprise-wide activity, characterized by a collection of IT-related activities emerging from and orchestrated by internal actors and external partners located across all of an organization's management levels and work (line and staff) units. Furthermore, a firm's IT management competencies are defined as the fundamental capabilities, skills, and tacit know-how that an organization develops over time to acquire, deploy, and leverage its investments effectively in pursuit of business strategies and in support of business activities.

The next section provides an explanation of the crucial role of these competencies in understanding effective, contemporary IT management practice. Then, distinct types of competencies are identified and described, along with evidence from our research projects that these competencies do indeed make a difference in a firm's success in applying IT. Finally, the chapter concludes by discussing different ways in which practitioners and researchers can make use of our ideas about IT management competencies.

The Role of IT Management Competencies

Contemporary thinking about the competitiveness of firms and about a firm's ability to sustain superior performance is perhaps best captured within the resource-based theory of the firm. Here, highly competitive firms are seen to consist of bundles of costly-to-imitate attributes; and these attributes are regarded as the fundamental drivers of the firms' economic performance (Penrose, 1995; Collis and Montgomery, 1995; Shrivastava, Huff, and Dutton, 1994). Such a view accords fundamental importance to the role of competencies, which it defines as the unique skills and knowledge that a firm possesses and that its rivals find difficult to imitate and replicate. Furthermore, product-market strategies are viewed as a reflection of a firm's maneuverings to enable its most valued competencies to exploit market opportunities and thus influence, perhaps even determine, the competitive terrain of the product market. Although competitive responses can occur in the form of imitation of specific product-market strategies, competencies confer on a firm the agility and flexibility to transform "industry recipes" continually (Spender, 1989) and to sustain a competitive edge. As Claudio Ciborra illustrates in Chapter Eleven through his ideas about a platform organization, competencies not only enable current market strategies but also are the basis for future strategies that the firm can evolve.

A similar logic undergirds the concept of IT management competencies as the fundamental basis for shaping IT management practice in firms. Figure 6.1 suggests that internal IT organizations are in the "business" of enabling business value by having an impact on important organizational competencies. IT enhances firms' competencies by transforming its business processes, enriching its organizational intelligence, enabling dynamic organizational structures, and supporting the delivery of new and improved products and services.

An examination of the manner in which the World Wide Web is affecting firm's competencies is a good case in point (Cronin, 1996).

Furthermore, as illustrated in Figure 6.1, a firm's internal IT activities depend on the creation and deployment of IT management roles and processes to convert IT "raw materials" into desirable IT outcomes. Some examples of roles and processes are systems acquisition and development, strategic planning, and data-center operations. Such IT management roles and processes fuse together data, IT artifacts, knowledge of the IT artifacts and business, and business threats and opportunities to allow IT to have an impact on the fundamental competencies of the firm. However, like product-market strategies, specific IT management roles and processes have a limited shelf life. For example, most internal IT organizations have evolved, experimented with, and used a variety of strategies for systems development (traditional systems-development life cycle, prototyping, object-oriented), strategic planning (top-down, bottom-up, inside-out), and user partnering (integrator roles, steering committees, service-level agreements) over time.

We believe that although organizations may change their IT management roles, structures, and processes in response to situation-specific exigencies (business changes, industry changes, reorganizations, process reengineering, outsourcing), their IT management competencies are relatively stable and, hence, represent the extent to which firms are poised to mobilize their IT assets and investments in effectively carrying out their business strategies. Thus, IT management competencies are the fundamental enabler of the nature of the "IT business" within an organization: they reflect the cumulative knowledge, experience, and skills developed by the firm to convert IT "raw materials" into valued IT outcomes. But, even more important, such a focus imbibes the "platform organization" thinking that Ciborra in Chapter Eleven portrays as a hallmark of future organizations: with appropriate competencies in a high state of development, a firm no longer considers strategic alignment as an overriding goal. As Janice Burn illustrates in Chapter Three, IT

Figure 6.1. Role of IT Management Competencies.

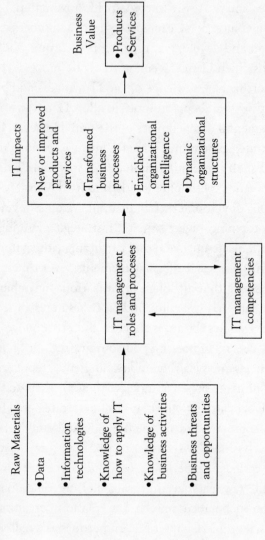

management competencies should enable a firm to produce both IT-lead and IT-lag business activities and strategies.

Finally, the ability to identify IT management competencies permits us to assess an organization's current ability to exploit IT for business advantage and to chart roadways for developing them further.

IT Management Competencies

The ideas about IT management competencies presented in this chapter are the product of a four-year program of research involving Delphi studies, questionnaire surveys, and case studies. Full details are available in Sambamurthy and Zmud (1992, 1994). Exhibit 6.1 describes the seven categories of IT management competencies that emerged from our research program. These competency categories reflect an enterprise perspective in that they span a wide variety of business-related and IT-infrastructure activities.

Business deployment refers to the capabilities involved in (1) enabling managers across an organization to envision the potential business value of existing and new IT and to recognize the benefits from working in multidisciplinary groups to fuse IT tightly to business processes, (2) devising policies and measurement systems to focus the IT-related efforts of organizational members, and (3) developing procedures and programs to facilitate both the acquisition of IT resources and their diffusion across the organization. The nine competencies that constitute business deployment relate to the creation and maintenance of organizational routines that enable individuals to envision new business applications of IT and rapidly transfer promising ideas and applications throughout the enterprise. These competencies are consistent with research findings that organizational routines, structures, and processes are key sources of innovation (Nelson and Winter, 1982).

External networks refers to an organization's capabilities in developing value-added partnerships with customers and suppliers and

Exhibit 6.1. IT Management Competencies.

Business Deployment
- Examination of the potential business value of new, emerging IT
- Utilization of multidisciplinary teams throughout the organization
- Effective working relationships among line managers and IT staff
- Technology transfer, where appropriate, of successful IT applications, platforms, and services
- Adequacy of IT-related knowledge of line managers throughout the organization
- Visualizing the value of IT investments throughout the organization
- Appropriateness of IT policies
- Appropriateness of IT sourcing decisions
- Effectiveness of IT measurement systems

External Networks
- Existence of electronic links with the organization's customers
- Existence of electronic links with the organization's suppliers
- Collaborative alliances with external partners (vendors, systems integrators, competitors) to develop IT-based products and processes

Line Technology Leadership
- Line managers' ownership of IT projects within their domains of business responsibility
- Propensity of employees throughout the organization to serve as "project champions"

Process Adaptiveness
- Propensity of employees throughout the organization to learn about and subsequently explore the functionality of installed IT tools and applications
- Restructuring of business processes, where appropriate, throughout the organization
- Visualizing organizational activities throughout the organization

IT Planning
- Integration of business strategic planning and IT strategic planning
- Clarity of vision regarding how IT contributes to business value
- Effectiveness of IT planning throughout the organization
- Effectiveness of project management practices

IT Infrastructure
- Restructuring of IT work processes, where appropriate
- Appropriateness of data architecture

Exhibit 6.1. IT Management Competencies, cont'd.

- Appropriateness of network architecture
- Knowledge of and adequacy of the organization's IT skill base
- Consistency of object (data, processes, rules) definitions
- Effectiveness of software development practices

Data Center Utility
- Appropriateness of processor architecture
- Adequacy of quality assurance and security controls

fostering collaborative alliances with a variety of external partners (customers, suppliers, vendors, competitors) targeted at the development of innovative IT-based products and processes. Three competencies—one directed at customers, one at suppliers, and one at collaborative alliances—make up this category. External actors have an important role in enabling firms to gain knowledge of emerging IT, innovative applications of IT, and the IT-related experiences of other companies (Pennings and Harianto, 1992). In today's fast-paced (and, at times, chaotic) business and technological environments, firms must develop relationships with relevant external partners in order to gain the advantages that can accrue from flexibility and agility (Davidow and Malone, 1992; Goldman, Nagel, and Preiss, 1995).

Line technology leadership consists of two competencies: cultivating a willingness by line managers and non-IT business professionals to (1) own and (2) champion IT-based business initiatives. Much research has stressed the necessity for users to actively participate in and sometimes take the lead in systems development projects (Ives and Olson, 1984; Hartwick and Barki, 1994). Yet not all organizations have empowered their line managers to own and champion those IT projects that have a significant impact on their business domains. Without a well-developed technology leadership capability, line management may be only too pleased to cede IT management responsibilities to the corporate IT group; resulting adverse consequences can be the increased alienation of line management from IT management activities, an inability to appreciate the transformational capabilities of the firm's IT investments, and adoption of a view that IT can only lag behind the firm's business activities.

Process adaptiveness refers to an organization's capability to instill within its members the ability to fabricate fresh views of business processes and to understand the potential of IT to transform these business processes. Although IT is a key enabler of efforts to redesign business processes, the development of a process-management capability is not without its challenges (Davenport, 1993). The three competencies in this category are the ability of a firm's managers to visualize organizationwide activities, the success the firm has achieved in restructuring its business processes, and the importance the firm attaches to creating an environment where members are encouraged to discover the functionality of IT tools and applications. As illustrated by Robert Galliers in Chapter Seven and by Jane Craig and Philip Yetton in Chapter Eight, firms possessing this category of competencies recognize the dangers of obliterating their intellectual heritage. To reiterate the point made by Craig and Yetton, these competencies allow firms to recognize that "the real event of reengineering occurs in the area of [business] competencies—roles, skills, management processes, and their fit with IT."

IT planning consists of four competencies that collectively represent capabilities involved in directing a firm's IT-related actions. The IT research literature has repeatedly underscored the critical importance of integrating business and IT planning (Earl, 1993), as well as providing a clear vision about the contributions of IT investments to the value of the business.

IT infrastructure comprises six competencies that enable a firm to devise, implement, and maintain a strong technological resource base. Surveys of IT managers reveal the critical importance of developing an infrastructure that is responsive to current and future business initiatives (Niederman, Brancheau, and Wetherbe, 1991); and Sambamurthy and Zmud (1996b) have found that an appropriate

IT infrastructure is a necessary enabling condition in firms that have been successful in conceiving and implementing "breakthrough" IT applications.

Finally, *data-center utility* refers to the capabilities involved in building, maintaining, and securing the information-processing facilities that handle an organization's "life-blood" business transactions. This category comprises two competencies. The first is the appropriateness of a firm's processor architecture (hardware capacities and connectivity), and the second is the adequacy of a firm's quality assurance and security controls. These competencies have consistently surfaced in research aimed at uncovering the critical factors in the success of corporate IT groups (Martin, 1982; Rockart, 1982; Guimaraes, 1984; Henderson, 1990; Saunders and Jones, 1992).

Effectiveness of IT Management Competencies

Do the seven categories of IT management competencies make a difference to the "IT business" of the organization? Our research program evaluated this issue through a questionnaire survey of 230 organizations. Respondents to the survey were senior IT executives who assessed their firms' current level of development of the twenty-nine specific competencies described in Exhibit 6.1. They also provided assessments of their firms' success with deploying IT in their business strategies and value-added activities (details are available in Sambamurthy and Zmud, 1994).

The data on firms' current state of development of the competencies were evaluated through the cluster-analysis technique to identify seven different clusters of firms, as described in Exhibit 6.2. These clusters were then compared with each other relative to their success with IT deployment. Table 6.1 discloses how each cluster of firms "scored" on its current state of development of the IT management competencies. The clusters of firms are arranged left to right in descending order of their development of these competencies. The firms belonging to cluster A have best developed all seven

Exhibit 6.2. Descriptions of IT Management Competency Clusters.

A   These firms report extremely high performance across all seven categories. The fewest number of firms are in this highest performing cluster.

B   These firms report high performance across all seven categories.

C   These firms report high performance across five of the competency categories, extremely high performance with line technology leadership, and average performance with external networks. The firms in this cluster are more "inwardly looking" in their IT management practices than those in cluster B.

D   These firms report high performance with business deployment and external networks, average performance with IT planning, and low performance with line technology leadership, process adaptiveness, IT infrastructure, and data-center utility. Although the firms in this cluster nicely focus their IT management practices on obtaining business value from their IT investments, their approach to IT management may not be sufficiently "forward looking" and may not sufficiently address IT infrastructure issues.

E   These firms report average performance with business deployment, external networks, line technology leadership, and process adaptiveness; low performance with IT planning and IT infrastructure; and extremely low performance with data-center utility. Essentially, these firms exhibit typical IT management practices except that they may not sufficiently address IT infrastructure issues.

F   These firms report average performance with IT planning, IT infrastructure, and data-center utility; low performance with business deployment, line technology leadership, and process adaptiveness; and extremely low performance with external networks. Although these firms' IT management practices seem typical regarding IT infrastructure issues, these practices may not be sufficiently "forward looking" and may not be sufficiently targeted on obtaining business value from IT investments.

G   These firms report low performance with external networks and data-center utility and extremely low performance on the other five competency categories. (The firms in this cluster are clearly the lowest performers with regard to their IT management practices.)

Table 6.1. Success with IT Deployment Across the Clusters of IT Management Competencies.

	A	B	C	D	E	F	G
Number of Firms	15	25	36	21	32	35	29
IT Management Competencies[a]							
Business deployment	1.97	2.69	2.60	2.89	2.93	3.11	3.41
External networks	2.07	2.29	2.90	2.43	2.99	3.61	3.38
Line technology leadership	1.77	2.42	1.82	2.83	2.64	2.87	3.48
Process adaptiveness	1.93	2.33	2.53	3.06	2.71	3.06	3.34
IT planning	1.73	2.34	2.26	2.72	3.05	2.82	3.53
IT infrastructure	1.83	2.34	2.37	2.86	2.81	2.56	3.13
Data-center utility	1.49	1.84	2.15	2.12	2.91	2.09	2.45
Success with IT Use[b]							
Business strategies	.983	.758	.073	.515	.135	−.262	−.750
Logistics/operations	.411	.648	.266	.082	−.158	−.200	−.313
Marketing/customer service	.557	.434	.289	.347	−.029	−.376	−.449

[a]Measures were aggregated on a five-point scale where 1 is high and 5 is low.

[b]Measures reported are factor scores, with high positive scores indicating superior use of IT.

categories, whereas firms in cluster G exhibit the lowest levels of development across all the categories. Firms in clusters E and F appear to develop particular sets of IT management competencies. Apparently, firms in cluster E do an average job on business-oriented competencies but a poor job on the IT-infrastructure competencies; and, firms in cluster F perform poorly on the business-oriented competencies but do an average job on the IT infrastructure competencies.

Table 6.1 displays the relative success of the firms in these clusters in deploying IT in their business strategies and value-chain activities. These IT performance variables were analyzed across the seven clusters using analysis of variance; significant differences were found across the clusters on all three indicators of the extent of IT deployment: IT use for strategies, IT use for logistics/operations, and IT use for marketing/customer service. One concern with relying on senior IT executives' assessments of their firms' success in applying IT is that they will be biased toward the area for which they are responsible. In order to obtain a different perspective, a subsequent extension of this research project obtained responses on the "success with IT" scales from members of these same firms' top management teams (for example, the CEO, president, COO, CFO, senior vice-president of a major business group). Usable responses from at least one member of the top management team were obtained from 123 of these firms. Using the perceptions of senior business executives (rather than senior IT executives), we found similarly significant results in the case of IT use for business strategies; similar but weaker significant results in IT use for logistics/operations; but no significant differences in marketing/customer service. Although these results are not as strong as those based on senior IT executives' perceptions, they do complement the earlier findings. Overall, we find adequate evidence that an association does indeed exist between a firm's IT management competency and its success in deploying IT in support of its business strategies and work processes.

The data in Table 6.1 confirm the quantitative analysis. The firms in the cluster characterized by the highest levels of IT management competency (cluster A) were also those exhibiting the highest success in IT deployment. Firms in the cluster characterized by the poorest levels of IT management competency (cluster G) were those exhibiting the least success in IT deployment. Generally, those firms that have apparently nurtured the development of IT management competencies outperformed those that have not.

Implications for Organizational Transformation

The focus of this chapter has been on identifying a set of IT management competencies that are salient to the success of contemporary organizations in using IT effectively. Building on the conclusions of related research that IT management skills are the single true source of sustained IT-related competitiveness, the research reported in this chapter identified seven categories of IT management competencies and demonstrated their significant association with firms' success in applying IT.

Venkatraman (1991) provides a rich set of ideas about the different avenues through which IT can facilitate fundamental transformations, such as business process redesign, business network redefinition, and business scope expansion. However, our position is that the most important activities for organizations desiring to apply IT to their transformational initiatives are evaluating and enhancing their IT management competencies. A focus on these competencies will enable senior IT managers to focus on the "IT business" of the firm and to develop an organizational IT capability that leads or enables business strategies and activities. More important, a focus on competencies shapes managerial attention away from pursuing strategic alignment and toward nurturing a platform of IT capabilities that will enhance business competencies and become the basis for competitive agility. In Chapter Two, Yetton describes three successful Australian firms that focused their energies on enhancing their organizational IT capability; in the process, they realized some of the new business transformation opportunities that Venkatraman (1991) describes. Our view is that as different industries become more competitive and use IT more intensively, the degree to which firms enhance IT management competencies will separate the winners from contenders as well as the contenders from losers!

If IT management competencies are crucial for senior IT executives, particularly in transformational contexts, it will be important for managers to monitor firms' development of these competencies. One of the products of our research is a self-assessment tool that an organization could use to assess the current level of its IT management competencies based on the responses of executives across the enterprise (Sambamurthy and Zmud, 1994). This tool provides an assessment of the current and desired levels of competency as well as the relative importance of the twenty-nine competencies. Our experiences in using this tool in eight different firms suggest that organizations can identify those IT management competencies most in need of incremental and radical enhancements. Additionally, the tool has proved to be especially valuable in promoting rich dialogues among a firm's IT managers and IT professionals and between the IT staff and managers and professionals throughout the enterprise.

We have also found that the local salience of the seven categories varies according to the firm's history, current situation, and business strategies. Managers must carefully judge the relative salience of each of these competencies. Our assessment tool has enabled IT management teams to identify specific competencies on which to focus their attention in order to best utilize available time and funding. For example, one of these firms (a public utility) discovered from its (internal) client responses that building external networks with key customers was an increasingly significant element of their rapidly transforming competitive landscape. However, the firm was not satisfied with the extent to which it had developed competencies targeted at external networks, and, as a consequence, it is now actively building such competencies.

We clearly recognize that our research results are preliminary, at best. Although the twenty-nine competencies identified are supported both by prior research and by current IT management trends, we strongly encourage others to undertake similar research and contrast their findings with ours. We undoubtedly have overlooked important competencies given the dynamic nature of today's business and technological environments; we expect that the "true" set of IT management competencies will constantly evolve. Some of these competencies may always be present, while the remainder will become less salient and will be replaced by others over time. We particularly encourage research aimed at understanding the evolving nature of this "portfolio" of IT management competencies.

Finally, we expect that the individual competencies within this portfolio will vary with regard to their influence on particular IT activities and the outcomes from these activities. Thus, we also encourage research aimed at understanding which organizational outcomes are most affected by specific IT management competencies, how these competency-outcome relationships unfold, and how these competencies complement one another in their effects on organizational performance outcomes.

Summary

In contemporary organizations, for IT to enable fundamental transformational initiatives aimed at business processes, business networks, or business scope, an understanding and acceptance of the networked mode of IT management will be required. In this regard, we recommend that both IT researchers and IT practitioners expand their view beyond the corporate IT organization to enterprisewide IT management competencies and initiatives. To do so IT practitioners will have to make active partners of business management, senior management, and influential external networks to develop their enterprises' IT management competencies. Researchers will have to reexamine their conceptual and methodological orientations. For example, future projects should tap responses about the status of IT management competencies not just from IT executives but also from business executives.

Although this chapter has identified seven categories of IT management competencies, we do not anticipate that all these categories will be equally important in all contexts. We still have much to learn. For example, we do not yet know the relative importance of these competencies across several contexts, such as industries (for example, manufacturing versus services), firms' competitive strategy orientations (for example, defenders versus prospectors), intensity of competitive rivalries, or the degree of information intensity in firms' products and services. We anticipate that the importance of each of these competencies will evolve over time as firms face dynamic challenges in their products, markets, organizational processes, and business networks. We need to give attention to how firms could anticipate important future IT management competencies and mobilize organizational attention and effort to develop those competencies. How should a firm "retire" competencies considered to be less important and "groom" competencies anticipated to be more important in the future? Furthermore, how should a firm leverage external alliances and partnerships to enhance its important competencies?

Finally, our ideas about IT management competencies build bridges to the larger stream of current thinking that embraces the resource-based view of the firm (Shrivastava, Huff, and Dutton, 1994), which examines the evolution of fundamental organizational competencies (Hamel and Prahalad, 1994). There are ample opportunities for examining the links between fundamental organizational competencies and important IT management competencies. One important direction for future research is to examine how an alignment between the firm's basic competencies and its IT management competencies influences business performance. What mechanisms should firms develop to nurture a strong synergy between their business and IT management competencies? Managers may need to find ways to leverage the development of business and IT management competencies off each other. We encourage researchers and managers alike to think in terms of the resource-based view of the firm and the notion of firm competencies in order to advance both the theory and the practice of IT-enabled business transformations.

For practicing managers, we offer three action-oriented guidelines:

1. Involve your firm's senior corporate and line management in discussions about the role that IT will play in future organizational transformation and renewal efforts, and about important IT management competencies that will be central to such efforts.

2. Conduct a self-assessment of your IT management competencies to evaluate current performance and to spotlight areas that need enhancement in order to reach the desired level of performance in the future.

3. Design and implement a strategy for competency enhancement that identifies specific action plans, time frames for action completion, responsibilities for actions, resources required, and criteria for evaluating success. Managers might consider the creation of a separate task force, consisting of IT and business managers, to oversee such an initiative. A few firms have used our self-assessment tool to embark on such competency-enhancement initiatives, and the early results of these initiatives are encouraging.

References

Brown, C. V., and Magill, S. L. "Alignment of the IS Functions with the Enterprise: Towards a Model of Antecedents." *MIS Quarterly*, 1994, 18(4), 371–404.

Collis, D. J., and Montgomery, C. A. "Competing on Resources: Strategy in the 1990s." *Harvard Business Review*, July-Aug. 1995, 118–128.

Cronin, M. J. *The Internet Strategy Handbook*. Boston: Harvard Business School Press, 1996.

Davenport, T. H. *Process Innovation: Reengineering Work Through Information Technology*. Boston: Harvard Business School Press, 1993.

Davidow, W. H., and Malone, M. S. *The Virtual Corporation: Structuring and Revitalizing the Corporation for the 21st Century*. New York: HarperCollins, 1992.

Earl, M. J. "Experiences in Strategic Information Systems Planning." *MIS Quarterly*, 1993, 17(1), 1–24.

Goldman, S. L., Nagel, R. N., and Preiss, K. *Agile Competitors and Virtual Organizations: Strategies for Enriching the Customer*. New York: Van Nostrand Reinhold, 1995.

Guimaraes, T. "Defining and Ranking MIS Critical Tasks." In *Proceedings of the Fifth International Conference on Information Systems*. Tucson, AZ, 1984.

Hamel, G., and Prahalad, C. K. *Competing for the Future: Breakthrough Strategies for Seizing Control of Your Industry and Creating the Markets of Tomorrow.* Boston: Harvard Business School Press, 1994.

Hartwick, J., and Barki, J. "Explaining the Role of User Participation in Information System Use." *Management Science*, 1994, 40(4), 440–465.

Henderson, J. C. "Plugging into Strategic Partnerships: The Critical IS Connection." *Sloan Management Review*, spring 1990, 7–18.

Ives, B., and Olson, M. H. "User Involvement in Information Systems: A Review of the Research." *Management Science*, 1984, 30(5), 586–603.

Martin, E. W. "Critical Success Factors of Chief MIS/DP Executives." *MIS Quarterly*, 1982, 6(2), 1–9.

Mata, F. J., Fuerst, W. L., and Barney, J. B. "Information Technology and Sustained Competitive Advantage: A Resource-Based Analysis." *MIS Quarterly*, 1995, 19(4), 487–505.

McKenney, J. L., Copeland, D., and Mason, R. O. *Waves of Change: Business Evolution Through Information Technology.* Boston: Harvard Business School Press, 1995.

Nelson, R. R., and Winter, S. G. *An Evolutionary Theory of Economic Change.* Cambridge, Mass.: Belknap Press, 1982.

Niederman, F., Brancheau, J. C., and Wetherbe, J. C. "Information Systems Management Issues for the 1990s." *MIS Quarterly*, 1991, 15(4), 475–502.

Pennings, J. M., and Harianto, F. "Technological Networking and Innovation Implementation." *Organization Science*, 1992, 3(3), 356–382.

Penrose, E. *The Theory of the Growth of the Firm.* (3rd ed.) New York: Oxford University Press, 1995.

Rockart, J. F. "The Changing Role of the Information Systems Executive: A Critical Success Factors Perspective." *Sloan Management Review*, 1982, 24(1), 3–13.

Rockart, J. F., and Short, J. E. "Information Technology in the 1990s: Managing Organizational Interdependence." *Sloan Management Review*, 1989, 30(2), 7–17.

Rockart, J. F., and Short, J. E. "The Networked Organization and the Management of Interdependence." In M. S. Scott Morton (ed.), *The Corporation of the 1990s: Information Technology and Organizational Transformation.* New York: Oxford University Press, 1991.

Sambamurthy, V., and Zmud, R. W. *Managing IT for Success: The Empowering Business Partnership.* Morristown, N.J.: Financial Executives Research Foundation, 1992.

Sambamurthy, V., and Zmud, R. W. *IT Management Competency Assessment: A Tool for Creating Business Value Through IT.* Morristown, N.J.: Financial Executives Research Foundation, 1994.

Sambamurthy, V., and Zmud, R. W. *Factors Influencing Information Technology Management Architectures in Organizations: A Theory of Multiple Contingencies.* Florida State University, unpublished manuscript, 1996a.

Sambamurthy, V., and Zmud, R. W. *Information Technology and Innovation: Strategies for Success.* Morristown, N.J.: Financial Executives Research Foundation, 1996b.

Saunders, C. S., and Jones, J. W. "Measuring the Performance of the Information Systems Function." *Journal of Management Information Systems*, 1992, 8(4), 63–82.

Shrivastava, P., Huff, A., and Dutton, J. *Advances in Strategic Management: Resource-Based View of the Firm.* Vol. 10a. Greenwich, Conn.: JAI Press, 1994.

Spender, J. C. *Industry Recipes: An Enquiry into the Nature and Sources of Managerial Judgement.* Oxford: Blackwell, 1989.

Tapscott, D., and Caston, A. *Paradigm Shift: The New Promise of Information Technology.* New York: McGraw-Hill, 1993.

Venkatraman, N. "IT-Enabled Business Reconfiguration." In M. S. Scott Morton (ed.), *The Corporation of the 1990s: Information Technology and Organizational Transformation.* New York: Oxford University Press, 1991.

Part III

Process Change

The two chapters in Part Three see process change as an important approach to organizational transformation but criticize the ultrarationalist ideology of the Business Process Reengineering (BPR) movement. Chapter Seven argues for a holistic approach to process change and stresses the value of existing organizational knowledge. Chapter Eight relocates the critical knowledge and competencies for process change in implementation activities rather than strategic design.

BPR has placed itself at the center of IT-based organizational transformation, but schisms have rapidly developed among its priesthood. One reason for division is the high risk entailed by the radical change BPR demands. Both chapters criticize this attachment to radical change as managerially misconceived.

In Chapter Seven Robert Galliers outlines an approach to controlled-risk process change centered on knowledge and learning. He rejects obliteration, the catchcry of Michael Hammer, because it ignores organizational knowledge and learning. He therefore argues for a holistic approach that recognizes the full range of organizational interests and elements involved in successful change. Particularly, he points to the sociotechnical movement, with its inclusive approach to organizational and individual factors, and to the University of Lancaster–based Soft Systems movement's approach to organizational change, which develops radical characterizations of problems from in-depth understanding. Galliers thus points the way to an alternative account of what it takes to achieve successful, radical, lower-risk process change and in doing so indicates characteristics of the competencies required.

In Chapter Eight Jane Craig and Philip Yetton advocate an approach they call *dynamic improvement*. Their view is that BPR has adopted ideas from the positioning school of strategy led by Michael Porter without examining the appropriateness of those ideas. BPR would do better to follow the school of thought promoting emergent strategy formation that is associated with J. Brian Quinn and Henry Mintzberg. They argue that the dominant organizational form since the mid-1970s has involved a strategy of differentiation implemented chiefly through a divisional structure. BPR, however, is about integration. Unlike divisionalization, which seeks to differentiate, process engineering requires changed competencies to effect integration. But the classic approach to BPR is top-down. It emphasizes strategic positioning and the careful design of strategy, structure, and IT. Not surprisingly, according to these authors, projects adopting this approach run into trouble. Extrapolation from the wrong theory leads to a misconceived approach. The real event of reengineering occurs in the area of competencies—roles, skills, management processes, and their fit with IT.

Craig and Yetton's solution, dynamic improvement, inverts the thinking of classic BPR. It prefers strategic intent to strategic positioning. The basic thrust of this approach is the learning and development of new competencies through performing new activities. This is what it takes to reengineer. Because new strategic opportunities emerge from the mastery of these activities, this approach is more bottom-up than top-down.

Both chapters emphasize the value of organizational knowledge and its acquisition through learning. They value the status quo and see change less as a designed process and more as an emergent, incremental activity that leverages off the existing organization. They reconceptualize organizational transformation as a transition to a new set of competencies with the help of the existing set. Thus, process change can be enabled by IT without the risks inherent in classic BPR.

7

Against Obliteration

Reducing Risk in Business Process Change

Robert D. Galliers

The business process change movement has been both its own best friend and its own worst enemy. It has some valuable ideas to offer, but they are often lost in the barrage of criticism business process change invites as a result of its narrow and outdated view of change. We refer to these narrow and often dogmatic ideas by the label under which they have been most popularly marketed—namely, Business Process Reengineering (BPR)—so as to distinguish them from the broader class of approaches to process change, which we refer to as *business process change*.

The more facile approach of BPR assumes a level of risk that is unacceptable in all but the most extreme circumstances, and BPR thereby detracts from the constructive and positive elements in process change. It does not just seek to obliterate existing processes, which is risky enough, but it also argues for a clean-slate start, which implies that most prior knowledge and experience have also to be obliterated. The obvious outcome is that BPR is particularly risky, and success, however measured, is elusive. Although its recommendations for change may well be rational, they fly in the face of hard-won and often not rational but organizationally realistic experience. Furthermore, the role of people and implementation issues tend to be downplayed. The focus is on strategy formulation (very much in the traditional, rational mode) rather than on strategic thinking with a concern for the realpolitik of organizational change.

In this chapter, we use an analysis of the different risks incurred by the more hot-headed approaches to BPR so as to reveal the characteristics necessary for a considered form of business process change, characteristics that we believe exist in some already established approaches. Our discussion emphasizes the value of business process change and the reasons why the best-known approaches to BPR are so risky. More constructively, we suggest ways in which the advantages of business process change may be gained without undue risk and without having to adopt untried and untested approaches.

We start by distinguishing the essence of business process change from its more extreme forms. We identify four sources of risk and argue that they represent an outdated approach to strategic thinking. We analyze the risks arising from the most dangerous (the term is used advisedly) of the assumptions on which BPR is based to reveal the requirements for a lower-risk approach to business process change. We then describe some of the elements of a more holistic and balanced approach by which to neutralize at least some of the risks.

The Essence of Business Process Change

To begin, let us identify what is so distinctive about, in fact what is the essence of, business process change. It is clearly about processes in the following sense: it is cross-functional, and it is end-to-end in that it relates all activity to the firm's customers. Although business process change may merely repackage existing concepts (Earl, 1994; Grint, 1994; Mumford, 1994), the focus on process is timely both because it promotes integration after years of differentiation through divisionalization and because the technology now exists to implement cross-functional integration. Business process change also provides the opportunity for organizations to review some of their long-established and sometimes dysfunctional processes without being subject to all the traditional constraints associated with what is considered politically achievable.

Business process change is also distinguished by the fact that it has top management's attention. Therefore the resources are often available to embark on BPR projects. Moreover, it is big—very big—business, reputedly a $51 billion industry in 1995 (Davenport, 1996). Getting those projects right is obviously economically very important.

Marketing of BPR

In developing the market for BPR (as a consultancy product), its most vocal proponents have saturated us with a rhetoric that has successfully obscured the inner essence of the process. Most people now view business process change as necessarily involving radical rethinking to achieve radical organizational change that will bring radical benefits. The stated intention of BPR is to produce radical improvements in cycle times and costs. For example, Rockart and Short (1989, p. 8) argue that "competitive pressures are now forcing almost all major firms to become global in scope, to decrease time to market, and to redouble their efforts to manage risk, service and cost." By focusing on a firm's business strategy and radically improving business processes to achieve strategic objectives with these competitive pressures in mind, BPR seeks considerable improvement in the firm's bottom line.

The radical rethinking to achieve these improvements is done at the strategic level and involves devising a new organizational world starting with a blank slate and none of the complications of the everyday world. Once creative strategists have worked out the design, armies of technologists set about developing and implementing the information technology (IT) that is to realize the design. The essential integrative character of business process change as a means to achieve redesigned cross-functional processes is obscured by the ultrarational rhetoric of BPR.

Roots of BPR

"Radical" is an overused (or, rather, misused) word in much of the BPR literature. It helps position BPR as progressive and as offering a new departure from existing approaches. By utilizing a framework devised by Whittington (1993, p. 3) to analyze the different schools of thought in the field of strategic management, we might come to precisely the opposite view however (see Figure 7.1).

Whittington (1993) identifies four schools of thought in the field of strategy and places them along two axes: (1) whether the strategy process is intended to have a single outcome (profit maximization) or a number of different outcomes and (2) whether the process itself is deliberate or emergent (compare Mintzberg and Waters, 1985). Whittington characterizes the *classical* school of thought (profit maximization/deliberate) as being concerned, through a process of rational analysis, with the development of plans for a single, defined, profit-maximizing end. The *evolutionary* school (profit maximization/emergent) is concerned more with survival in the marketplace through optimizing the fit between the organization and its environment. The *processual* school (pluralistic/

Figure 7.1. Approaches to Business Strategy.

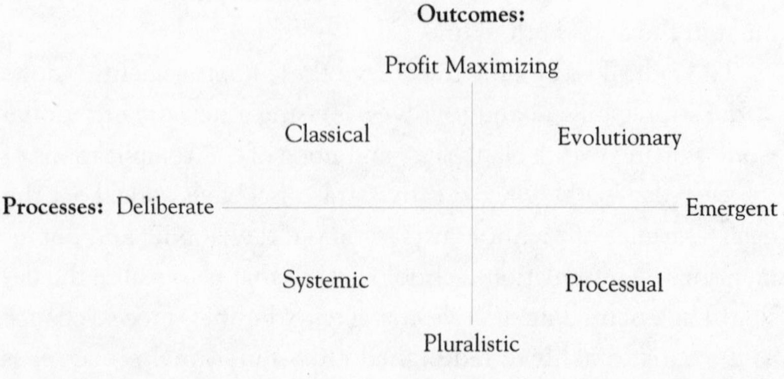

Outcomes:

Profit Maximizing

	Classical		Evolutionary	
Processes: Deliberate				Emergent
	Systemic		Processual	

Pluralistic

Whittington (1993, p. 3).

emergent) takes a contrary stance. Here, strategy emerges not from the business environment but as a result of individual actions. The *systemic* school (pluralistic/deliberate) recognizes plurality in strategic outcomes and the impact of cultural influences on these outcomes. Whittington sees the development of strategic management as being influenced by each of these schools of thought, with the classical school having its heyday in the 1960s, giving way to the processual school in the 1970s, the evolutionary school in the 1980s, and the systemic school in the 1990s.

If we accept Whittington's analysis, we can locate BPR in his matrix. Profit maximization would appear to be its major object, with other outcomes not even being mentioned. Profit maximization is to be achieved through a deliberate, rational analysis of business processes and clean-slate design. BPR thus belongs in the classical quadrant, which represents earlier strategic-management thinking. This analysis is further confirmed by noting the absence of concern in BPR for cultural or contextual issues other than as obstacles that must be overcome. (In BPR change is almost by definition desirable.) Moreover, the notion that process change could emerge incrementally is not even considered.

Being based in classical strategic thinking dating back to the 1960s, BPR incorporates little or nothing of what we have learned in the intervening period. This anachronistic thinking and the apparent lack of concern for implementation issues result in BPR assuming unnecessarily high levels of risk.

Risks in BPR

It seems strange that while most organizations devote considerable energy and resources to managing risks associated with their existing endeavors, many seem so willing to try BPR without a second thought. In other circumstances they may well take calculated risks but only when those risks are carefully weighed and consciously accepted. With BPR, firms seem to accept the risks with intemperate haste. What are the BPR beliefs that increase risk, and how might they be moderated?

Belief in the Centrality of Business Processes and IT

Business processes and IT are together the primary focus in BPR projects. Davenport and Short (1990) propose a recursive, mutually reinforcing relationship between business processes and IT. Scarbrough (1995), in a critique of the sociotechnical movement, with its emphasis on user participation in the design of technology, refers to the work of Zuboff (1988) in arguing that IT can itself create nonroutine work and pooled interdependencies that in turn have widespread social and organizational ramifications. In line with this kind of thinking, business processes and IT are seen by the proponents of BPR as being at the heart of strategic change and business innovation.

Davenport and Short (1990) propose a fairly typical five-step approach:

1. Develop business vision and process objectives.
2. Identify processes to be redesigned.
3. Understand and measure existing processes.
4. Identify IT levers.
5. Design and build prototype of new process(es).

The approach is clearly in the classical mold, exhibiting no awareness of the social and organizational side of technology.

To think that IT alone is necessary to identify needed change denies the importance of opportunities in the business environment. More important, it does not take into account an organization's ability to harness the opportunities that may arise from the astute utilization of IT. Strange as it may seem to the ardent proponents of BPR, yet as Chapter Six shows, some organizations are better able to gain and sustain advantage from IT than others! Those less able run serious risks of failure when they attempt to couple radical change with a technology they do not fully understand. In much the same way that IT-capable organizations gain most from outsourcing, so too it is likely that the same organizations have a greater chance of succeeding with business process change than their less capable counterparts. This correlation may seem blindingly obvious, but when did you hear a BPR consultant or writer counsel caution in this regard?

A perspective that focuses on more than processes and IT alone is required given the complexity of organizational change. Notwithstanding Scarbrough's criticisms, the sociotechnical school (Leavitt, 1965, for example) provides such a perspective. Although the variation on Leavitt's model presented in Figure 7.2 necessarily limits the analysis to some degree, it takes account of a wider range of elements than the approach advocated by Davenport and Short (1990) and others of the same school.

Although process engineers recognize the likely impact on structure—and even people—of introducing a new technology or process change, there is a tendency to relegate these issues to an implementation phase. They become something of an afterthought rather than being seen as an integral part of the process itself.

To think that an organization can be transformed without interactions among structure, culture, roles, norms, skills, and so on is to risk resistance and rejection both in the process of identifying the required change and in its implementation. Such lack of forethought is dangerous because it encourages an undervaluing of other crucial elements of the organization. Admittedly, process engineers may occasionally acknowledge that social and organizational issues could have been given more attention. Baxter and Lisburn (1994, p. 15) state, for example, "Maybe more time could have been spent preparing the people involved for the change." However, the grudging way in which such admissions are made demonstrates that the

Figure 7.2. Variation of Leavitt's Model.

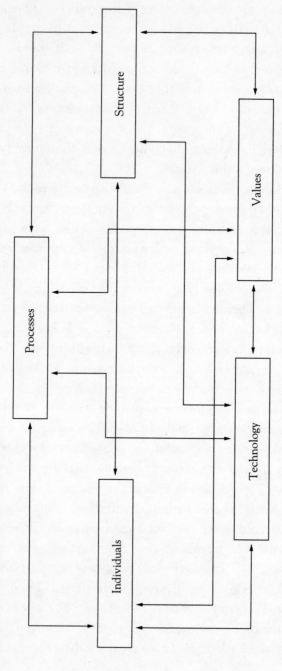

Adapted from G. Davis and M. Olson, *Management Information Systems: Conceptual Foundations, Structure, and Development*, 1985, p. 355. Reprinted by permission of the McGraw-Hill Companies.

importance of these issues is still not recognized by committed process engineers.

Belief in the Necessity of Radical Process Changes

Proponents of BPR would have us believe that only radical change
can bring radical improvements in business performance. For example, Venkatraman (1991) argues that only revolutionary, IT-induced
business transformation can ensure large-scale benefits. As we shall
see, plenty of evidence demonstrates that this is not the case. Moreover, the risk attached to revolutionary change is high. The greater
the magnitude of the change, the greater the chance that it will not
work out as intended. It is harder to get the design right when there
are many aspects of change to think of. Also, implementation of the
proposed change is more likely to meet with resistance because it
imposes too many new burdens on individuals and challenges the
power structure. When the proposed change brings with it a requirement to downsize, both these problems become even more acute.
Furthermore, radical change can cause radical damage and may well
result in an irretrievable disaster.

Two problems are associated with linking radical change with
radical improvements. First, the desired outcome can be confused
with the process required to achieve this end. Does radical improvement always require radically changed processes? In the field of
strategic information systems, Senn (1992) reminds us that competitive advantage from IT most often arises from incremental
change in existing information systems. Copeland and McKenney's
(1988) study of airline reservation systems, which are so often held
up as examples of radical transformation, reminds us that in fact
they emerge from consistent exploitation of opportunities rather
than extraordinary vision. Second, radical change may not always
be either necessary or desirable.

The risks associated with large-scale change are clearly considerable. Organizations must judge whether the risks are justified and

must also seriously consider whether incremental change might not be a better alternative in certain circumstances. BPR does not emphasize such a risk assessment.

Belief in Obliteration as a First Step

The exhortation to begin anew, to forget the past, to "unlearn," to obliterate (see Hammer, 1990) adds further risks to those already identified. Existing processes embody years of otherwise uncodified organizational learning. Changes may well have been initiated by staff long since departed, with the rationale for such changes having disappeared with them. Moreover, existing processes may provide the only way of learning about particular aspects of the organization's business. People understand their role within the business in relation to these processes: they can most often tell you what they do, not why they do it. To obliterate, then, is to gratuitously discard much useful knowledge and risk its not being appreciated or in any way incorporated in a new, blank-slate design.

In effect, the blitzkrieg mentality of obliteration derives from a false dichotomy that process engineers have set up. The alternative to obliteration is incrementalism, but process engineers view incrementalism as inevitably rooted in and chained to the past and therefore unable to generate radical change. The incrementalist perspective is characterized by Davenport (1993) as being focused on existing processes and structures, based on bottom-up approaches, informed by statistical data, and motivated by a perceived need for increased control. Contrast this characterization with Quinn's (1980) theory of logical incrementalism or Checkland's (1981) soft-systems methodology. Although both Quinn and Checkland argue, albeit from quite different perspectives, that current circumstances need to be taken into account, neither suggests that these should in fact be the starting point for analysis. And Checkland in particular has explicitly sought radical reconceptualizations of organizational problems.

The clean-slate approach also seems to argue against what de Gues (1988), among others, describes as planning as learning. Here, the view is that strategy formulation can benefit from lessons drawn from the past—a view echoed by Baker (1995) in stressing the importance of feedback in the information systems planning process, a point that is developed below.

Belief in Unitary, Deterministic Strategic Change as the Only Approach

The unitary, deterministic view of strategic change represented by BPR emphasizes design. Other successful approaches to change are disregarded. BPR assumes that all that is necessary for successful design and implementation can be known in advance by the designers. The crucial role of organizational knowledge and learning is ignored. Learning is reduced to training people to operate the newly designed process(es). Although ostensibly rational, this central tenet of BPR flies in the face of past lessons. Change is far too complex to be fully understood prior to its implementation. To suppose otherwise is to risk implementation failure.

This worldview might reasonably be contrasted with that in the field of strategic management, where strategy is viewed as being both deterministic and emergent; Mintzberg and Waters (1985) provide perhaps the best-known exposition of this view. Others, such as Pettigrew (1973), view organizations in micropolitical terms, as coalitions of individuals rather than homogeneous entities that might be malleable given rational, goal-seeking behavior. The deterministic viewpoint can also be compared with the view of those who see the outcome of strategic change in pluralistic terms, such as Granovetter (1985). He argues that the process of strategic goal setting and associated activities are bound up in the social values of players in the organization. As Whittington (1993, p. 4) puts it, "Strategists often deviate from the profit-maximizing norm quite deliberately. . . . The pursuit of . . . different objectives, even at the cost of profit maximization, [can be] therefore perfectly rational." The development of approaches to strategy since the early 1970s has been characterized by an increasingly sophisticated understanding of the subtleties of strategic change, yet BPR fails to recognize any value in this learning. As a result it attracts much of the now unnecessary risk typical of the classical approach to strategic change.

Despite all these criticisms of BPR, the purpose of this chapter is not to dismiss business process change out of hand but to paint a more realistic picture of what strategic change involves by drawing on the literature about sociotechnical systems, soft-systems methodology, strategic change, and information management. The aim is to go beyond mere reengineering, as commonly described in the literature and as commonly practiced, toward a more holistic approach to business transformation and strategic change that reduces the risk in change projects.

Toward a More Holistic Approach

Our analysis shows that BPR could learn a lot from developments in related fields such as strategic management. A systemic and balanced perspective is needed given the difficulties often encountered in implementing (radical) change. An approach incorporating such a perspective would allow for both radical and evolutionary or incremental change, would take into account a range of viewpoints and allow for pluralistic outcomes, would consider the role that IT might play without necessarily placing it center stage, and would attempt to identify implementation issues as part of the process of strategy formulation. One such approach, based on soft-systems methodology (Checkland, 1981), is illustrated in Figure 7.3.

Space limitations preclude describing the approach in detail, and, in any event, this detail is provided elsewhere (see Galliers and Baker, 1995). However, a number of features of the approach can be highlighted:

Figure 7.3. A Systemic Approach to Business Innovation and IT.

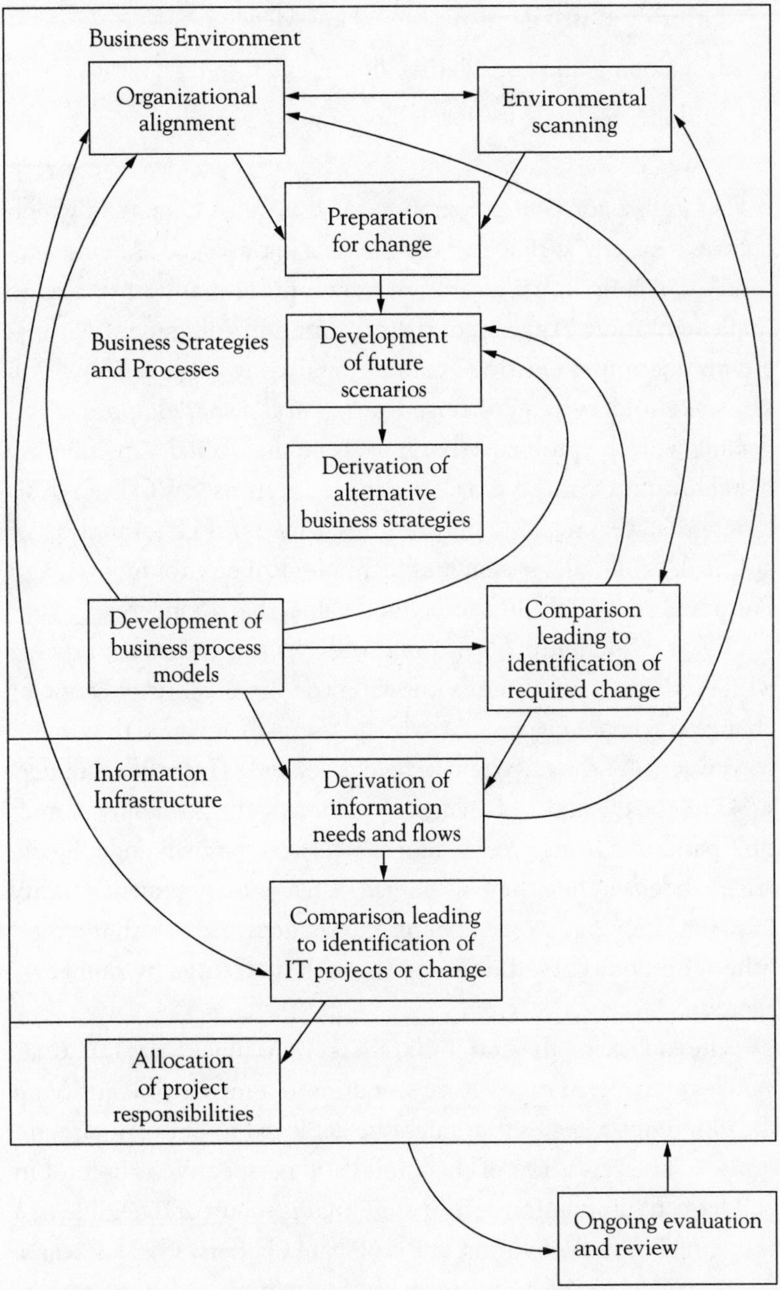

Adapted from Galliers and Baker (1995, p. 269).

Preparing for change

Utilizing existing organizational knowledge

Developing and considering alternative future scenarios

Building multiple feedback loops into the process

Let us first consider preparation for change. A climate in which change is eagerly anticipated or at least acknowledged as being necessary can help considerably in overcoming many obstacles to implementation. Analysis of the organization's alignment with its environment uses existing organizational knowledge to help bring key stakeholders to a concerted action and a shared approach to dealing with the problems that have been uncovered. Any number of techniques can be employed here, such as SWOT analysis (strengths, weaknesses, opportunities, threats), PEST (analysis of political, economic, social, and technological environments), and Porter's (1980, 1985) five forces and value-chain concepts.

Two key elements allow organizations to prepare for change while reducing risk. One is knowing the dimensions or scope of change (compare Figure 7.2), which lessens the chance that major constituents of the change will be overlooked. The other is understanding the dynamics of change by admitting the possibility of multiple paths and being prepared for the barriers that will undoubtedly arise. Understanding these dynamics increases management's ability to manage change as it happens and reduces the risk that would otherwise be involved in going through a "change by numbers" exercise.

After analyzing the current business environment, organizations can develop alternative future scenarios as a means of identifying the different strategies that might be deployed in different circumstances. The retention of this pluralistic perspective is helpful in building an information architecture that is robust and flexible in a changing business environment (compare Galliers, 1993). Clearly, greater risk would be associated with the creation of an architecture based on a single view of the future, which may well turn out to be inappropriate in today's turbulent times.

A technique that can be employed to good effect in creating different scenarios is to identify facts (those elements that may be assumed to remain fairly constant throughout the planning period), trends (those that may be assumed to continue), and issues (those elements about which there may be considerable debate or uncertainty). Counterintuitive scenarios can also be included by changing facts and trends and considering what the organization's response might be in such radically different circumstances. An architecture that provides the information necessary to support and question the alternative strategies that arise from such considerations as these enables a flexible response to changing circumstances and conditions and thereby reduces the risk associated with a single, taken-for-granted view of the future—a view often associated with an organization's IT strategy and most BPR projects.

The development of business process models is aided by Checkland's (1981) concept of root definitions. Here, the objective is to produce a succinct statement that captures the essence of what the activity is meant to do and achieve in the context of the chosen scenarios. Checkland uses the mnemonic CATWOE (customers, actors, transformation process, worldview, owner, environment) to achieve comprehensive coverage of the key features in producing alternative root definitions. Organizational knowledge is essential in this context because, although a root definition may represent a radical reinterpretation of the status quo (for example, perceiving a charitable organization as an educational system rather than a collection and distribution system) or a radical response to possible future scenarios, there is a clear expectation that it should be based on a solid understanding of the organization's actual and potential goals and raison d'être. Business process models comprise the processes that are necessary to enable the system of activity described in the root definition to take form (compare Checkland's concept of a human-activity system). Information needed for each process to take place and to be monitored and information needed to question the taken-for-granted assumptions on which alternative strategies are based can then be identified and mapped onto the business process model. Required information can then be compared with the information currently available and decisions made to rectify any shortfall.

Ongoing evaluation and review is enabled by this information architecture and includes an assessment of both longitudinal perspectives in the context of changed circumstances and newly available information and any strategies that might have emerged from the actions of individuals outside the stated plans.

The inclusion of multiple feedback loops helps to institutionalize learning so that change is informed by earlier change. Under such circumstances incrementalism is facilitated while at the same time not precluding more radical change. Informed judgments and decisions are made, and the risk associated with one-time, radical change based on a clean-slate approach is reduced significantly.

Summary

This contribution to the debate about IT and the dynamics of organizational transformation has attempted to provide a critique of some of the key features of business process change as it is often practiced (as BPR) in order to devise an approach that builds on existing knowledge in the fields of strategic management, organizational change, sociotechnical systems, and information management. It is easy to dismiss BPR out of hand given its reversion to aspects of the classical, rational school of strategic thinking popularized in the 1960s. In this chapter I have tried to avoid this temptation however. By utilizing hard-won knowledge from related fields, I have outlined an approach that retains the strengths of business process change while recognizing and doing something to correct the more crass elements that have emerged in popular writings on the topic.

By arguing against obliteration of existing processes and knowledge (both within the organization and with respect to related disciplines) and by offering some useful alternatives to the task of implementing change, this chapter has sought to make business process change more attractive than it usually is by reducing the risks associated with BPR.

References

Baker, B.S.H. "The Role of Feedback in Assessing Information Systems Planning Effectiveness." *Journal of Strategic Information Systems*, 1995, 4(1), 61–80.

Baxter, S., and Lisburn, D. *Reengineering Information Technology: Success Through Empowerment*. Englewood Cliffs, N.J.: Prentice-Hall, 1994.

Checkland, P. *Systems Thinking, Systems Practice*. New York: Wiley, 1981.

Copeland, D. G., and McKenney, J. L. "Airline Reservations Systems: Lessons from History." *MIS Quarterly*, 1988, 12(3), 353–370.

Davenport, T. H. *Process Innovation: Reengineering Work Through Information Technology*. Boston: Harvard Business School Press, 1993.

Davenport, T. H. "Why Reengineering Failed: The Fad That Forgot People." *Fast Company*, 1996, 1(1)70–74.

Davenport, T. H., and Short, J. E. "The New Industrial Engineering: Information Technology and Business Process Redesign." *Sloan Management Review*, summer 1990, 11–27. Reprinted in R. D. Galliers and B.S.H. Baker (eds.), *Strategic Information Management: Challenges and Strategies in Managing Information Systems*. Oxford: Butterworth-Heinemann, 1994.

Davis, G. B., and Olson, M. H. *Management Information Systems: Conceptual Foundations, Structure, and Development*. New York: McGraw Hill, 1985.

de Gues, A. "Planning as Learning." *Harvard Business Review*, 1988, 66(2), 70–74.

Earl, M. J. "The New and the Old of Business Process Redesign." *Journal of Strategic Information Systems*, 1994, 3(1), 5–22.

Galliers, R. D. "Towards a Flexible Information Architecture: Integrating Business Strategies, Information Systems Strategies and Business Process Redesign." *Journal of Information Systems*, 1993, 3(3), 199–213.

Galliers, R. D., and Baker, B.S.H. "An Approach to Business Process Reengineering: The Contribution of Socio-technical and Soft OR Concepts." *INFOR*, 1995, 33(4), 263–278.

Granovetter, M. "Economic Action and Social Structure: The Problem of Embeddedness." *American Journal of Sociology*, 1985, 91(3), 481–510.

Grint, K. "Reengineering the Labyrinth: The Ariadne Solution." *Focus on Change Management*, 1994, 1, 21–23.

Hammer, M. "Reengineering Work: Don't Automate, Obliterate." *Harvard Business Review*, 1990, 68(4), 104–112.

Leavitt, H. J. "Applying Organizational Change in Industry: Structural, Technological and Humanistic Approaches." In J. G. March (ed.), *Handbook of Organizations*. Skokie, Ill.: Rand McNally, 1965.

Mintzberg, H., and Waters, J. A. "Of Strategies, Deliberate and Emergent." *Strategic Management Journal*, 1985, 6, 257–272.

Mumford, E. "New Treatments or Old Remedies: Is Business Process Reengineering Really Socio-technical Design?" *Journal of Strategic Information Systems*, 1994, 3(4), 313–326.

Pettigrew, A. M. *The Politics of Organizational Decision-Making*. New York: Tavistock, 1973.

Porter, M. E. *Competitive Strategy: Techniques for Analyzing Industries and Competitors*. New York: Free Press, 1980.

Porter, M. E. *Competitive Advantage: Creating and Sustaining Superior Performance*. New York: Free Press, 1985.

Quinn, J. B. *Strategies for Change: Logical Incrementalism*. Burr Ridge, Ill.: Irwin, 1980.

Rockart, J. F., and Short, J. E. "Information Technology in the 1990s: Managing Organizational Interdependence." *Sloan Management Review*, 1989, 30(2), 7–17. Reproduced in R. D. Galliers and B.S.H. Baker (eds.), *Strategic Information Management: Challenges and Strategies in Managing Information Systems*. Oxford: Butterworth-Heinemann, 1994.

Scarbrough, H., 1995. "Review of Eric Trist and Hugh Murray (eds.), 'The Social Engagement of Social Science: A Tavistock Anthology (Vol. II),'" *Human Relations*, 1993, 48(1), 23–33.

Senn, J. A. "The Myths of Strategic Information Systems: What Defines True Competitive Advantage?" *Journal of Information Systems Management*, summer 1992, pp. 7–12.

Venkatraman, N. "IT-Enabled Business Reconfiguration." In M. S. Scott Morton (ed.), *The Corporation of the 1990s: Information Technology and Organizational Transformation*. New York: Oxford University Press, 1991.

Whittington, R. *What Is Strategy—and Does It Matter?* New York: Routledge, 1993.

Zuboff, S. *In the Age of the Smart Machine: The Future of Work and Power*. New York: Basic Books, 1988.

8

The Real Event of Reengineering

Jane Craig and Philip W. Yetton

In a competitive environment that is both dynamic and complex, firms now need an operating core that is at once flexible and cost effective and that simultaneously takes account of customer demands and production requirements. For firms to meet these exacting conditions requires extensive lateral cooperation (integration) as well as precise functional control. Business Process Reengineering (BPR) is the implementation approach many firms are taking in their efforts to achieve such a conjunction of cooperation and control. BPR can be described as follows. Firms should actively manage the set of business processes that are central to competitive success in their industry. Each process will have at least one of three generic objectives—to reduce time, to reduce cost, or to increase quality and flexibility of delivery—with the specific aim of improving performance to meet customer expectations. This process orientation involves spanning traditional functional boundaries to eliminate redundancies and streamline processes.

The BPR movement was initially practice-driven. This gave rise to a large amount of literature by both consultants and academics, but because its roots were in practice rather than theory, newcomers to the field have had a hard time developing a clear picture of what BPR entails or what its distinctive and defining characteristics are. Jones (1994) provides a good overview of this complexity.

One issue on which all writers do generally agree is that information technology (IT) is now important for organizational effectiveness in a way it has not previously been. IT is universally identified as one of a handful of enablers for reengineering. Writers also agree that managing IT is one of several problems that arises with undertaking BPR but it is by no means the only problem. The purpose of this chapter is both to explain the underlying causes for the problem encountered in managing IT—specifically, coping with radical, discontinuous change—and to identify one solution.

One of the strengths of the existing, practitioner-oriented literature is its focus on successes. Unfortunately, however, a theoretical framework that would permit the core issues to be identified from among all the details reported is missing. Writers about BPR are therefore unable to interrogate the practice or to make tractable the issues they acknowledge as unresolved. We begin here by describing the MIT90s model as the basis for developing such an analytical framework. We identify the implicit theories of strategy (the positioning school of Porter, 1980) and change (transformational leadership) that have been directly incorporated into the practice of BPR. We use Davenport (1993) and Hammer and Champy (1993) as the sources for the characteristics of BPR. We then reconfigure the MIT90s model to highlight the central role of IT in BPR and the limitations imposed by the uncritical acceptance of the positioning strategy and the need for radical change. Finally, we consider *emergent strategies* and *strategic intent* combined with *organizational learning* as theories that would support rather than sabotage BPR.

Analytical Framework

The MIT90s framework (Scott Morton, 1991), reproduced in Figure 8.1, enjoys widespread acceptance and recognition in the IT literature. Here it provides a theoretical structure for examining BPR. All the elements identified as relevant for reengineering can be captured within this one contingency framework—strategy as a

Figure 8.1. MIT90s Model.

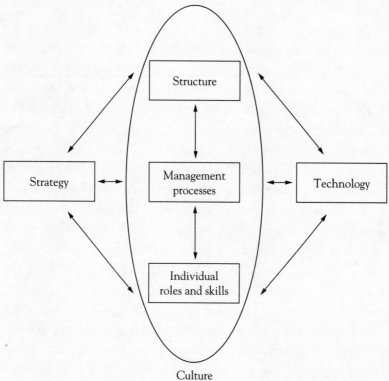

Culture

Adapted from Scott Morton (1991, p. 20).

determinant, IT (technology), human resources (individual roles and skills), and structure and culture as organizational enablers and constraints.

Implicit Foundations

The BPR literature makes three important assumptions, often implicitly. Figure 8.1 illustrates the first of these—the theory of organizational fit. This states that fit contributes to superior performance and that optimal performance will occur only if there is a fit among all organizational elements (Miles and Snow, 1984).

The second implicit assumption relates to the dynamic by which firms move into fit. Although the idea of fit and a framework such as this one are essentially static and do not themselves imply any sequencing, most applications of such models assume that determining the strategy is the first step in establishing fit. Indeed, the idea that fit leads to high performance has been most comprehensively developed around the link between strategy and structure. The strategic-management and organization-theory literatures have long held that changes in business strategy precede structural adaptation (Chandler, 1962; Rumelt, 1974), with structural adaptation driving a realignment of management processes (Miles and Snow, 1984).

Researchers into the management of IT also implicitly adopt this dominant view about the dynamics of strategic change. They add IT to the conventional model at two separate points. First, they advocate an active role for IT in strategy formation by emphasizing the potential benefits it offers in reconfiguring the business or competition (Henderson and Venkatraman, 1992; Keen, 1991; McFarlan, 1984). Second, the literature recommends that IT be incorporated into the strategy-structure fit by aligning it to the dominant organizational design. The federal IT structure, in which IT is aligned with the existing divisional structure, with IT units at each of the corporate, business group, and business unit levels (see Chapter Two), is the most sophisticated and elegant of the solutions for the alignment of IT management.

The third implicit assumption concerns the positioning approach to strategy that predominated in the 1970s and 1980s. This approach sees strategy formation as a controlled, conscious process that produces full-blown strategies, which are made explicit before they are implemented (Mintzberg, 1991). It is predicated on a formal strategic-planning model in which senior managers generate and review options, analyze the options, formulate a position on the basis of that analysis, and then implement the strategy. This approach is consistent with Porter's (1980) notion (derived from economics and the theory of industrial organization) that because some industries are more attractive than others it is desirable to establish a position in them.

These implicit assumptions about the dynamic path to fit together imply that once the strategy-structure configuration is right, all the other elements should be aligned to it. These assumptions are apparent in the BPR literature, which, at the broadest level, describes and recommends two procedural steps—to develop a radically different idea for a process and then to implement it. For the design phase, being courageous and imaginative is seen as the key issue. What is and what should be are assumed to be widely divergent. Many BPR authors argue that the new process should be guided by what exists only insofar as current processes indicate problems. Sticking with these processes is a trap and will typically lead to a failed BPR effort. Indeed, Hammer and Champy claim that "one of the hardest parts of reengineering lies in recognizing the new, unfamiliar capabilities of technology instead of its familiar ones" (1993, p. 85). Thus BPR suggests discontinuous, major change. IT has a starring role in the design stage, where it is claimed to dramatically expand the range of the possible. According to most BPR authors, the possibilities of IT should be the primary determinant of where to reposition.

Once the new orientation or strategy has been decided, implementation involves the management of a number of factors, including structure, management processes, and individuals' skills, roles, and responsibilities. Hammer and Champy baldly state that "reengineering determines first *what* a company must do, then *how* to do it" (1993, p. 33). Thus, when the BPR literature deals with the implementation phase, it emphasizes steps and procedures. The focus is on structured, planned, rational project management as the primary mechanism for dealing with the large-scale change that will be required over a period of up to five years. IT has at least two parts to play in this implementation stage. Because it is one of the elements that needs to be aligned with the new strategy, it has to shift from its current emphasis on supporting separate vertical systems within organizational functions, or silos as they have come to be called, to flowing horizontally across the organization. IT also has a second part in the implementation problem in the sense that it is a project that has to be brought in to specification, on time and on budget.

Reconfiguring the MIT90s Model

This two-step process for BPR and the twofold role of IT in both the design and the implementation phase can be illustrated by reconfiguring the MIT90s model to form two triangles, as shown in Figure 8.2.

Figure 8.2 places technology (IT) at the center, highlighting that technology has two roles—as a determinant of what new strategy might be attractive and as an element to be aligned with the new strategy-structure configuration.

The BPR literature focuses on the top triangle, which comprises strategy, technology, and structure, as the source of major strategic gains, taking an essentially top-down approach. Attention is automatically directed toward this grouping by the implicit theoretical combination of a positioning view of strategy formation and the dominant dynamic for achieving fit. The real substance, including the cleverest use of IT, is considered to lie here. At the same time, the issues about managing BPR that all authors identify as needing resolution lie in the bottom triangle—technology, management processes, and individuals' skills and roles. However, because most practitioners come to the table thinking, "Step one, design the top triangle; step two, implement the bottom triangle," the difficulties that arise in relation to the bottom triangle are seen as implementation problems that occur after the event and thus as a nuisance. The question automatically becomes "How do we fix the implementation problems?" and the intuitive answer is "We make sure the design is really good so everyone will have a clear picture of what they're supposed to be doing." In other words, the solution to

Figure 8.2. Different Focuses of BPR Literature and BPR Activity.

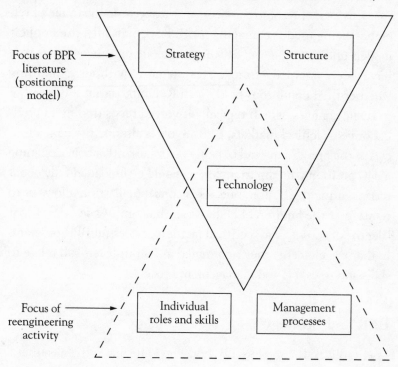

solving problems that occur in the bottom triangle is to specify the top one better—both more clearly and more accurately. Consequently, many of the checklists, watch points, and procedures suggested in the BPR literature relate to controlling and planning the design process better in order to guarantee a more specific and more nearly optimal design.

We do not mean to suggest that the BPR literature does not address or attempt to deal with any of the issues relating to the bottom triangle. It does, and at great length, but with no real success. Most of the issues are acknowledged as difficult and not yet resolved by organizations. Experience bears out this analysis: few firms capture the expected dramatic gains from BPR (Hall, Rosenthal, and Wade, 1993; Hammer and Champy, 1993). Rather than claiming we can solve the problems that have frustrated others, we propose that this lack of resolution occurs in part because the frame of reference being used is damaging for BPR. Specifically, the implicit models underpinning the BPR literature are contingent ones that have been imported from other domains without examining whether their conditions hold for BPR. Unlike most of the earlier strategic changes, which typically involved repositioning in product or geographical markets, BPR involves altering the competencies of the firm. So instead of being predominantly about designing a new position (the top triangle), it should be fundamentally about reconfiguring the bottom one. This conceptualization allows us to reinterpret the findings of Hall, Rosenthal, and Wade (1993) that "depth" of activity was a critical factor in successful BPR programs in that the elements they nominated as "depth levers" all relate to skills and roles, IT, and management processes.

BPR and Strategy

Essentially, BPR combines two concepts. The first is the idea that a few key processes will determine the competitive success of a company. The second is that the entire set of activities involved in delivering a business process should be managed as one unit or flow of work and that the customer's expectations should determine the objectives of that process. Neither of these concepts represents a unique insight. The first is part of the core skill, or competency-capability, approach to strategy (Hamel and Prahalad, 1989), and the second derives from the approach now advocated for most quality programs (Eagleson and Sheather, 1993). In effect, the innovation of BPR lies in rolling together into one activity the two steps of conducting a strategic analysis (identifying core business processes) and developing a detailed blueprint for the new vision (redesigning those processes). But this task, by definition, requires new competencies: elements in the bottom triangle (Figure 8.2) must be substantially reconfigured in order to reintegrate elements that were previously separate.

By contrast, most of the strategic changes made in the 1970s and 1980s, when the dominant-dynamic and positioning models emerged, involved increasing the organization's sensitivity and responsiveness to one (product or geographical) segment or another. The emphasis was on increasing focus and control, typically by driving bottom-line accountability further down the organization. Doing so reduced the need for a complex management hierarchy to deal with a complex external world (that is, multiple products or regions). The basic competencies needed to perform in each of the separate markets were assumed to exist. The design activity primarily involved bundling the resources differently and dedicating them to that segment. So performance losses in the implementation phase could be minimized, particularly by making the changes quickly. And then, over time, separate business units grew increasingly different as they acquired market-specific skills and developed particular versions of what had been generic firm competencies. In population ecology terms (Hannan and Freeman, 1984), such restructuring involved minimal liability of newness because it largely entailed replication, with some regrouping, rather than invention of new forms.

In this world, restructuring was the critical issue because it was the vehicle for dedicating resources and fine tuning. Thus a fundamental assumption of the positioning model and of the dominant dynamic for moving into fit is that the firm does not need new competencies. The empirical evidence in the strategy and structural-contingency literatures tends to support this conclusion. Firms that undertook related diversification performed better than those that moved into unrelated areas, which, by definition, call for new competencies. Consequently, when firms were differentiating markets, it was appropriate to take a top-down approach, beginning with elements in the top triangle and subsequently aligning those in the bottom one, because the bottom triangle contained the requisite set of competencies to function in the new groupings. However, when, as they now do, firms seek to reintegrate elements that are common and not specific to market segments, the real activity involves creating new competencies by substantially reconfiguring the elements in the bottom triangle. Dealing with these elements is not the problem that comes after the event. It is the real event of reengineering. And the substance of the BPR literature confirms this observation.

While a new product or market strategy or a new structure can be determined off-line on the basis of *ex ante* analysis and then implemented on a certain date, BPR is typically not so straightforward. Reengineering requires that an organization master a new set of competencies which are a composite not only of new technological capabilities but also of new individual skills and roles and of complex interactions of subprocesses. Because of the complexity, interdependence, and novelty of this configuration, designing it all in advance is simply not possible. Nor, because it involves at a minimum individuals learning new skills and roles, can it all be implemented at a single point in time. In effect, the new management competencies simply do not exist. In turn, without the management processes that would easily provide accurate, timely data on the new skill sets, the organization cannot monitor performance data and continually adjust. So adopting a positioning model for BPR necessarily means that all the problems will lie in implementing the new design rather than developing it.

Thus the framework in Figure 8.2 makes clear where the literature says the problems with BPR occur (in implementation—the bottom triangle), where the solution they advocate lies (in better design, using strategic analysis and planning—the top triangle), and the tension between them. It also shows that the nature of BPR, which involves creating new core competencies, suggests that problem definition should treat the bottom triangle as the real event and that solutions deriving from the top triangle may not be helpful.

BPR and Radical Change

As well as showing where the problem with the current approaches to BPR lies, Figure 8.2 also sheds light on the form and nature of the problem. While the positioning approach and dominant dy-namic for moving into fit prevailed in the strategy and organization literature, transformational leadership, which emphasizes having a new vision and implementing it, was favored in the change world. This framework reinforces the positioning model and, again, focuses on the top triangle. It emphasizes that the organization is going to be different from how it is now. Consequently, the transition from the current location (A) to the preferred position (B) is the central problem. The proposed solution involves developing and commu-nicating a detailed vision of what B looks like. In this context, A is important only because it is undesirable and to be avoided. Indeed, the more different B is from A the better.

This implicit mind-set is also clearly apparent in the BPR liter-ature, which does not equivocate about the need for radical reposi-tioning of most American firms. "Reengineering is about inventing new approaches to process structure that bear little or no resem-blance to those of previous eras. . . . Reengineering takes nothing for granted. It ignores what *is* and concentrates on what *should be*" (Hammer and Champy, 1993, pp. 33, 49). This observation is also universally extended to the normative proposition that a radically different competitive position can be reached only by a wrenching, discontinuous change process. Davenport (1993), for example, explicitly rejects incremental changes, which he terms "process improvement," in favor of "process innovation"; Hammer and Champy's (1993) term for this type of innovation is "reinvention."

Certainly the emphasis on inventing new approaches is appro-priate in light of the changed competitive environment organiza-tions now face in most industries. If a firm is to respond by becoming a customer-driven organization with the value chain or subchains directly linked to adding value to the customer, then the traditional, functionally structured organization is not a desirable starting point because the bases of expertise, control systems, recruitment, pro-motion, training, and IT all run vertically within functions. The goal of reengineering is to build such a new and different organiza-tion that the old one is discounted as a possible starting place for change. In contrast, there is no obvious sense in which the elements or the characteristics of the bottom triangle, where the reengineering is conducted, indicate that the change process has to be discontinuous and radical rather than continuous and incremental.

This issue is important because, although radical change is strongly advocated, the current approaches to BPR do not deal effectively with the risk of introducing the dramatic changes they advocate (see Chapter Seven). Problems derive partly from the incompleteness of the vision, partly from the complexity of the change activity, and partly from the fact that the effort may not yield significant results until most of the change is in place, which typically takes three to five years. Unfortunately, by then the new processes may be obsolete.

The high risks and delayed payoff result in a preoccupation with managing the change itself. Determining how to disaggregate the vision into its component actionable elements and devising a workable sequence are daunting tasks. The usual response is a combination of planning and process activities designed to coordinate across and generate ownership throughout the organization. This timetable and breakdown of activities for implementation are driven primarily by the technical considerations related to the design of the end product rather than being influenced by the organization's existing capacities. As the track record of most major change programs shows, this approach rarely guarantees success.

We also find that the assumption that radical change is necessary, which underpins uniformly strong recommendations to strike out bravely, spurning all that currently exists, is never critically evaluated in the BPR literature. For instance, the major authors all point out that continuous improvement objectives of 5 or 10 percent each year are insufficient in the face of intense business competition; only innovation or invention can deliver improvements in performance levels in the needed order of 50 to 100 percent. But, being very simplistic, 10 percent a year compounded for five years represents a gain of 61 percent. Why go for "radical" change of only 50 percent? More important, why subject the organization to all the risks of a major change that will take three to five years to deliver any real benefits and that may not work in any case? Which CEO would not prefer the certain and slightly more modest but still substantial return of 61 percent at the end of the period, with some gains accruing along the way? These issues are left unaddressed in the BPR literature, yet for all but organizations in the most dire circumstances, which have no choice but to make one last roll of the dice, they are arguably crucial. That the relative merits of alternative risk profiles are not explored suggests that the BPR movement has a blind spot with respect to incremental models of process change.

Conceptualizing the literature's distinction between process innovation/invention and process improvement (Davenport, 1993) in terms of the MIT90s model illustrates the contrast. The recommended radical, discontinuous shift can be represented as identifying a new fit and achieving it by uncoupling all the elements and reconfiguring them. By contrast, process improvement, or working on what is, would be equivalent to tightening the links between the existing elements in the existing configuration. But BPR assumes that such a configuration is uncompetitive.

Alternative Theoretical Context for BPR

As a result, the BPR literature leaves firms with few options. The net effect of implicitly adopting the conventional positioning-model logic is that firms are presented with two unpalatable alternatives. The only approach that offers the potential for competitive repositioning (process innovation or invention—focus on the top triangle) entails high risks and all the apparently unresolvable problems of managing large-scale change. The only approach that avoids the risks associated with change on that scale by proceeding incrementally (process improvement—focus on the bottom triangle) will not result in strategic repositioning, and the existing strategic position is assumed not to be viable.

However, a third route to competitive repositioning, by making different theoretical assumptions, does not have to regard working on the top or the bottom triangle as mutually exclusive. Critics of rational approaches to strategy formation have consistently pointed to gaps between observed practice in organizations and the descriptive and normative theories of strategy development and implementation (Lindblom, 1959; Quinn, 1980; Mintzberg, 1991). They argue that strategy formation is an emergent process, rather than a rational one, involving small steps that provide information and a new basis for action and that, over time, gradually foreclose alternative courses of action and limit what is possible. Thus, instead of strategy preceding and determining structure and the other elements of fit, the whole configuration evolves together. Strategic options emerge over a period of time as the firm gains mastery. More recently, and specifically in response to the increasingly dynamic and complex competitive environment faced by most firms, Hamel and Prahalad (1989) have argued that static positioning and fit models are a liability. Firms should instead accelerate organizational learning to outpace competitors in building new advantages.

A theory of organizational learning and mastery, and thus incremental change, is a co-requirement of these models of emergent strategy and strategic intent. Effective learning requires goals and feedback and is necessarily an incremental process. In a complex system in which many variables have been changed, as with a redesigned business process, it is difficult, if not impossible, to pinpoint the cause if something does not work. But if the activity proceeds one step at a time, then possible causes of failure can be tested for, even with complex interactions. Such an approach makes the interpretation of outcomes meaningful and accessible both to the individuals and to the organization, and learning is possible. By contrast, it is extremely difficult to learn in a world that is discontinuous.

The alternative model of "dynamic improvement" (Craig and Yetton, 1992) draws on these different theories to formulate an approach to BPR that provides firms with the capacity to relocate competitively with few of the risks associated with radical process innovation/invention. Here, both triangles from Figure 8.2 are simultaneously important. The top one, however, expresses a broad strategic intent rather than a highly specified particular vision, while the bottom one is the starting point for a learning process that seeks performance gains from the largely neglected and therefore unexploited realm of integration across existing internal boundaries. Thus, instead of beginning with a strategic vision, firms may be able to start anywhere in the bottom configuration, with all their action framed by their strategic intent. This possibility explicitly acknowledges that BPR is challenging not only because some of the activities in a process are new or because treating a particular process as a coherent set of related activities is new but also because each process entails the complex crossing and recrossing of many functional boundaries.

These different theoretical approaches to strategy formation and the change process have empirical support in the IT area, where suggestions have begun to surface that successful firms follow different dynamics in achieving fit. It may be that at times strategic repositioning has been a bottom-up process, and the top has simply adopted the win. Ciborra (1991), for example, plausibly reinterprets some familiar war stories, traditionally presented as examples of organizations' rationally devising radical, new IT-centered strategies, from the perspective of a more emergent development process for the strategic IT. On this reinterpretation, innovations such as SABRE or American Hospital Supply's network of terminals were made into the core of a deliberate strategy only after they had emerged within their organizations and been recognized as a transformation.

Summary

In this chapter we have argued that the implicit selection of theories by BPR authors from the strategy and change domains leads to a framing of BPR that limits the likelihood of finding workable solutions for it. The combination of the positioning model with the dominant dynamic generates an intuitive focus on implementation as the problem and design as the response. But the detailed design required is not feasible given the newness of and complex interrelatedness entailed in reengineering processes. Similarly, the focus on radical change, which is consistent with these strategic frameworks and picks up transformational models from the change area, exposes organizations to high levels of risk without providing effective means of managing those risks.

Importantly, nothing in any of the descriptions of BPR activity that appear in the literature suggests that these models are appropriate, let alone the best available. The substance of BPR activity involves complex reconfiguration of elements in the bottom triangle. The strongly, almost stridently, normative prescriptions to focus on design as a first step and to act radically, not incrementally, are simply a "rational" overlay on the phenomena that are reported rather than an orientation that flows naturally from them.

It is understandable that these theoretical models were taken up, particularly when that adoption was implicit rather than explicit. Each represents the prevailing wisdom in its field. But both have historical antecedents different from those that precipitated BPR. One would not expect models that worked for differentiation and rebundling of existing competencies to work well for creation of new competencies through reintegration.

Yet within both the strategy and the change fields, competing theoretical frameworks exist that are appropriate to such activity. Here we have argued that drawing on these by taking an emergent and strategic-intent approach to strategy formation, in combination with an organizational learning model, transforms BPR into an activity that is tractable, with an increased certainty of yielding the anticipated results. When this dynamic improvement orientation is adopted, the firm can proceed incrementally, thereby avoiding the risks involved in instituting major, discontinuous change, and still achieve a radically different outcome. In this conceptualization, the firm's current position simply represents the first step on a long march rather than the take-off point for a leap into the unknown.

References

Chandler, A. D., Jr. *Strategy and Structure: Chapters in the History of American Industrial Enterprise.* Cambridge, Mass.: MIT Press, 1962.

Ciborra, C. U. "From Thinking to Tinkering: The Grassroots of Strategic Information Systems." *Proceedings of the Twelfth International Conference on Information Systems.* New York, 1991.

Craig, J., and Yetton, P. W. "Business Process Redesign: A Critique of Process Innovation by Thomas Davenport as a Case Study in the Literature." *Australian Journal of Management,* 1992, 17(2), 286–306.

Davenport, T. H. *Process Innovation: Reengineering Work Through Information Technology.* Boston: Harvard Business School Press, 1993.

Eagleson, G., and Sheather, S. *Total Quality Management.* Sydney: Australian Open Learning Program, 1993.

Hall, G., Rosenthal, J., and Wade, J. "How to Make Reengineering Really Work." *Harvard Business Review,* 1993, 71(6), 119–131.

Hamel, G., and Prahalad, C. K. "Strategic Intent." *Harvard Business Review,* 1989, 67(3), 63–76.

Hammer, M., and Champy, J. *Reengineering the Corporation: A Manifesto for Business Revolution.* New York: HarperCollins, 1993.

Hannan, M., and Freeman, J. "Structural Inertia and Organizational Change." *American Sociological Review,* 1984, 49, 149–164.

Henderson, J. C., and Venkatraman, N. "Strategic Alignment: A Model for Organizational Transformation Through Information Technology." In T. A. Kochan and M. Useem (eds.), *Transforming Organizations.* New York: Oxford University Press, 1992, pp. 97–117.

Jones, M. "Don't Emancipate, Exaggerate: Rhetoric, Reality and Reengineering." In R. Baskerville, S. Smithson, O. Ngwenyama, and J. DeGross (eds.), *Transforming Organizations with Information Technology.* New York: Elsevier, 1994.

Keen, P. *Shaping the Future: Business Design Through Information Technology.* Boston: Harvard Business School Press, 1991.

Lindblom, C. "The Science of 'Muddling Through.'" *Public Administration Review*, 1959, 19(*1*), 79–88.

McFarlan, F. W. "Information Technology Changes the Way You Compete." *Harvard Business Review*, 1984, 62(3), 98–103.

Miles, R. E., and Snow, C. C. "Fit, Failure and the Hall of Fame." *California Management Review*, 1984, 26(3), 10–28.

Mintzberg, H. "Strategy Formation: Schools of Thought." In J. W. Fredrickson (ed.), *Perspectives on Strategic Management*. New York: HarperCollins, 1991.

Porter, M. E. *Competitive Strategy: Techniques for Analyzing Industries and Competitors*. New York: Free Press, 1980.

Quinn, J. B. *Strategies for Change: Logical Incrementalism*. Burr Ridge, Ill.: Irwin, 1980.

Rumelt, R. *Strategy, Structure and Economic Performance*. Boston: Graduate School of Business Administration, Harvard University, 1974.

Scott Morton, M. S. (ed.). *The Corporation of the 1990s: Information Technology and Organizational Transformation*. New York: Oxford University Press, 1991.

Part IV

New Interpretations

The three chapters in Part Four issue fundamental challenges to traditional thinking. Chapter Nine concentrates on theories that use countervailing forces for explaining and understanding paradoxical and unpredicted outcomes of IT-based transformation projects. Chapter Ten emphasizes that technological and organizational outcomes are joint products of one process rather than one being the result of the other. Chapter Eleven reconceptualizes transformation, presenting a future in which organizations are in a continual state of partial transformation.

Daniel Robey starts with the paradox of the potential versus the actual performance of IT-based change (Chapter Nine). The question this paradox has led managers and technologists to ask is what makes the difference between those cases where the technology does deliver and those where it does not.

Robey takes a step back to look at what we know before advancing to how we might learn more. There is no point in inspecting more cases, carrying out more surveys if the research so far does not make sense. He reviews existing research and finds that the only consistent result is that the results are inconsistent!

As a first step forward, he argues that we have relied too heavily on the technological determinism criticized elsewhere in this book rather than on the logic of contradiction—organizational outcomes from IT-based change are the result of the contradictory forces of persistence and change. No wonder there is variability in the outcomes.

His second step is to identify forces of persistence. He finds four: political interests, organizational culture, institutional factors, and organizational memory. Each is tractable to some degree within its own framework, but there is no available integrating theory. The best we can do is acknowledge the logic of contradiction and look out for the forces of persistence when we are seeking to manage IT-based change, but we cannot expect to be able to achieve consistently successful results.

In Chapter Ten, Rod Coombs agrees with Robey that we are always likely to encounter unanticipated outcomes, although his route to this conclusion is different. He presents a summary account of an eight-year research project that has studied IT-based organizational change in several economic sectors in the United Kingdom. Coombs's project is unusual in that it deployed several strands from contemporary European sociological thought. The reader will be struck by the marked similarities between his conclusions and those of authors in this book while at the same time recognizing some real differences of insight.

Like others in this volume, Coombs rejects technological determinism and hence the idea that IT has specific effects. His own approach, derived from the relatively new actor-network theory, is both similar and different. He altogether rejects the distinction between IT and the business: the technological is not to be distinguished from the organizational because this distinction leads us into thinking in simplistic terms about cause and effect. Instead, IT and organizational change are joint outcomes of the same set of processes.

Unlike others, Coombs lingers over the distinctive nature of IT as a representational medium. IT allows us to represent organizational reality in many and various ways that can be quickly reconfigured. This quality makes IT both a powerful resource in organizational change and the focus for conflict over what that change should be.

Chapter Eleven is different from the rest of the book because it does not explicitly deal with IT-based organizational transformation. Claudio Ciborra muses on the special conditions that currently apply in high-tech industries with an eye to ascertaining whether they could become a model for future organization. Ciborra sees a world in which organizations do not measure up to textbook strategy-structure forms because they inhabit such a turbulent and complex environment. What could be less stable than having to perpetually ask "What is my business?" and "What industry am I in?" Yet these are the questions the most technologically advanced companies face.

How do these companies respond? They become what Ciborra calls *platform organizations*, which are characterized according to a resource-based view as collections of recombinable resources. Contrary to classic management theory, the "engine of recombination"—in other words, the way they are deployed—is improvisation, not planned decision making. The platform is not an existing, ideal organizational type but may be a combination of different structures in different parts of the same organization. Such organizations are shapeless in the sense that they have no single, enduring form. The central competency for the platform organization is to be able to operate in such an apparently anarchic situation, to be able to change structures, even industries, in less time than other organizations take to introduce a new product. The reason organizations like Olivetti are able to succeed is because the essence of this competency lies not in structures, roles, management processes, and task routines but in the underlying cognitive framework by which successful managers operate.

The story Ciborra tells seems almost like science fiction, but it is real enough in one economic sector. The issues he does not address here are how long it will be before the platform organization comes to dominate in other sectors, and what would that mean for

IT-based change. Not only is improvisation not the basis for today's information systems, but we do not even pretend to know how to design for improvisation. What will be the fate of the classic, multi-year project cycle with extended periods of identifying user requirements, long-drawn-out development, and five-year paybacks? The answer is that success in such a turbulent world will not be achieved by designs and plans but by experience, knowledge, learning, structures, and processes combined into competencies. Drawing on the chapters in Part Four, organizations will be able to improvise responses to competing forces and unanticipated turns of event so as to fashion technological and organizational outcomes rather than trying to decide them and plan them fully in advance.

9

The Paradoxes of Transformation

Daniel Robey

The potential of information technology (IT) to transform organizations has been a consistent theme in management circles since computers were first introduced commercially in the 1950s. Yet the reported experiences of different companies suggest that the outcomes are not consistent across organizations, and in many cases a single organization has experienced paradoxical and ironic outcomes. The objectives of this chapter are to identify such paradoxical outcomes and to guide managers in how to cope with them. Fresh ideas for managing paradoxical changes can be found in four emerging theoretical areas: organizational politics, organizational culture, institutional theory, and organizational learning. Whereas more conventional theories employ a logic of determination, each of these approaches accounts for both organizational persistence and change by incorporating a logic of contradiction. Each approach provides useful guidance for the practicing manager by stimulating questions about change and opposition to change.

The Logic of Determination
Beneath Visions of Tomorrow's Organizations

Each new generation of technology and each major technological advance is invariably ushered in with energetic claims that

---

Note: Earlier versions of this chapter were presented at the National Meeting of the Academy of Management, 1995, in Vancouver, and at the Sixteenth International Conference on Information Systems, 1995, in Amsterdam.

organizations as we know them will be radically and fundamentally altered. Leavitt and Whisler's (1958) early forecast set the tone for later speculations, each of which offered compelling visions of organizations in the future. For Leavitt and Whisler, organizations would leverage their mainframe computing power to reduce middle management and push decision making upward to a small executive elite. With the advent of desktop computing in the 1980s, this vision shifted to focus on a workforce of autonomous knowledge workers and empowered clerical staff. As microcomputers became linked within and across organizations, new predictions of "virtual corporations" emerged. More recently, the World Wide Web has spawned still another set of forecasts for electronic commerce among boundaryless organizations and "intranet systems" within them. Programs of Business Process Reengineering proceed apace as newer technologies like workflow management tools enter the picture with their own implications for revised structural forms. These visions are typically accompanied by claims that new organizational forms must be adopted en masse in order to prevent business failure (see, for example, Applegate, Cash, and Mills, 1988; Hammer and Champy, 1993; Lucas, 1996; Scott Morton, 1991).

Although the range of technologies that has fueled these visions has been tremendous, the logic employed by their advocates is usually deterministic. Most such arguments place technology in the role of causal agent, capable of transforming organizations directly through the sheer necessity of using new technologies. Writers who describe IT as a "force," "driver," or "imperative" are advising managers that they must adjust to the demands of this external agent of change. To do otherwise would be to court economic disaster. A more moderate, yet equally deterministic argument portrays managers as designers using information technologies as tools to make new organizational designs possible. Writers who refer to the "enabling" role of IT place managers in the role of causal agent and expect them to make wise judgments about new technology.

The logic underlying these arguments about IT and organizational change can be labeled the *logic of determination*. Both the imperative argument and the enabler argument share the assumption that organizational change is determined by a set of factors whose influence can be identified. The imperative argument implies that determining factors act on their own and cannot be controlled. The enabler argument is more moderate because it provides for control over the forces driving organizational change. But both arguments are essentially deterministic.

The matching of a particular technology with new organizational forms is actually a profound theoretical statement. It means that IT accounts for variations in organizational structure across organizations and that new structures can be expected when technologies change. Equally profound is the statement that managers employ technologies as tools to accomplish business objectives. Few people dispute that managers are responsible for deploying technologies and other resources in the service of organizational goals, yet most managers would admit that the process is not simple. Nonetheless, many books and articles continue to treat both advanced information technologies and managerial intentions as determinants of organizational transformation, reinforcing the simple causal logic linking IT with organizational change.

What Happens in the Real World

The actual experiences of companies trying to transform themselves with IT do not support the deterministic account of how transformation is accomplished. The outcomes these companies have experienced are cataloged both in comparative research studies and in studies of individual firms.

Results from Comparative Research

Accumulated studies produce no consistent picture of the effects of advanced technologies on organizational structures or processes, according to every major review of research (Attewell and Rule, 1984; Huber, 1984; Kling, 1980; Markus and Robey, 1988; Nelson, 1990; Robey, 1977; Swanson, 1987). In fact, the only consistent conclusion we can derive from the research literature is that the impact of IT on organizations is inconsistent! Since the mid-1950s, researchers have discovered IT to be associated with a diverse range of outcomes: highly centralized and decentralized structures, oppressed and empowered employees, hierarchical and nonhierarchical decision processes, and both increases in staff and radical downsizing.

An increasing number of studies indicate that comparable organizations employing identical technologies may experience sharply contrasting consequences. For example, Barley's (1986) study of computerized tomography showed different effects on social roles in two hospitals. Robey and Sahay (1996) found completely different social consequences resulting from the introduction of geographical information systems in two county-government organizations. In addition, Orlikowski (1993) showed that tools for computer-aided software engineering (CASE) produced different degrees of change in adopting organizations. Studies of this type undermine the notion of the technological imperative by showing contradictory outcomes where uniform effects might have been expected.

Armed with such evidence, one finds it hard to support a logic of determination. Research findings provide little basis for predicting what will happen when organizations embark on programs of change with the latest information technologies in their tool kits.

The orthodox response of researchers confronted with such inconsistent results is to refine research methods and to continue the search for the determinants of organizational form. Simple causal arguments are made increasingly elaborate with the inclusion of additional variables. This strategy was nicely articulated by Attewell and Rule (1984, p. 1189): "We must identify those variables that can account for differential outcomes and examine them in a comparative study of a stratified sample of organizations. Variables include organizational size, industry type, degree of prior routinization or variability of work, degree of dependence upon a professional or high-skilled work force, and the patterns of information usage and information flow associated with the technologies in use." By including neglected variables with presumed causal strength, researchers may be able to explain why differences in the impact of technology occur between studies. This strategy employs a more elaborate logic of determination, one that recognizes complexity and previously overlooked variables, but one that also rests on faith in an underlying order within the phenomenon being investigated: IT is still presumed to have predictable consequences for organizations.

Paradoxical Consequences

The faithful search for orderly relations between organizations and IT is further challenged by the findings of several studies that suggest paradoxical consequences of technology. In a paradox, two seemingly opposite statements are simultaneously true. Paradoxes are just one form of contradiction; irony, oxymoron, hypocrisy, double bind, and dilemma are others. Contradictions are commonly used as rhetorical devices to create (and later resolve) tension in a story, expose novel insights, and produce humor. The existence of a tension between two apparently incongruous statements forces creative thinking about how logically opposed statements can coexist in reality. For example, the apparently paradoxical, yet profound, wisdom of "doing more with less" stimulates the creative search for ways to overcome resource limitations. Likewise, foolish and self-defeating practices may be exposed in oxymorons such as "wildlife management." Removal of an apparent paradox resolves the contradiction through either logical manipulation or empirical demonstration.

Examples abound of the paradoxical outcomes of IT in organizations. In February, 1995, Denver International Airport (DIA) opened for passenger service. Built at a total cost of $4.2 billion, DIA was the first new airport to be constructed in the United States in twenty years. IT played a central role in the design of DIA, especially in the automated baggage-handling system. Unfortunately, airlines using DIA had such low confidence in the automated system that they refused to use it, forcing DIA to implement a manual baggage-handling system operating in parallel with the automated system. Ironically, rather than saving money through investments in technology, DIA had to spend more to provide the redundant manual system. DIA's cost-per-passenger after opening was estimated to be the second highest of all U.S. airports. Although new, DIA was the least cost-efficient airport in the country apart from New York's Kennedy Airport (Hoverston, 1995).

Such ironies and contradictions are common in the modern world of work. The wide proliferation of electronic communications, in particular, has led to curious practices with paradoxical outcomes. The daily ritual of well-dressed commuters fighting traffic jams to reach their central-city offices, only to interact hour after hour with their co-workers on electronic mail systems, seems both curious and counterproductive. Likewise, the provision of e-mail services at trade shows and conventions seems inconsistent with the idea of business travel for the purpose of meeting other people. In one study of e-mail use, Markus (1994) found users to be so sensitized to the need to communicate electronically that their face-to-face meetings were frequently interrupted by beeping terminals that signaled incoming electronic messages. Many face-to-face meetings were thereby rendered ineffective despite their supposed superiority in handling equivocal communication. Markus also reported that users found electronic media to be ideal for storing and organizing the trail of documentation needed to justify decisions. Ironically, "such compulsive documentation detracted from the very productivity it was designed to increase" (Markus, 1994, p. 142).

Numerous other studies of a variety of applications of IT support this picture. For example, Orlikowski (1991) argued that the use of CASE tools by a consulting firm resulted in the ironic outcome of standardizing the work of consultants as they simultaneously promised innovative technological solutions to their clients. Elsewhere, Star and Ruhleder (1996) explored the double binds and paradoxes within a community of scientists who were provided with an electronic infrastructure to support their communication with remote laboratories. Among the contradictions experienced was the disincentive for scientists to use their network for sharing preliminary results; they saw electronic sharing as less prestigious than more traditional journals and newsletters. In other research, Kraut, Dumais, and Koch (1989) found that users of a computerized record system ingeniously created a clandestine note-passing facility where no formal electronic messaging had been provided. By leaving notes in a field of the database record intended for customer comments, users were able to communicate with each other through the system. Ironically, one of management's apparent intentions in implementing the system was to increase efficiency by removing such opportunities for social interaction. Finally, Zuboff (1988) reported a case where "open" electronic communication networks were endowed with structures and controls that removed their threat to the traditional hierarchy.

In each of these studies, IT was associated with consequences that were inherently contradictory, even paradoxical. In retrospect, rational explanations could be provided to account for the behavior of individuals and groups that subverted the technology's original purpose, thereby producing the contradictions. I am not suggesting that such behavior is irrational or impossible to understand. Rather, such contrary motives are not easily accommodated by the simple causal logic of determination. In each case where paradoxes of technology use have been reported, more complex causal forces are at work. Theories that anticipate these complexities are potentially more valuable for understanding IT's role in organizational transformation than deterministic explanations offered in hindsight.

Theories That Employ a Logic of Contradiction

In the face of contradictory evidence pertaining to the role of IT in organizational transformation, it is worthwhile to identify theories that employ a logic of contradiction in place of a logic of determination. Theories that incorporate a logic of contradiction are constructed to include two kinds of forces: those that promote organizational change and those that oppose it (Ford and Ford, 1994). Such theories view organizational change as a process in which transformative actions are pitted against persistent structures. As plans for new structures are greeted by opposing forces, strange new contradictory forms may emerge. Such theories are better equipped to explain these emergent paradoxes and contradictions than theories with more deterministic assumptions about change (Poole and Van de Ven, 1989).

Four theories are offered here as fresh perspectives on the old problem of understanding how IT is linked to organizational transformation: political theory, organizational culture, institutional theory, and organizational learning. For each theory, we suggest how information technologies are implicated in the dynamics of persistence and change and how managers might use the theory to guide their thinking and action. Table 9.1 summarizes these theories and contrasts them with the more deterministic theories mentioned earlier.

Political Theory

Political theory uses contradiction as the underlying motivation for social change (Benson, 1977). Organizations are regarded as structures in which the contributions and rewards of multiple parties are permanently misaligned. The resulting tension becomes the source of energy from which efforts to transform organizations arise. However, any attempt to align the contributions of one party more fairly with its rewards is likely to create imbalance for other parties. For example, denial of opportunities for nonmanagerial workers to participate as they desire in organizational decision processes may cause them to oppose managerial attempts to design new structures. However, allowing participation by nonmanagerial workers may prevent managers from realizing important economic objectives and shareholder benefits. Instead of transforming organizations, therefore,

**Table 9.1. Summary of Theories Used
to Explain Organizational Transformation.**

Theories Using a Logic of Determination	*Organizational Outcomes Are Determined by Causal Forces, or Imperatives*
Technological imperative	IT directly accounts for changes in organizational form.
Managerial rationalism	Managerial intentions for changes in organizational form are enabled by IT.

Theories Using a Logic of Contradiction	*Forces Promoting Change Are Contradicted by Opposing Forces Favoring Persistence*
Political theory	Using IT as a resource, groups with incompatible opposing interests engage in political activity, from which organizational changes emerge.
Organizational culture	Cultural persistence opposes cultural change; information technologies are produced and interpreted as cultural artifacts that may symbolize a variety of values, beliefs, and assumptions.
Institutional theory	Institutionalized patterns and practices sustain an organization's legitimacy and are unlikely to change. IT may be adapted to institutional practices or used to reform them.
Organizational learning	Existing organizational memory cannot be obliterated by IT, although technology may be used to support organizational learning.

managers may merely incite opposition from disgruntled workers who are more concerned about their jobs being eliminated than about meeting managerial goals. The collision of transformational goals and political resistance may produce a negotiated compromise. For example, nonmanagerial staff may concede to reorganization plans only if current jobs are not threatened. Such a negotiated solution may be contradictory—perhaps analogous to the practice of retaining firemen on diesel locomotives.

Political contradictions are best understood as dynamic processes, in which currently observable forms of organization are viewed as unstable and temporary solutions to political struggle. Thus, we should never expect to find political equilibrium, just an ongoing contest among groups, each seeking to promote its own interests. At any point in time during the interaction among interested parties, a manager may detect outcomes from the implementation of IT that seem paradoxical. For example, the findings of Zuboff (1988) seem comprehensible only when accompanied by the political interpretations provided by the researcher. In case after case, the "informating" potential of Zuboff's "smart machine" is frustrated by interest groups who wish to preserve their political positions.

As dismal as these results sound, managers interested in using technology to transform organizations must be aware of both the interests of those promoting particular objectives of transformation (usually the managers themselves) and the interests of those opposing them (usually those who will be economically disadvantaged by transformation). Political theory directs attention to these opposing positions and sensitizes the manager to the political dynamics underlying change. It cautions managers promoting change and new technologies to assess potential sources of opposition and to formulate strategies for counteracting them. These goals may be accomplished through more open communication and an invitation to other parties to participate in outlining the dimensions of the new organization. Alternatively, opposition can be dealt with more crudely by reducing options available to resistant parties. Whichever route is taken, managers guided by political considerations will approach organizational transformation with a realistic appreciation for the prospect of opposition to their plans.

Organizational Culture

Organizational culture has been a popular approach to understanding organizations since the early 1980s (Smircich, 1983). Organizational culture is usually defined as patterns of basic values and assumptions that unconsciously guide the behavior of organizational members (Schein, 1992). Because the basic concept of culture was formulated to explain those aspects of social organization that persist rather than change, cultural theories help to remind managers of the difficulty of transforming organizations. Cultural "drag" may be too difficult to overcome even when concerted efforts are made to change culture. Change that is truly "cultural" is made incrementally because old assumptions and values tend not to be given up easily.

Only relatively recently has organizational culture been suggested as an approach to understanding the organizational consequences of IT (Robey and Azevedo, 1994). Cultural theory regards applications of IT as artifacts that reflect social values and assumptions. From this theoretical perspective, even the same technologies can acquire diverse meanings depending on the particular cultural setting in which they are implemented. Consequently, IT's social meanings may be more useful than the technology itself as an explanation of why organizational transformations do or do not occur. Cultural interpretations may prevent even the most ambitious transformation projects from achieving full results, or they may allow ironic partial transformation to emerge. Organizational culture thus provides an explanation for many of the observed contradictions in the empirical literature. The consequences of IT may include revised organizational practices, where new technologies are implemented and used but where users may cling to old assumptions about relative autonomy and control.

When organizational culture first appeared as a viable theory in the field of management, managers were led to think that cultures could be designed and micromanaged. Although such simplistic treatments drew needed attention to cultural symbols and their meaning, it is unlikely that serious managers ever thought of themselves as creators of organizational cultures. More realistically, a focus on culture draws attention to the forces of cultural persistence: shared assumptions, values, and practices are likely to continue in spite of structural and technical changes. When new technologies are introduced behind an agenda of transformational change, cultures find ways to preserve old forms even as the array of artifacts changes. For example, the rituals of old-fashioned face-to-face meetings are often replicated in electronic meeting systems for no other reason than that they are familiar and comforting to the members of an organization. Rituals of dress and appearance are likewise preserved even where contact with colleagues and customers is electronic. Managers must appreciate the logic of contradiction embedded in cultural theory and acknowledge the persistence of a culture even after transformation has occurred. Preventing cultural persistence is unlikely, even in the most radical programs of change.

Institutional Theory

Like theories of organizational culture, institutional theory is generally regarded as a means of explaining why organizational structures and values endure, even in the face of strong reasons and elaborate programs to change them (Scott, 1987). Organizations acquire institutional properties by drawing from abstract ideals that a society shares, such as competition, progress, and efficiency. This "institutional environment" both supports an organization and places demands on it to perform in a legitimate fashion. For example, business organizations are governed by rules that reflect societal expectations about appropriate business conduct. To achieve and sustain legitimacy, organizations tend to conform to institutional models while seeking minor variations to produce competitive advantages.

Nonetheless, seeds of organizational change can be found in institutional theory. Where sources of institutionalized values conflict, contradictory structural arrangements may arise (Meyer and Rowan, 1977). For example, the values of economic performance and efficiency, considered fundamental to the functioning of a free-market economy, may conflict with societal expectations that business provide meaningful employment, wages, and benefits for citizens. These conflicting pressures may lead to paradoxical human resource policies; loyal members of an organization may be laid off or transferred to another organization, as when in-house IT staff are transferred to an outsourcing vendor.

Institutional theory has informed a small amount of research on information systems. King and his colleagues (1994) have identified a broad range of institutional pressures on IT innovation in organizations. Among them are national policies, cultural and religious influences, and economic pressures. Clearly, such a variety can create contradictory signals and lead to contradictory outcomes. For example, companies operating within the European Economic Community were influenced by the policies of the ESPRIT program, which provided incentives for technological initiatives but discouraged sharing of innovations with firms in other countries. This exclusionary policy led multinational firms based in other countries (the United States and Japan, for example) to buy out the smaller European firms to obtain the results of their efforts. By responding only to the local policy initiatives of ESPRIT, the smaller firms lost both their newly developed trade secrets and their sovereignty.

Some researchers have claimed that information systems themselves can take on institutional characteristics (Kling and Iacono, 1989, for example). Institutionalized information systems may resist any attempts to modify them, despite the clear technical advantages of upgrades, conversions, and enhancements. As a result, technically meaningful advances may be avoided in the interests of preserving familiar, institutionalized systems features. Firms may paradoxically support obsolete operating systems that are less effective than cheaper ones available in the market.

Applied to the question of IT and organizational transformation, institutional theory can address contradictions among ideals such as efficiency, rights to privacy, and autonomy, and deeply embedded notions of bureaucratic and hierarchical structures. Although systems may be ostensibly designed to advance one of these valued ideals, usually efficiency, they may inadvertently affect others. Resulting organizational forms are likely to reflect the contradictions among competing values. For example, the persistence of occupational status differences in computer conferences, which have removed visible symbols of status, suggests the durability of our institutionalized notions of social structure (Saunders, Robey, and Vaverek, 1994).

As with organizational culture theory, a manager guided by institutional theory should be impressed by the difficulty of changing institutionalized practices. Institutions evolve over long periods of time, as do cultures. Organizational change, therefore, may produce paradoxes of the sort described earlier in this chapter rather than clean transformations. The logic of contradiction underlying institutional theory draws attention simultaneously to the forces promoting change and those promoting persistence.

Organizational Learning

Organizational learning considers organizations to be cognitive entities, capable of reflecting on their own behavior and modifying it. Thus, unlike theories of culture and institutions, organizational learning adopts an active and optimistic posture toward the prospect of organizational change (Fiol and Lyles, 1985). Organizational change is conceived as revisions to "organizational memory," which consists of shared understandings about the identity of the organization, shared mental maps that relate causes to effects, and stored routines for behavior (Duncan and Weiss, 1979; Walsh and Ungson, 1991). Changes in these shared understandings are not accomplished by the simple exchange of old knowledge for new, particularly where organizational memory is widely distributed among members. As with every theory employing the logic of contradiction, organizational learning theory focuses on the role of existing memory and knowledge in impeding the acquisition of new knowledge. Residual memory may prevent new learning unless there are established norms for experimentation and change. Contradictory outcomes from IT may be understood as evidence of partial learning, where parts of existing memory refuse to be eradicated despite infusions of IT.

The link between IT and organizational learning has barely begun to be explored. Clearly, IT may support the learning process as well as provide electronic repositories for certain types of knowledge (Stein and Zwass, 1995). Also, as more components of organizational memory become embedded within information systems, future learning may be impeded. Gill (1995) has looked again at the experience of Mrs. Fields Cookies, a company whose strategic use of information technologies has become legendary. By employing centralized systems for controlling production and inventory, Mrs. Fields Cookies was able to operate hundreds of small stores as it had run its original store. The company had no middle management, and it achieved prominence as an example of organizational transformation that could occur using IT. However, Gill attributes the strategic and financial demise of Mrs. Fields Cookies to the systems that were responsible for its successes. The flattened hierarchy eventually disabled its ability to respond to changing local markets. Its vaunted systems, designed to remove "unnecessary" layers of management, prevented top management from being aware of needed change. With no middle-management conduit for information other than that which the systems were programmed to convey, top management was unable receive bad news from individual stores and unable to react to the market changes taking place. Paradoxically, the same technology applications that enabled the innovative centralized structure that led to corporate success also disabled management's ability to learn how to change (Gill, 1995).

Managing these contradictions can be accomplished by adopting mechanisms and policies that promote learning. Much has been written about "learning organizations," which pursue experiments continuously to test their assumptions and validate their causal mental maps (Wishart, Elam, and Robey, 1996). Learning organizations can utilize IT, but they must prepare to modify systems and structures on short notice. Learning organizations do not need to have radically innovative structures as long as they allow for experimentation and modification (Wishart, Elam, and Robey, 1996). IT often plays a central role in learning organizations, but it is the learning process that is most important, not the presence of the technology itself. Organizational learning also requires a careful balance between the exploration for new knowledge and the exploitation of existing knowledge (March, 1991); imbalance may result in contradictory IT outcomes.

Organizational learning also provides a fresh perspective on existing methods of achieving organizational transformation, particularly the popular practice of Business Process Reengineering (Robey, Wishart, and Rodriguez-Diaz, 1995). While reengineering is premised on the ability to obliterate existing processes and to begin anew with "blank slates" (Hammer and Champy, 1993), learning acknowledges the value of existing memory. Managers may use existing memory as a baseline for setting learning objectives before they employ the methods of reengineering to produce alternative scenarios. By comparing learning objectives with a variety of plausible future plans, managers can use organizational learning and process reengineering together.

Summary

The theories described above address the common requirement that contradictions be explained rather than removed. Such theories are likely to be useful in accounting for the observed contradictions in research on organizational transformation. Each theory, in its own way, incorporates a logic of contradiction by including forces that both promote and oppose organizational change. Each theory sees organizational change as a process in which transformative actions must overcome persistent practices and structures. As intended new structures are greeted by political opposition, cultural and institutional lag, or existing organizational memory, strange new contradictory forms may appear, defying explanation with deterministic theories.

Table 9.2 summarizes the managerial implications of each of the theories described in this chapter. Common to these explanations is the realization that managers are not in a position to determine outcomes unilaterally. Deterministic logic is antithetical to the theories considered here. Rather, managerial action may be conceived as one of the forces in a dialectical, contradictory process of change. In the case of political theory, the contradicting forces are likely to be familiar; managers have always dealt with political resistance to change and have learned the importance of negotiation and compromise. In the cases of organizational culture theory and institutional theory, managers often cannot overcome cultural and institutional persistence with new technology. If organizational practices are deeply

Table 9.2. Managerial Implications of Four Theoretical Perspectives.

Political theory	Use power and political action to effect change, but plan on resistance to unilateral change. Political resistance to technology-enabled transformations can be managed through negotiation and compromise.
Organizational culture	Cultural persistence cannot be eliminated by technological intervention. Use longer-term strategies of transformation that give time for new organizational practices to become a part of the culture.
Institutional theory	Institutional persistence cannot be eliminated by technological intervention. Use longer-term strategies of transformation that respect the organization's external sources of legitimacy.
Organizational learning	Organizational transformation must honor existing organizational memory. Design technology applications that enable organizational learning, and avoid those that disable learning.

influenced by historical traditions and enduring values, and if they are supported by societal sources of legitimacy, it would be foolish to expect IT to effect transformation. Appreciation and understanding of cultures and institutions may, however, stimulate thinking about longer-term strategies for organizational change. Finally, organizational learning is most likely to lead to a realistic role for IT in organizational change. By drawing on the metaphor of learning to explain organizations, managers may see how information technologies both enable and disable organizational learning. By designing flexible systems that are capable of adjusting to external changes, managers may harness technology in the service of organizational learning. However, existing memory must be dealt with realistically, not as a knowledge base that should be obliterated but rather as a repository of rich historical knowledge.

Efforts to encompass contradiction within the predominant paradigm of deterministic theory are not likely to be successful. In this chapter we have explored four theories that employ a different logic, the logic of contradiction. The search for more complex explanations than we now have of technology's consequences for organizations pushes us in the direction of greater conceptual and methodological diversity. Accordingly, the theories presented here offer little comfort to those seeking to establish or preserve a unified theoretical perspective for information systems or management. Both managers and researchers require a closer match between theory and observed phenomena, and the logic of contradiction contained in each theory is attuned to the paradoxes and contradictions actually experienced when IT is used to transform organizations.

Rather than perpetuating the misleading assumption that IT drives, or even enables, organizational transformation, this chapter directs us toward a different way of thinking about IT. Managers should examine their plans for new structures and processes, and assess their prospects in light of countervailing forces and actions. Where opposing forces are ignored or underestimated, puzzling and paradoxical consequences are likely to ensue. Managing the organizational impacts of new technology requires new theories that acknowledge contradiction instead of insisting on determination. Such a fresh approach should become an integral part of every manager's thinking about organizational transformation with and through IT.

References

Applegate, L. M., Cash, J. I., and Mills, Q. F. "Information Technology and Tomorrow's Manager." *Harvard Business Review*, Nov.-Dec. 1988, 128–136.

Attewell, P., and Rule, J. "Computing and Organizations: What We Know and What We Don't Know." *Communications of the ACM*, 1984, 27, 1184–1192.

Barley, S. "Technology as an Occasion for Structuring: Evidence from Observation of CT Scanners and the Social Order of Radiology Departments." *Administrative Science Quarterly*, 1986, 31, 78–108.

Benson, J. K. "Organizations: A Dialectical View." *Administrative Science Quarterly*, 1977, 22, 2–21.

Duncan, R., and Weiss, A. "Organizational Learning: Implications for Organizational Design." *Research in Organizational Behavior*, 1979, 1, 75–123.

Fiol, C. M., and Lyles, M. A. "Organizational Learning." *Academy of Management Review*, 1985, 10, 803–813.

Ford, J. D., and Ford, L. W. "Logics of Identity, Contradiction, and Attraction in Change." *Academy of Management Review*, 1994, 19, 756–785.

Gill, T. G. "High-Tech Hidebound: Case Studies of Information Technologies That Inhibited Organizational Learning." *Accounting, Management and Information Technologies*, 1995, 5, 41–60.

Hammer, M., and Champy, J. *Reengineering the Corporation: A Manifesto for Business Revolution.* New York: HarperCollins, 1993.

Hoverston, P. "Backers Hope Amenities Will Quiet Critics." *USA Today*, Feb. 22, 1995, pp. 1–2.

Huber, G. P. "The Nature and Design of Post-industrial Organizations." *Management Science*, 1984, 30, 928–951.

King, J. L., and others. "Institutional Factors in Information Technology Innovation." *Information Systems Research*, 1994, 5, 139–169.

Kling, R. "Social Analyses of Computing: Theoretical Perspectives in Recent Empirical Research." *Computing Surveys*, 1980, 12(1), 61–110.

Kling, R., and Iacono, S. "The Institutional Character of Computerized Information Systems." *Office: Technology and People*, 1989, 5, 7–28.

Kraut, R., Dumais, S., and Koch, S. "Computerization, Productivity, and Quality of Work-Life." *Communications of the ACM*, 1989, 32, 220–238.

Leavitt, H. J., and Whisler, T. L. "Management in the 1980s." *Harvard Business Review*, Nov.-Dec. 1958, 41–48.

Lucas, H. C., Jr. *The T-Form Organization: Using Technology to Design Organizations for the 21st Century*. San Francisco: Jossey-Bass, 1996.

March, J. G. "Exploration and Exploitation in Organizational Learning." *Organization Science*, 1991, 2(1), 71–87.

Markus, M. L. "Finding a Happy Medium: Explaining the Negative Effects of Electronic Communication on Social Life at Work." ACM *Transactions on Information Systems*, 1994, 12, 119–149.

Markus, M. L., and Robey, D. "Information Technology and Organizational Change: Causal Structure in Theory and Research." *Management Science*, 1988, 34(5), 583–598.

Meyer, J. W., and Rowan, B. "Institutionalized Organizations: Formal Structure as Myth and Ceremony." *American Journal of Sociology*, 1977, 83, 340–363.

Nelson, D. L. "Individual Adjustment to Information-Driven Technologies: A Critical Review." *MIS Quarterly*, 1990, 14, 79–98.

Orlikowski, W. J. "Integrated Information Environment or Matrix of Control? The Contradictory Implications of Information Technology." *Accounting, Management and Information Technologies*, 1991, 1, 9–42.

Orlikowski, W. J. "CASE Tools as Organizational Change: Investigating Incremental and Radical Changes in Systems Development." *MIS Quarterly*, 1993, 17, 309–340.

Poole, M. S., and Van de Ven, A. H. "Using Paradox to Build Management and Organization Theories." *Academy of Management Review*, 1989, 14, 562–578.

Robey, D. "Computers and Management Structure: Some Empirical Findings Re-examined." *Human Relations*, 1977, 30, 963–976.

Robey, D., and Azevedo, A. "Cultural Analysis of the Organizational Consequences of Information Technology." *Accounting, Management and Information Technologies*, 1994, 4, 23–37.

Robey, D., and Sahay, S. "Transforming Work Through Information Technology: A Study of Geographic Information Systems." *Information Systems Research*, 1996, 7, 93–110.

Robey, D., Wishart, N. A., and Rodriguez-Diaz, A. G. "Merging the Metaphors for Organizational Improvement: Business Process Reengineering as a Component of Organizational Learning." *Accounting, Management and Information Technologies*, 1995, 5, 23–39.

Saunders, C. S., Robey, D., and Vaverek, K. A. "The Persistence of Status Differentials in Computer Conferencing." *Human Communication Research,* 1994, 20, 443–472.

Schein, E. H. *Organizational Culture and Leadership.* (2nd ed.) San Francisco: Jossey-Bass, 1992.

Scott, W. R. "The Adolescence of Institutional Theory." *Administrative Science Quarterly,* 1987, 32, 493–511.

Scott Morton, M. S. (ed.). *The Corporation of the 1990s: Information Technology and Organizational Transformation.* New York: Oxford University Press, 1991.

Smircich, L. "Concepts of Culture and Organizational Analysis." *Administrative Science Quarterly,* 1983, 28, 339–358.

Star, S. L., and Ruhleder, K. "Steps to an Ecology of Infrastructure: Design and Access for Large Information Spaces." *Information Systems Research,* 1996, 7, 111–134.

Stein, E. W., and Zwass, V. "Actualizing Organizational Memory with Information Systems." *Information Systems Research,* 1995, 6, 85–117.

Swanson, E. B. "Information Systems in Organization Theory: A Review." In R. J. Boland and R. A. Hirschheim (eds.), *Critical Issues in Information Systems Research.* New York: Wiley, 1987.

Walsh, J. R., and Ungson, G. R. "Organizational Memory." *Academy of Management Review,* 1991, 16, 57–91.

Wishart, N. A., Elam, J. J., and Robey, D. "Redrawing the Portrait of a Learning Organization: Inside Knight-Ridder, Inc." *Academy of Management Executive,* 1996, 10, 7–20.

Zuboff, S. *In the Age of the Smart Machine: The Future of Work and Power.* New York: Basic Books, 1988.

10

Joint Outcomes

The Coproduction of IT and Organizational Change

Rod Coombs

Information technology (IT) is frequently promoted as bringing the benefits of change to organizations through its ability to support existing organizational processes and to create new processes that provide them with a competitive edge. It is typically assumed that IT can be straightforwardly managed so as to achieve these promised benefits. At one extreme, so to speak, it is thought to be sufficient to implement the technology to achieve the benefits, a view somewhat discredited but not entirely abandoned. At the other extreme, it is thought that the organization, or groups within it, will appropriate the technology to serve organizationally entrenched interests. All such views, which see technology as a simple and objective item, as an "instrument," are fundamentally too

---

Note: This chapter is based on research carried out at the Centre for Research on Organisations, Management and Technical Change (CROMTEC), in the Manchester School of Management, University of Manchester Institute of Science and Technology. The work was funded by the Economic and Social Research Council (ESRC) through its Programme on Information and Communication Technology. The author acknowledges both the ESRC support and the contributions of the rest of the CROMTEC research team. This chapter draws in particular on the work of Brian Bloomfield, Richard Hull, David Knights, Fergus Murray, Theo Vurdubakis, and Hugh Willmott.

simplistic both in their understanding of technology and in their appreciation of the dynamics of organizational life.

Were organizations more content with the results they have achieved from IT investment, it would be harder to justify our adopting an alternative, more critical approach. As it is, organizations and their managers are often, even usually, disappointed. We believe therefore that it is both justified and timely to subject existing thinking and existing practice to a different scrutiny—through the lens of the social sciences rather than that of conventional management theory.

This chapter presents results from an eight-year program of research conducted from 1987 to 1995 at the Manchester School of Management in the United Kingdom. The Programme on Information and Communication Technology (PICT) focused on the organizational processes involved in the design, development, and use of IT in management information systems and in other strategic areas. Based on a variety of detailed case studies conducted over several years during the course of our research program, the chapter advances some of the distinctive theoretical perspectives through which we have achieved our insights. It is not possible to present in full the theory that informs us and all the results we have obtained. We therefore offer a flavor of our work through a sketch of the theoretical background and its distinctive characteristics, some cameos of our research, and a summary of a number of our more important results. As social scientists using recent social science theories, we are most concerned to understand and explain, rather than to prescribe. Nevertheless, we believe that our results are relevant to managers and that the understandings we offer can help managers obtain more satisfactory results when they seek organizational change with IT.

We offer several contributions and insights. The theoretical background itself is a salutary counterbalance to traditional IT management thinking. The value of this background is best seen in the way it has revealed the joint character of the processes through which organizations and technologies change and evolve. Neither IT nor organization is a lever that can be manipulated to obtain planned organizational benefits; rather IT and organization are joint outcomes of a set of organizational processes. If we understand the processes, we may better understand the outcomes. We also reconceptualize the technology of IT by drawing attention to its special informational character, so as to improve our understanding of the unusual relationship between IT and organization. It also helps us to comprehend the nature of some of the practices surrounding IT, such as IT consulting and systems development methods, and to recognize that they are not neutral tools for achieving an independently specified result but are part of the way organization is represented in its relationship to IT.

We start this chapter by highlighting some underlying assumptions about power in traditional thinking about IT. We then sketch the three distinct theoretical perspectives from which we draw our understandings; the first of these perspectives, the disciplinary view of power, contrasts with the assumptions of traditional thinking. We briefly describe a number of our areas of research, including studies of IT use in different economic sectors; analyses of practices surrounding IT design, development, and use; and reassessment of currently popular thinking relating to networked organizations and Business Process Reengineering. We draw together our results to develop some conclusions for both further theory development and practical application. Finally, we draw a clear distinction between both prior and current thinking about IT and the alternative perspective we present.

Two Accounts of Power in IT

The central issue with which we are concerned is the way in which power relationships between groups of people in organizations interact with decisions concerning the design and use of information systems. This issue has often been presented as variations of two oversimplified accounts. Caricaturing somewhat, we can describe these two accounts as follows.

Information Systems as Pliable Tools

In the first case, the account begins from an analysis of (or even simply the assumption of) an existing "distribution" of power in an organization: certain characteristics, such as structural arrangements, roles, and control of resources, confer power on individuals and positions. Given this distribution of power, the design of an information system, even if it is done using some democratic and participative mechanism, will somehow embed these power relations in the technology that emerges. In this model, then, distinctive patterns of monitoring and control (including patterns characterized more by the absence of monitoring and control than by their presence) will be incorporated into an information system during the systems development process, which is seen as structured by existing power distributions.

In a more dynamic version of this account, an organization's information systems may be seen by one group as having the potential to enhance its power position. Such a group might then use information systems as the cutting edge of a process of organizational change that alters work routines, the division of labor, and levels of visibility of work performance. In this case, the information system and its development process constitute an instrumental device that acts as a new resource in the maintenance or reinforcement of power relations, and thus the technology within the information systems is configured in a particular way to reflect that instrumental role.

Information Systems as Disrupters of Power Distributions

In the second approach, many aspects of the analysis are the same as in the first case: a presumed distribution of power and a set of intentions written into the systems development process that are designed to alter that power distribution. The difference in this account is that the technology is not seen as simply a passive reflector of organizational forces. Instead, it is seen as having some "intrinsic" properties that are not completely overwritten by the organizational factors. These properties structure the outcome in ways that do not derive entirely from the intentions of the human actors. Examples of such alleged intrinsic properties are the notion that information systems decentralize organizations; or that they empower individuals; or indeed, as some suggest, that they do the opposite.

The difference between these two perspectives, then, is that in one case the technology is seen as directly "shaped" by preexisting organizational factors, while, in the other case, the technology is seen as having a degree of specificity that can shape organizational processes. However—and this is particularly important for the argument we develop in this chapter—both perspectives share a concept of power in organizations that is static. Power is seen as a property of a position in a structure or as a commodity that can be accumulated and reinforced by one individual or group at the expense of another. Thus the two perspectives artificially force us to view power as residing either in the organization or in the technology itself. Indeed this treatment of power as a commodity or as a positional phenomenon in a sense forces the treatment of information systems into one or the other of the two accounts described above. The work done at Manchester in the PICT program has adopted a different approach, one that depends on the use of some distinct theoretical perspectives, which are outlined in the next section.

Theoretical Perspectives

In our critical study of IT and organizational change we have employed three theoretical lenses to gain new perspectives. They are all different from traditional management theory, having their roots in contemporary European social theory. Each on its own challenges us to see IT adoption and use rather differently. Together they represent an important alternative basis for understanding.

Disciplinary Concept of Power

This view has at its heart the notion that power in organizations does not derive from certain individuals coercing or exerting direct control over others. Rather power results from "self-disciplining" individuals and groups controlling their own behavior because they have internalized deeply embedded constructs and understandings that originate in the organization's "politics." This view draws on a number of strands in the literature on organizations and social theory, especially the writings of Michel Foucault on power/knowledge, the work of Anthony Giddens on structuration, and the trend in organization studies to see power as a relational phenomenon rather than as a property of one agent or another.

In this approach individuals play a part in the exercise of power because their subjective experience interacts with organizational phenomena in ways that lead to their disciplining themselves. Consequently, we focus here on the interaction between subjectivity and organizational phenomena, and the part this interaction plays in the creation and maintenance of power relationships. This approach was deployed in our research in the analysis of the development of major IT systems in private and public organizations, with the focus initially on the dynamics of the relationships between different functional groupings within each enterprise.

Here is a brief example of how this perspective works in practice. Hospital doctors in the United Kingdom have traditionally had no control over the "supply" of patients who are referred to them for treatment. They also have a strong set of values and a professional culture that require them to treat all patients in the best possible way and to make their own judgments on these matters. At the risk of some oversimplification we can therefore say that the expenditure incurred is a result of treatment decisions rather than a factor which influences decisions. But when government and health authorities seek to control expenditure, they encounter the clinical freedom of doctors as a "problem." Information systems appear to provide one element of a solution to this problem because they at least enable the cost of treatment per patient to be tracked, calculated, and made visible, whereas before they were invisible.

But what should be done with these data once they are collected? One approach is to give them to managers and then assume that the managers will have additional power with which to coerce changes in the behavior of doctors. This approach rarely gains the results intended because this purely instrumental view of power is too simplistic. But the alternative approach is to place the information in the hands of the doctors themselves and allow them to consider its significance as a point of comparison between doctors. Our research suggests that doctors will then begin to change their value systems and conceptions of "appropriate" professional practice. The result is that their framework for decision making shifts, and they "discipline" their own behavior in ways that are subtly different from before.

This is not a case of the doctors or the managers using the technology as a tool with which to further entrench their own positions of power. Rather, the doctors do indeed make some changes to their behavior that are consistent with managers' goals. But they do not do so because of an exercise of power by the managers; instead, they "discipline" their own behavior.

Actor-Network Perspective

The actor-network perspective, which originated in the work of Michel Callon and Bruno Latour, is now a well-established approach to the study of processes of innovation and technological change. In some respects it can be regarded as a particular strand of analysis within the broader family of approaches to the creation of technology that have been christened "social shaping." Its principal axiom is that, when studying the emergence of a technology, it is necessary to systematically avoid making a priori distinctions between "the technical" and "the social." This methodological principle enables nonjudgmental observation of the practices through which some actors present an issue as being "social," while other actors present the same issue as being "technical."

To give the simplest example: a computer system that was being underutilized or ill-regarded by staff could be diagnosed as either a problem of bad staff attitudes and poor training or as a badly designed system that no amount of training would make any more acceptable. The point here is not to try to find which diagnosis is "right" but to examine the consequences of such claims for what actually gets done to change the system, the training regimes, or both.

The idea of an actor-network centers on the notion that the development of technology involves the building of networks of alliances among various actors, including individuals and groups, as well as among "natural entities," forces, and machines, there being no prior distinction between people and technology in this approach. Building networks involves "enrolling" actors into a network. In one particular "enrolling" maneuver some individuals or groups may seek to persuade others that they share a common cause or interest. They may try to convince the other actors that they have a solution to a problem that matters for the others, and thus that they in a sense represent an "obligatory passage point" on the road (through the network) to a solution. In this framework, "social interests" are not seen as the force or explanation behind social actions but rather as one of the outcomes.

In the example of the underutilization of a computer system, different coalitions of actors may succeed or fail in their attempts to change either the system or the training programs. In so doing, a new, more or less stable situation will emerge in which both the technology and the actors' perceptions of their interests with respect to that technology will have changed. That new situation is not determined in advance either by the "logic of the technology" or by the "power distribution in the organization." Causation is inherently more open than that and may be influenced by the mobilization of other factors from outside, such as appeals to the importance of "upskilling the workforce" or to the "importance of formal systems design processes." Thus, a network of actors forms itself around the situation with the coalitions and interests being an outcome of this process of formation rather than a determinant of it. Inasmuch as management information systems in organizations are complex pieces of technology but are simultaneously woven into the fabric of the organization, they present appropriate opportunities to apply the actor-network approach.

Representational Properties of IT

This perspective is concerned with exploring the significance, for actors' understandings of organizational reality, of the special "representational properties" of IT. These properties lie in IT's claimed ability to produce ever more mobile and combinable "inscriptions" that can represent organizational reality "at a distance." These properties, which emphasize the informational dimension of IT, can be seen as part of its current historical distinctiveness. Thus, while IT can be partly analyzed using received concepts and approaches in the economics and sociology of technical change, it also deserves some analysis that is *sui generis*. This analysis aims to penetrate the point of interaction between the informational content of IT systems and the role of information in the construction and conduct of organizational life. Understanding this interaction is important because control in modern organizations depends heavily on textual forms—written documents using paper or computer media, including reports, letters, memoranda, and policy and procedure manuals—and IT can render these forms more mobile and combinable than they were before. As a result the informational component of IT can and does affect what is perceived as "organizational reality."

The importance of this perspective can be seen in the previous example of cost data in medical practice. The factor that causes the change in the doctors' practice is not their engagement with the technology (indeed they may never see the IT) but with the information that is generated. Through detailed arguments about how medical procedures are costed out, how overheads are calculated, and how comparisons between doctors are made, doctors are drawn into a new calculus of cost effectiveness that then becomes part of the organizational reality of hospitals. The ability of IT to work and rework the data and present it in alternative forms is an important novel feature in the situation.

A further dimension of this perspective on IT is its capacity to help us to examine various discursive practices or "intermediaries" such as consultants' reports, systems methodologies, and project management tools that exemplify the generic attempt to use IT in the creation of organizational rationality. In short then, this perspective highlights the relationships among IT, information, and "meaning" in the organization.

Common Themes

The common themes running through these three perspectives employed in our research program are significant. All three approaches give prominence to the subjective understandings of organizational and technical "facts" that are formed by actors. The processes that generate these understandings are important objects of inquiry, as are the consequences of these understandings for behavior. The connections between actors' understandings and specific instances of IT are twofold. First, there is the (now familiar) possibility that the technology will be the site of contested understandings that influence its evolution and pattern of use. This is a property that IT shares with other technologies. Second, there is the possibility that information systems will be bound up with the creation and mobilization of new understandings of organizational reality. This is a property distinctive to IT. The two instances are not mutually exclusive but can occur in combination.

In summary, our research differs in a number of significant ways from the received perspectives discussed at the beginning of this section. Rather than making a priori assumptions about where power "resides," we focus on the fluid relations between power and understandings within specific networks. We see information systems and new organizational arrangements as being jointly produced within these networks, a process that is understood as one of maneuvering and negotiation rather than of the "exercise of power." The three theoretical perspectives outlined above can be used singly or in combination to examine specific cases of IT use and to provide powerful analytical insights.

Application of the Theoretical Perspectives

This section provides a brief synopsis of selected pieces of our empirical work using the approaches described in the previous section. We include research conducted in the financial services and health sectors, research on management consulting and systems development techniques, and analyses of some popular management ideas relating to IT. Much detail has been excluded for reasons of space but can be accessed through the references provided. Our intention is to give an idea of the type of analysis that emerged so that we can then draw some broader conclusions for both the theory and the practice of innovation in IT.

Financial-Services Sector

The financial-services sector was studied intensively through detailed case studies of particular companies over several years, which were backed up by industrywide surveys. Some of the findings that emerged are described here.

There are profound interactions between the use of IT systems and the progress of deregulation in the industry. One feature of this interaction is that the particular types of managerial expertise needed at the senior level shifted from actuarial and professional skills to marketing, operational, IT, and functional integration skills. Many companies found this transition difficult, and their development of

IT was hindered by this difficulty, as organizational functions competed for influence over IT. In particular, IT strategies were frequently split between market-driven paradigms and operational efficiency paradigms. Thus, rather than IT systems emerging as a distinct reflection of power relations in the organizations, they were the territory within which contested understandings of the industry confronted each other (Knights and Murray, 1994).

These politics of IT development, which occur within most organizations, were found to be greater than average in the financial-services sector because of the larger than average proportion of systems that are industrywide rather than firm-specific. The number and range of interests competing to define and build systems was therefore larger, and the competition was exacerbated by the intense turbulence caused by deregulation and the move to trans-European markets.

The work in this sector illustrated particularly well the notion that "interests" emerges as an outcome of organizational change rather than as the explanatory force behind it (Knights, Murray, and Willmott, 1993).

National Health Service

The National Health Service (NHS) in the United Kingdom is another sector in which our work continued over a long period, and consequently our findings are several. Here we focus on only one major issue.

Information systems and the reports they generate were seen in some sections of the NHS as useful instruments for maneuvering doctors into accepting responsibility for some management decisions. This attempt has been effective to only a limited extent. Doctors have not fully become managers, but they have become more involved in management because of the combined effects of organizational changes that preceded the internal market reforms (a series of reforms designed to create a market between different parts of the health system such as doctors, pathologists, and hospitals), the market reforms themselves, and (to a lesser extent) the enabling role of information systems. But this complex picture has made the design and development of these information systems conflictual and difficult (Bloomfield, Coombs, Cooper, and Rea, 1992; Bloomfield and Coombs, 1992).

We have analyzed this period of change in the position of doctors using all three of the perspectives described above. First, we can view both the attempted shift in their position and the final and rather less dramatic shift as a change in their own self-disciplining behavior, thus reflecting the notion of power as mediated through deep-seated understandings of organizational reality. Second, we can analyze the tortuous processes through which particular information systems were configured and particular job roles linked to them as attempts to build actor-networks. Third, the whole history of NHS information systems is bound up with the unique opportunity to make a major leap in the transparency of the organization and the visibility of the consequences of medical practice for the deployment of scarce financial and other resources through the special representational properties of IT.

Our findings in the financial-services and health sectors are not a neat accumulation of results that permit simple generalizations. Rather, they illustrate our themes of understanding IT-based activity and outcomes in organizations as activities around which actor-networks coalesce, through which interests emerge in ways that allow IT and organizational outcomes to be jointly produced, in which outcomes can be explained as actors disciplining themselves, and in which the information part of IT has the capacity to represent organizational "reality" in different ways.

Management Consulting and Systems Development Techniques

Next we consider some findings that were not related to particular industries or organizations but were specific to particular management practices.

One of the consequences of the more simplistic approaches to IT and power is the belief that desired systems outcomes can be achieved without being disrupted by the "messy" social and political interactions we have described. This misconception is made apparent in our work on management consulting and systems development techniques.

Management consulting firms are important suppliers of expertise in the development of IT systems for customer organizations. Commonly their assignments tie together in an intimate way the design and commissioning of an IT system and the redesign of the client's organizational structures and work practices to mesh with the IT system. Somehow it is felt that even if the client organization itself cannot implement the system cleanly to achieve organizational benefits in a straightforward fashion, consultants can. Therefore, an important feature of the tacit contract between the client and the consulting firm is that the consultants can stand outside the internal politics of the client organization and thus both identify and facilitate an IT-organizational solution superior to that which would be internally generated (Bloomfield and Danieli, 1995). However, while this assignment may appear possible in principle, in practice our research using the actor-network perspective shows that the work of the consulting firm can be carried out only through engagement with the organizational politics of the client.

In the actor-network perspective, in order to get things done consultants have to enroll those actors whose compliance is deemed a necessity, while mollifying those actors whose sensitivities must not be infringed. These demands frequently result in a clear intellectual gap between private views of desirable solutions and public stances, which are couched in terms of what can be "sold" to (the dominant actors within) the client organization. This is not a situation where techniques are "not yet fully perfected"; still less is there any suggestion of bad faith on the part of the actors. Rather the consultants' sensitivity to the power structure of the client organization demonstrates an ineradicable feature of the assembling of technologies in organizations (Bloomfield and Vurdubakis, 1994). Actors cannot stand outside the actor-network and at the same time influence outcomes.

Another finding of our research concerns the techniques deployed in the introduction of IT, such as project management methods, systems development methodologies, and tools for determining information requirements. The use of such techniques and tools presupposes that the organization can be represented in the particular ways that they facilitate. More specifically, the development of an organization in any particular direction through the deployment of IT represents a particular "vision of organizing" that embodies both a critique of existing organizational practice as well as recipes for its radical overhaul (for example, decentralization, efficiency, empowerment). In turn, this "vision" presupposes the use of particular tools for analyzing the organization in information-theoretic terms—an "organization of vision" in the form of specific representational practices such as data modeling and information engineering (Bloomfield and Vurdubakis, 1994). But these practices are employed precisely because they are consistent with the kind of "vision" proposed. They are therefore not neutral but directly supportive of an IT-enabled organization.

Our research on management consulting and systems development techniques leads us to conclude that there are no neutral instruments for developing IT-organizational "solutions"; the use of these techniques constitutes a displacement rather than an avoidance of organizational politics. They are relevant elements of the actor-network.

New Organizational and Management Practices

Some of our research findings relate to new organizational and management practices in which there is deemed to be a special role for IT. These developments, which include "networked organizations" and Business Process Reengineering (BPR), were explicitly studied both through analysis of management literature and discourses and through other empirically based projects. In particular, case studies in large manufacturing organizations cast significant light on the issue of BPR.

The Networked Organization. The networked organization is a loosely defined concept that acts as a flag of convenience for a wide variety of ideas relating to flattening existing organizations, decentralizing responsibility, empowering individuals, and creating immensely flexible relationships among organizations so that ever-changing combinations of productive resources can be assembled rapidly to meet opportunities in the market. Our analysis traces the lineage of the concept back through separate management discourses about firm structure, about technical change, and about cultural change. Lying behind these discourses are long-acting socioeconomic and geopolitical factors such as multinational localization of competitive processes and shifts in the basis of competition from commodities to service packages and from factor costs to the orchestration of knowledge resources.

However, despite the potential of these deep roots to provide a useful explanatory analysis of new directions, including the networked organization, on the whole the literature is unconvincing and contradictory. In particular, two weaknesses can be seen in these ideas. First, despite the years of scholarship that have undermined common-sense beliefs in technological determinism, the view persists that the sheer logic and power of information and communication-network technology will drag organizations toward the "network paradigm." In practice, our reading of the situation is that the implementation of interunit networks often intensifies monitoring and control as much as the reverse. This observation indicates to us that there is more potential for conflict and resistance in relation to the "network paradigm" than is normally acknowledged. Second, the perceptions and attitudes of managers are assumed to be unitary; such a belief implies that "management" will in general be an unproblematical vector for networking and that any resistance will be at other levels of the organization. This view grossly underestimates sources of friction inherent in the internal fragmentation of management into subunits, layers, and specialties.

In sum, behind the rhetoric of "empowerment" through networks, change processes oriented toward a "networked reality" need to be seen as depending on significant amounts of coercion. It therefore seems likely that progress toward the "networked organization" as a widespread phenomenon will not be smooth but will involve a sometimes sharp conflict between the genuine competitive pressures that underlie the trend and the so-far-underestimated potential for conflict and resistance within organizations (Knights, Murray, and Willmott, 1993).

Business Process Reengineering. BPR, a currently popular approach to reorganization of businesses, is characterized by a number of basic principles including the reduction of functional specialization, the promotion of multiskilling of individuals and multiskill teams, the collapsing of previously differentiated tasks and responsibilities into larger and more holistic tasks to be undertaken by individuals, and the targeting of business processes on clearly identified goals external to the employees involved and related directly to customer needs. The early impetus for BPR came in large part from the idea that applications of IT could be a stimulus. IT is often seen as the enabling technology that allows the "horizontal" reconfiguration of workflows and information flows, cutting across vertical functional specializations in an organization. However, some of those involved in the beginnings of BPR realized that allowing IT to be the enabler was dangerous; instead, organizational rearrangements needed to be planned and enacted prior to the final commissioning of new IT systems. To do otherwise would be to commit all the old sins of trying to use the IT systems to push through the organizational changes, with all the attendant possibility for conflict and unpredictable outcomes (Coombs and Hull, 1995).

Despite the attempt to detach BPR from its early image as an "IT-led" approach, most BPR practice remains denuded of any serious treatment of issues in human resource management (HRM) and organizational culture—issues that are normally associated with attempts to change organizational structures and work processes (Willmott, 1995). Lack of attention to these matters continues despite the fact that many other relatively recent management initiatives, such as Total Quality Management, have shifted from an operations management orientation to a focus on "people" issues. One explanation for the persistence of this IT-led approach is that the prevailing economic and political climate results in a tacit view that BPR changes can be implemented without the necessity of HRM lubrication because employees will feel obliged to accept such changes. If this is the case it calls into question the extent to which management thinking has genuinely internalized the value of HRM-based empowerment strategies as sources of performance improvement.

This apparent contradiction was partly exemplified in some of our case studies. We encountered examples of the application of BPR techniques in an environment in which the overarching purpose was strategic reorientation of the business and reduction of the power of functional groups. Commitment from staff to BPR was sought on the basis of the merits of this business strategy. However, a general trend toward cost cutting, downsizing, and increased financial control was affecting the organization in parallel with the shift in business strategy. The two trends, cost cutting and "strategic BPR," interfered with each other to the point where they came to be seen as related. This perceived relationship compromised the success of both approaches and exacerbated HRM problems. This case exemplifies and underlines the problems identified in our analysis of the wider BPR scene.

Implications for Theory and Practice

Our studies of IT in organizations have permitted us to develop a new understanding of power, particularly in its relation to IT. The key has been recognizing the role of information. The specific informational content of management information systems becomes a powerful representation of organizational reality once constructed. But even before that, the process of designing and developing IT provides a means and a focus for questioning inherited organizational structures and practices. This agenda is understood by the participants and therefore shapes their engagement with both the development and the use of IT.

Our work with the disciplinary concept of power marks a major shift in our understanding of the relationship between IT and power, but also more generally it extends our understanding of the nature of management control in organizations. This conceptualization improves on earlier theories that conceive of power as a "property" attaching to individuals, roles, or technology, and that therefore conceive of the role of information in power as merely that of an additional "resource." This new conceptualization helps us to understand why simplistic accounts of power in relation to IT fail to shed light on the varied outcomes from IT and organizational change. Power is not simply a magic ingredient that can be applied to determine organizational outcomes.

The study of IT has therefore created an opportunity to advance organization theory to better accommodate the role of information. This is more than simply an improvement in understanding of a general kind. It is an improvement with sharp contemporary significance because the evolution of organizations in modern society is increasingly bringing the incidence and importance of these kinds of "information-mediated" power relations to the fore.

Although we believe that our major breakthrough was the recognition that the relationship between IT and organizational change has to be conceived in terms of disciplinary power, this breakthrough came only in the context of our work on the IT innovation process. And although our new understandings emerged in part through paying attention to the specificity of IT as a technology—that is, to its distinctive representational character—it was natural that our research program, based as it was on an actor-network perspective that denies any a priori separation between the technical and the social, should focus also on the theoretical fundamentals of organizations and management.

Where Are We Now?

How do we locate our ideas in the historical development and use of IT and its associated thinking? We start from three pervasive understandings, or "frameworks of computing," that have characterized most of the debate, the thinking, and the research and development about computers, people, and organizations since the mid-1960s. These frameworks are not, however, a purely "internal" feature of computing; in many respects they both reflect and affect wider debates about and developments in the relationships among people, technology, and organizations (Hull, 1994a, 1994b, 1995).

The first framework is the "technical" framework that was predominant in the early years of computing. It was characterized by a naïve belief in the possibility of optimizing organizational systems by building them around the power and accuracy of the computing hardware.

The second framework could be termed the "partnership" framework. It takes the view that building human activity around computers does not work because of fundamental incompatibilities between the nature of the two objects. Thus it argues that computer systems have to be carefully redesigned so that they are "configured" to the human user's needs and thus enable the user to see the computer as a tool and an adjunct rather than a master. The user in this framework is still predominantly seen as an individual user.

The third framework is now emerging powerfully; it can be described by the slogan "the organization is the IT and the IT is the organization": in shorthand, the "informated organization" framework. This approach can be seen currently in trends such as computer-supported cooperative work, in some aspects of BPR, and at a broader level in the superhighway debates. The distinctive feature of this framework is that it treats the organization and IT systems as more of an integrated entity and less as two discrete entities. It even acknowledges the substitutability of IT- and non-IT-enabled processes.

At first sight, it might seem that the emergence of this third framework is a small step in the direction of the theoretical stances toward technology and organization that we have described. To the extent that the framework "problematizes" the relationship between the organizational and the technical this characterization may be true. The third framework is emerging, at least in part, from the intellectual and practical engagement of technologists and nontechnologists over how to use IT adequately. In this engagement knowledge from social science is playing its part. However, this framework still presents the relationship between organizational change and technical change in the context of a reformulated determinism centered on the "intrinsic" dynamic of technical change. There is also a further problem. The third framework does not automatically displace the first and second. It would be more accurate to say that the three frameworks are layered on and folded into each other in contradictory ways. The "politically incorrect" technical framework can still burst through from time to time, especially where powerful economic forces appear to demand radical change rather than incremental progress. This layering of frameworks is perhaps part of the problems surrounding BPR. More fundamentally, the third framework, while acknowledging the necessity of a closer integration of IT and organizational issues, still on the whole has an underdeveloped appreciation of the issues of power and representation.

Consequently, at the practitioner level and even in much academic writing, the approach to IT and organizational design is still instrumental. This approach considers the problems of IT and organization as inherently soluble through the application of "rational" principles shared by all participants. In some cases reality does approximate this view. But we have shown that in many cases it does not—not because of bad faith or irrationality but because of the inevitability and intractability of politics and the uncertainties in organizational life (Knights and Murray, 1994; Murray and Willmott, 1993).

Summary

Our approach has resulted in several advances. First, IT can not be *known* as such, as if it were a given and readily understandable object. Rather, it is made known, and therefore available for managerial action, through the deployment of particular intermediaries: for example, consultants' IT strategy reports, user and "how to" guides, systems development methodologies, user manuals, academic texts (including case studies of organizations and IT!). Because IT enters the organizational landscape only through such intermediaries and because we have found the intermediaries not to be neutral means of representing organizational reality, we see the intermediaries as important participants in the actor networks through which organizational and technology outcomes are fashioned. In other words, contrary to the assumptions of traditional IT thinking, the intermediaries are not transparent and cannot be taken for granted in the transition from design ideas to realized organizational benefits.

Second, we have shown that new organizational arrangements and new technological artifacts are frequently joint products of the innovation process and cannot be produced independently of each other. This finding contrasts with positions that see the relationships between technical artifacts and organizational arrangements as the result of power residing in one or the other and hence having deterministic effects in one direction or the other. It also contrasts with bland "interactionist" models that simply place both technological and organizational determinism in a spurious cycle. In fact we would argue that innovation presupposes organizational change but does not determine either its nature or its details.

Third, we have shown that this mutual dependence of organizational and technological innovation extends outside individual organizations to sectoral levels and beyond. Just as our point about intermediaries is that they do not permit us to evade messy conflicts of interest and the like in order to yield "clean" outcomes, so too reorganizing into "networked organizations" does not get us out of the mire. And here is the real force of our findings: there are no ways of escape. It is an inescapable fact of innovation in organizations and particularly IT innovation that there are no simple, clean and neat, cause-effect pairings of technology and organizational change.

Fourth, from evidence across organizations in different sectors, we conclude that a persistent gap between theory and practice means that a species of technicism subsists in the conceptualization and operationalization of the relationship between organizations and IT. However, this gap is not accidental; the common-sense assumption of boundaries between the technical and the social is a primary means through which actors make sense of "technology" and "organization." This boundary is a useful political resource in actor-networks when efforts are made to achieve closure concerning the possibilities and limits of particular projects.

Finally, despite the best efforts of more radical approaches to systems development—for instance, bringing users into the frame in a serious way—they still tend to rely on techniques that undermine their stated intentions. Thus, both "objective" (conventional) and "subjective" (soft systems, for example) approaches to systems development assume the adequacy and therefore the objectivity of received approaches to representation: the social/subjective (user view, for example) becomes translated into the technical/objective (information requirements, data models, for example). But as we have noted, such technical intermediaries, by virtue of their specific representational characteristics, already assume certain kinds of organizational "reality" that may be at odds with the "realities" of users. These implications of our analysis can be summarized as follows:

- Our understandings of a particular piece of IT always come to us through intermediaries such as a consultant report, a manual, or a "received" view.

- Organizational change and IT change are joint products of one process. It is fundamentally wrong to see one kind of change as causing the other.

- Common-sense definitions of what is technical and what is social are not objective. They are claims made as part of maneuvers to achieve a desired outcome in change efforts.

- More participative approaches to systems development do not dilute the effects of the above points.

We have outlined some new academic views on IT and organizations that have emerged from our research. How might we expect managers and IT professionals to view their problems differently as a result of their encounter with these academic perspectives? We would hope that shifts in their perspectives might be reflected in their being prepared to espouse two different views.

First, the important issues in information systems design do not have to do primarily with the hardware or the software but with the way the organization is portrayed to the users through the terms and concepts that the system employs as everyday language. These terms and portrayals of reality actually create the reality. Choosing them and using them is therefore very much bound up with alternative "political readings" of what the organization is doing. The perceived "success" of an IT system will depend crucially on these non-IT features.

Second, we should not see the resolution of the problem of IT systems and organizational structures as "getting them to fit together." That solution implies a clear separation between them. In fact, the organizational characteristics and the IT characteristics have to be conceptualized and changed together. An attempt to use change in one to "pull through" change in the other will usually lead to conflict and failure.

Accepting the two previous points and acting accordingly is difficult. Although we are trying to look at the IT systems and the organization as intimately connected, strong cultural pressures in both the technical and the managerial communities tend to make us continue to see the evolution of the technology as an autonomous force and to see our efforts at organizational change as delayed responses to the challenge of exploiting this potential. Arguably, this view is upside down. We should aim to change the technology and the organizational factors together. To be fully pragmatic, we must be prepared for the fact that unintentional outcomes and clashes of interests will still not be eradicated.

If these views do resonate with practitioners and take root, then we will have made the case for social scientists to play an increasing role in the development and use of IT in the future. We can summarize these practical implications as follows.

- The most critical feature of an IT system is the picture of the organization that it requires the user to accept. This picture affects compliance, resistance, creativity.

- Using IT to "pull through" organizational change will never work.

- Using prior organizational change to create the conditions for successful IT implementation has a better chance of working but is still based on flawed logic.

- IT change and organizational change always take place together and always have some unpredictable dimensions and unintentional outcomes.

- IT professionals need to be organizational theory professionals too!

References

Bloomfield, B., and Coombs, R. "Information Technology Control and Power: The Centralization and Decentralization Debate Revisited." *Journal of Management Studies*, 1992, 29(4), 454.

Bloomfield, B., Coombs, R., Cooper, D., and Rea, D. "Machines and Maneuvers: Responsibility Accounting and the Construction of Hospital Information Systems." *Accounting, Management and Information Technology*, 1992, 2(4), 197–219.

Bloomfield, B., and Danieli, A. "The Role of Management Consultants in the Development of Information Technology: The Indissoluble Nature of Sociopolitical and Technical Skills." *Journal of Management Studies*, 1995, 32(1), 23–46.

Bloomfield, B., and Vurdubakis, T. "The Social and the Technical: An Introduction." *Information Technology and People*, 1994, 17(1), 4–8.

Coombs, R., and Hull, R. "BPR as 'IT-Enabled Organizational Change': An Assessment." *New Technology, Work and Employment*, 1995, 10(2), 121–131.

Hull, R. "The Governance of Computing: Computer Science and the Social Sciences." Paper presented at the Economic and Social Research Council Seminar Series on the "Transformation of the Professions," Manchester, Oct. 1994a.

Hull, R. "Information Management: The Convergence of Diverse Frameworks of Computing." Paper presented to the annual conference of the British Academy of Management, Working Paper Sessions, Lancaster, Sept. 1994b.

Hull, R. "Techno-Subjective Frameworks: The Spaces Between People and Things." Paper presented to the 3rd international Advances in Sociological and Economic Analysis of Technology conference, on "Managing New Technology into the 21st Century," Manchester, Sept. 6–8, 1995.

Knights, D., and Murray, F. *Managers Divided: Organizational Politics and Information Technology Management.* New York: Wiley, 1994.

Knights, D., Murray, F., and Willmott, H. "Networking as Knowledge Work: A Study of Strategic Interorganizational Development in the Financial Services Industry." *Journal of Management Studies*, 1993, 30(6), 975.

Murray, F., and Willmott, H. "The Communication Problem in Information Systems Development: Towards a Relational Approach." In P. Quintas (ed.), *The Social Dimensions of Systems Engineering: People, Processes, Policy and Software Development.* Hemel Hempstead, England: Ellis Horwood, 1993.

Willmott, H. "The Odd Couple: Reengineering Business Processes, Managing Human Resources." *New Technology, Work and Employment*, 1995, 10(2), 89–98.

11

Improvising in the Shapeless Organization of the Future

Claudio U. Ciborra

Try for a moment to put into brackets your current efforts at restructuring or streamlining your organization. You may currently be engaged in Business Process Reengineering, lean manufacturing, or customer reorientation. Try to abstract from all that and reflect on what is fundamental in what you are doing while engaged in business transformation. For sure, you do not want to focus on a specific methodology or the latest managerial formula: you have tried so many in the past, and you know you are going to try out many more in the future, probably at an ever-faster rate. Thus, what is fundamental cannot be the methods and approaches with which you have experimented. We submit that what is fundamental is the "trying out" itself, the relentless experimenting and not the specific object of or approach to transformation. We should extrapolate from this behavior in order to envision the workaday in the organization of the future. Forget process as an object you design and redesign according to the latest reengineering methodology. Rather, reflect on the business process you live through daily: a process of unceasing recombination of resources. Recombination is the main business around which competing and organizing will revolve in the future.

In this chapter we introduce two concepts to portray work as the recombining and organizing of resources. *Improvisation* is the engine of recombination, and the *platform organization* is the context for continuous reinvention of organizational structures. Improvisation turns out to be the key competency in the complex, dynamic, and shapeless organizations that we picture as "platforms."

We anchor our study in what is happening today in those organizations operating in the high-tech sectors, in particular the information technology industry itself. We investigate the nature of the transformation processes that characterize these firms and show that certain practices like "betting," "*bricolage*" or "tinkering" (Lévi-Strauss, 1966), and "improvising" play a key role in their "temporary" survival, while the contours and the structure of the industries where they operate are continuously undergoing radical changes. After an investigation of the cognitive and practical nature of improvisation in various types of organizations, we turn to the issue of organizational design and address the following questions: What kind of organizational "structures" are available to host and enable improvisation, and conversely what kind of outcomes does improvisation generate in organizational routines and arrangements? Our answer suggests that the shapeless platform organization is the outcome of and the context for effective economic recombination of resources.

Lessons from the High-Tech Industries

After the classic descriptions of structural configurations aimed at generating innovation, such as the adhocracy (Mintzberg, 1983) and the self-renewing organizational "tents" (Hedberg, Nystrom, and Starbuck, 1976), three organizational forms have been discussed in the literature in an attempt to capture the dynamics of the flexible firm operating in the turbulent high-tech industries.

Miles and Snow (1992) and Thorelli (1986) were among the first to identify the network as a flexible cluster of firms or specialized units coordinated by market mechanisms instead of by a vertical chain of command. Many high-tech firms, like IBM and Microsoft, can be regarded as dynamic networks that are continually building an "indecipherable maze of international agreements and alliances to protect market share, enter new arenas, seek for technical innovations, and promote the adoption of technical and/or systems standards" (Miles and Snow, 1992, p. 67).

Because product life cycles in these industries are relatively short and unpredictable, it makes sense to base the design of organizations on process capabilities that are general-purpose, flexible, generic, and relatively stable. Boynton and Victor (1991), in their model of "dynamic stability," propose a different definition of a firm: a "treasury of process knowledge." Management is able to apply organizational knowledge to a variety of end products (Prahalad and Hamel, 1990), which allows organizations to decouple process management capabilities from the generation of a whole array of product innovations. The dynamically stable organization contains two levels: the product level (frequently changing) and the process level (changing more slowly).

Finally, Bahrami (1992) describes high-tech firms as "structured and yet chaotic." These firms have developed "dualistic organizational systems" made up of a "bedrock" and a few temporary arrangements. The bedrock is the formal structure, which only periodically undergoes major transformations. The overlays of project teams and multifunctional groups change frequently. Such dualistic arrangements enable these firms to achieve a crucial foundation through creating a relatively stable setting within which people and resources can be flexibly deployed.

A somewhat different model emerges from the study of one of the largest European computer manufacturers (Olivetti) during its period of major growth in the 1980s (Ciborra, 1996). This firm continually switches between sharply different technology life cycles instead of evolving through successive product generations. Thus, Olivetti originally assembled mechanical typewriters, then electrical ones, then electromechanical systems, electronic typewriters, PCs and minis; today it is assembling generic computer platforms and is engaged in multimedia and telecommunications. During each period in which one technology was clearly dominant within the firm, management had a focused approach to product life cycles in setting, say, a technology strategy.

The key goal during the period of dominance of each technology has always been to build the firm's identity (culture, mission, market position, design skills, customers, suppliers) as a major player in that industry. The special case, however, of Olivetti and other companies that operate in the same industry and share similar histories—for example, NCR—is that the technology—as distinct from the product—life cycle is extremely short and is becoming shorter. Thus, such companies have to migrate from one industry to another and even create new industries at a pace that would be fast even for implementing product changes within a stable technological horizon. And the most frustrating implication of this "identity-building" process is that a new identity may have to be trashed just when one would like to keep it—that is, after a painful learning process when one has become not only a pioneer but a leader.

In such a rapidly changing world the problem of, for example, defining the mission and direction of research and development and, more generally, the global technology strategy is not a matter of choosing one alternative among various product lines or markets. Rather it is a matter of repeatedly asking the question, What business are we in? What, the firm must ask, is the identity of the product, what is the market, what is the production process, and what are the boundaries between those activities that should be performed internally and those that have to be procured externally? Such questions must be answered with the knowledge that many of the firm's core innovations are in the hands of external suppliers and that whatever combination, or mix, of answers the firm lights on will be temporary, regardless of its "success," as discussed below.

Hence, organizational structures in the high-tech industries are designed to cope simultaneously with significant discontinuities and incremental innovation. Over time, these dual demands put a premium on the firm's ability to develop multiple, often inconsistent competencies to deal with emerging, divergent technological and organizational requirements (Burgelman, 1983). As a result, structures, procedures, and frames that influence action are usually under severe strain. Managers feel they are operating in a fuzzy organizational environment: for example, even if structures are in place to guide behavior and there is an effort to revise them radically each year, everyone knows that they are only marginally relevant at the moment of action, and what matters to you, the organizational actor, is the possibility of relying on your own network of colleagues located in other departments.

In sum, the extraordinary complexities of operating in the high-tech industries affect not only the nature of the primary task to be accomplished but the very identity of the business. Coping with identity uncertainty requires responses that are at least one order of magnitude more sophisticated than dealing with "simple" task or product uncertainty. And though managers picture themselves as busy in decision making (forecasting, planning, and selecting alternative courses of action), they might be better described as engaged in "sense-making" (Weick, 1979)—that is, in endlessly picking up the pieces from the "identity crises" and "broken strategies" (previous plans, marketing choices, goals, and visions) and trying to paste them together in order to make new sense of emerging technologies, markets, and industries. The rapid succession of identities puts strain on the strategy-structure link, and, as a result, formal structures appear continually to be revised, fragmented, and trumped up. However, an underlying continuity is maintained, and so there must be a hidden context that keeps providing sense to managerial action.

Before attempting to address the complex issue of how to design an organization in such a turbulent environment, we need to investigate what managers do daily in these complex and changing structures so that we can figure out how they can reconcile in management action temporary fragmentation and volatility with hidden, underlying "bedrock" practices and frames.

Improvisation: The Engine of Recombination

In the new knowledge economy our ability to play with virtually limitless possibilities for ever better ways of doing things lies at the heart of industrial development. Economic growth is generated through ideas like the interchangeability of product parts or organizational activities and the capacity to continually try out new combinations of resources. Indeed, radical shifts in the organization of work, from the factory system to mass production and then to flexible manufacturing, have lead to quantum jumps in productivity (Romer, 1986). Today, modern forms of economic organization, such as alliances or networked, federated firms, are the latest combination of routines and transactions that can deliver increased efficiency in the new economy. But our investigation so far suggests that the uncertainty, speed, and frequency of recombinations are issues as important as the particular efficient configuration of resources that emerges at a given point in time. On the one hand, the birthrate of the new organizational forms that populate the industrial landscape can be measured in decades, if not half centuries. On the other, the current pace of competition and technological development requires a much faster generation (and elimination) of new arrangements, at least in the high-tech industries.

The economics of growth and change are characterized by many unexpected, paradoxical manifestations; Schumpeter (1942) remains unsurpassed in describing it as a process of "creative destruction." For example, in the information technology industry surprise and *bricolage*, or tinkering, seem to play a role at least as important as the specific contractual arrangements selected by management for many strategic alliances and even acquisitions. Sometimes, an acquisition is carried out to appropriate certain standardized assets that turn out to be volatile or simply not there; invisible assets are discovered subsequently and appropriated instead. The particular contractual form, far from being selected intentionally to permit the appropriation of the unanticipated asset, contingently happens to allow the transfer of skills and know-how. Surprises, rather than strategy, determine structure. Structures happen to be there, or, if not ready at hand, they are the flexible outcome of the artful recombination of what is at hand in the local circumstances.

What is the essence and nature of this phenomenon of recombination? Bahrami (1992), studying a sample of high-tech firms in Silicon Valley, suggests that they must cope frequently with "kaleidoscopic change," where a small, apparently insignificant variation can dramatically alter the entire action set (the task, the market, the business) of the organization. Growth patterns are volatile, it is hard to capitalize on early success, periodic readjustments will not do, and crises cannot be solved once and for all. In such an environment, the firm, in order to survive, must sport a variety of flexible responses: ability to react quickly, resilience in the face of disturbances, and readiness to face the radical surprises that are the consequences of chaotic change. We call this capability for coping with surprises not by planning and anticipation but by the extemporaneous recombination of resources at hand *improvisation*.

Improvisation is situated performance where thinking and action occur simultaneously and on the spur of the moment. It is purposeful human behavior with the paradoxical characteristic of seeming to be ruled at the same time by chance, intuition, competence, and outright design. Improvisation is intentional but extemporaneous—that is, almost unexpected (*ex tempore*, outside the flow of time)—and apparently without known causes or relationships. Improvisation can be found in a variety of organizational settings.

Improvisation in Emergencies

Improvisation can hold together a faltering organization in extreme situations. An original study of the aftermath of an earthquake in southern Italy shows how improvisation, rather than planned organization, led to the establishment of an effective network of local rescue organizations (Lanzara, 1983). The network started when an ordinary citizen opened a makeshift coffee bar (actually a bench) on the main square of an isolated village that was in ruins after an earthquake. The coffee bar proved to be a primary support for the survivors and an important coordination point for the first local rescue operations, before the army and the official rescue forces were able to reach the disaster area. While the official forces came late and proceeded slowly, if not clumsily, the improvised coffee bar became a knowledge brokerage house, allowing the quick allocation of resources available locally to those who needed them most. It effectively decreased the transaction costs of coordination and provided an essential organizational continuity to the community.

Improvisation is not just an individual or collective antidote to panic and disruption (Weick, 1993a). If this were the case, its role would be confined to the design of ad hoc organizations in emergencies or disasters. We submit, instead, that improvisation is part of the everyday behavior in important economic institutions. If we look closely, we discover that it is the very stuff of which market choices and hierarchical routines are made.

Improvisation and Market Behavior

Hayek (1945) is unsurpassed in portraying the functioning of the market institution, or price system. He characterizes the market as essentially a discovery process, where new opportunities and innovations are relentlessly brought to the surface and where the news of such findings is transmitted instantaneously through the price system. Decision making in markets is, like any relevant economic process, linked to change (Knight, 1964). And change can happen at any moment. Thus, looking at the behavior of agents in a market one can find the key components of improvisation: immediacy; situatedness; importance of idiosyncratic, local knowledge; and access to and deployment of the resources at hand. Take, for example, situatedness. Improvisation occurs through decisions based on knowledge of the particular circumstances of time and place. Relevant knowledge is ultimately in the hands of those actors "who are familiar with such circumstances, who know directly of the relevant changes and the resources immediately available to them" (Hayek, 1945, p. 524). So the behavior of agents in a market is bound to be highly situated, adapted to changing circumstances, and, because it must be reactive to the latest incoming item of information, improvised.

Improvisation in Hierarchies

At first glance, it is hard to imagine a role for improvisation in hierarchies. We exit the world of relentless exploration of new opportunities (the market), and we enter the world of exploitation of the already known and carefully planned, the world of hierarchical routines (March, 1991). Thanks to the division of labor and specialization, work routines are generated to freeze both the explicit and the tacit knowledge necessary to make decisions and carry out activities (Nelson and Winter, 1982). Organizational structures influence, sometimes in the minutest detail, decision making at all levels of the hierarchy, through sophisticated mechanisms of planning, communication, and authority (March and Simon, 1958). This picture of organizational decision making, which seems to rule out improvisation, has its basis in a bundle of assumptions embedded in a particular way of analyzing and designing organizations—the information-processing perspective (Simon, 1976; Galbraith, 1977). The adoption of other perspectives (for example, that which looks at organizations as interpretive systems; see Daft and Weick, 1984), coupled with close observation of the organizing processes that take place daily in any work organization, would result in a quite different picture in which routines are virtual and improvisation is for real. Here we can only refer to those empirical studies on the role of "practical thinking" in the execution of mundane, highly routinized tasks in, for example, dairies (Scribner, 1984), supermarkets (Lave and Wenger, 1991), offices (Wynn, 1979), and when using and repairing new technologies (Suchman, 1987; Orr, 1990). These studies conclude that in hierarchies, "contrary to much conventional wisdom, people continually learn and improvise while working" (Brown and Duguid, 1991).

Improvisation Versus Planned Decision Making

A thorough understanding of improvisation needs to emphasize its difference from planned, boundedly rational decision making (Winograd and Flores, 1986; Vera and Simon, 1993). Boundedly rational decision making is about the choice of an appropriate means-ends chain to achieve a preset goal. As a conscious, future-oriented activity, decision making is improvisational only in those circumstances where planning is impossible—that is, in the presence of contingencies of high uncertainty and unpredictability (the realm of nonprogrammable decisions) (Simon, 1976). Decision making and, more generally, action are for Weber ([1947] 1964) and Simon (1976) discrete means deployed to achieve a goal. However, the phenomenological study of choice processes (Husserl, [1931] 1962; Schutz, 1967) indicates that decision making and action are intrinsically subjective and transient—in Hayek's (1945) words, "linked to the here and now." More precisely, for Weber and Simon the meaning of a decision can be grounded in its objective circumstances, in the value premises and preferences of the actor, in the act of selecting alternatives, and so on. Phenomenologists advise us differently. For them, although any choice process is grounded in preceding programs of actions and derives its unity (sense) from the range and scope of such programs, choices are highly dependent on the here and now of their formulation and evocation. Hence, the meaning of an action is merely relative to a particular moment in time and to the recollections of the actor in those particular circumstances (Schutz, 1967). One may recall, however, our definition of improvisation as purposeful behavior that contains elements of planning and design even if "on the fly." How can an orientation to the future, which seems to characterize both improvisation and planned decisions, be reconciled with a view in which subjective, highly circumstantial interpretation of the past gives the ultimate meaning to action?

Every action is carried out according to a project, which contains a vision of the act as if already accomplished in the future. The unity of the action (its meaning) is constituted by the image of that project: the actor-in-action is led by the vision of the accomplished project. The meaning embedded in such a project and its constituent elements (plans, goals, means) represent what Schutz calls the "in-order-to" motives of action. And the in-order-to motives are the object of the analysis and design of rational decision-making processes (Simon, 1976). However, the in-order-to component is just the tip of the decision-making iceberg. Below are the actor's past experiences, selectively evoked according to the existential circumstances present at the moment of making and implementing the decision. Such a deeper and wide-ranging bundle of motives is called the "because-of" component of the action. This multilayered bundle conveys the ultimate meaning and motivational thrust to the devising and performing of the action. The in-order-to project deals with the explicit and conscious meaning of the actor's solution to a problematic situation, while the because-of motives can explain why and how the actor has perceived the situation as problematical in the first place.

The asymmetry between the orientation of attention to the past and to the future, intrinsic to any decision or action, has important implications for the study of improvisation. The because-of motives are tacit and lie in the background of the explicit project at hand (the "bedrock" of choice processes). They fall outside the glance of rational, awake attention, especially during action. They could be inferred by an outsider or made explicit by the actor as a result of a reflection after the fact. But that very act of interpretation of the because-of motives may well be "improvised," for it is in itself an act based on yet different bundles of because-of and in-order-to motives, some of which fall outside the awake attention of the actor doing the planning. The same action performed in the past may reveal new meanings depending on the circumstances in which the actor or the observer reconsiders it.

Here, improvisation begins to disclose for us the extemporaneous nature of "structured" decision making. The improvised component present in structured decision making comes from the highly circumstantial fashion in which the bottom of the iceberg (be-cause-of motives) is brought to bear on the situation at hand, the relevant problem formulation, and the solution chosen. The bottom is there, but we are not aware of its selective influences on our plans and projects at the moment of action. Hence, even a carefully planned and explicit decision can be regarded as extemporaneous and pasted up because it is based ultimately on motives that are opaque and remote. Structured analysis and design methodologies in the various fields of management science assume that plans and decisions can be analyzed and executed objectively, and deny the intrinsically improvised nature of decision making and action. Such methods are ineffective because they create artificial worlds (such as the "enterprise models") made of deceptively hard, objective "entities," "data," "processes," and "activities." Of course, improvisation is only apparently ruled out from such artificial worlds. Decision makers and designers who implement solutions according to abstract models and illusionary visions are bound to be surprised and possibly puzzled by the unpredictable events generated by the gaps between artificial routines, programs, and structures and their practical use. In fact, the surprises are so common that a sign of competent organizational behavior is not to panic in the face of them but to acknowledge that automated procedures, instructions, and the information in manuals should not be followed blindly but regarded as one way, not always reliable, to get the job done (Zimmerman, 1973; Suchman, 1987).

The Platform: Toward the Shapeless Organization

We look now at the qualities of an organization that let improvisation-based recombinations take place without too much stress on its members. Organizational structures can be compared on the basis of their efficiency in dealing with transaction or coordination costs. The multidivisional form, the matrix, and the network are selected on the basis of their relative ability to coordinate businesses efficiently (Williamson, 1985). The efficiency perspective, however, assumes implicitly that the technology of products and processes remains relatively stable, so that organizations have time to set up a new structure, fine-tune it, and evaluate its results; in other words, if the technology and the task are known and stable, firms can engage in exercises of vertical integration versus market externalization and then compare the results at the margin (Williamson, 1975). In industries such as information technology, however, the rules of the game are quite different. We enter the world of dynamic technologies (Ciborra and Lanzara, 1994): it is hard to tell what operating system will prevail in two years time or what chip architecture will be the industry standard. Firms are uncertain about the technology trajectory they are on (Dosi, 1984) and consequently about the boundaries of their industry and their business identity. Whenever perceptions change, the business mission and primary task can shift abruptly. For example, is a firm like Olivetti in PCs or computer platforms? Should it become a low-cost manufacturer or a system integrator (Ciborra, 1996)? In such a turbulent environment, plans to vertically integrate or disaggregate in order to lower transaction costs miss the point. The issue may be not so much whether to integrate but with whom, in what industry—with a telecom company, a chip maker, a large software vendor, a media company, a consumer electronics giant, or a mix thereof? Prescriptions for setting up efficient organizational structures around a complex, primary task lose part of their normative relevance, for one cannot know in advance the complexity of the task or its precise nature and contours.

Indeed, one major source of uncertainty in defining a strategy is the rapid succession of technological discontinuities, which may involve not only the dismantling of assembly lines or product teams but also a deeper transformation of the bundle of cognitive frames, cultural views, and structural arrangements linked to the very technology that has to be abandoned. In brief, a shift in technology paradigms, especially when they are, as in this case, competency-destroying (Anderson and Tushman, 1990), requires the abandonment of the extant "formative context" (Unger, 1987) that generates the firm's prevailing identity (that is, its design approaches, production organization, and marketing strategies) and the rapid establishment of a new one. Note, however, that such a transformation can never be achieved completely. With each new technological generation, management and the organization do not start from scratch: the company that today manufactures PCs cannot be considered a start-up in relation to the company that until yesterday used to build typewriters. Because the extant, dominant designs are difficult to dislodge, the prevailing organizational arrangement at any point in time is a pasted-up combination, a sedimentation of successive formative contexts; in such an organization the people who sell PCs and minis may be still imprisoned in the typewriter salesperson mind-set. In this trumped-up combination of frames and organizations, where the old can hardly be distinguished from the new, surprises are inevitable. In that context the managerial competency in strong demand is the ability to improvise—that is, to quickly respond to and learn from surprises and, with artful courage, to expose oneself to new situations that may trigger knowledge creation (Nonaka and Takeuchi, 1995). An example is the various external links that high-tech firms' management teams have been busily setting up and dismantling since the mid-1970s.

Characteristics of the Platform Organization

In a rapidly changing environment none of the well-known organizational arrangements may optimize resource utilization. We submit that one can only settle, at best, for a shapeless organization that keeps generating new forms through frequent recombinations: we call this a *platform organization*. The platform may be the model of the organizations of the future because of its intrinsic potential to efficiently generate new combinations of resources, routines, and structures that are able to match turbulent circumstances. From the structural point of view the platform is a resilient outcome manufactured from the ingenious reconciliation of existing organizational mechanisms and forms that have been selected by management according to subjective and situated plans and interpretations (improvisation and *bricolage*) (see Lévi-Strauss, 1966; Weick, 1993b). The platform's most distinctive qualities are its flexibility, movement, and transformation, which derive from the intersecting, penetrating, and collating of different organizational arrangements such as the network, the matrix, and even the hierarchy. It is at the same time fragmented and intertwined, and may be the only form able to survive in those industries where a monolithic, rigid business identity cannot respond to the frantic pace of technological change.

From a cognitive point of view the platform works as a collective, cognitive engine driven by a pool of flexible human resources in order to explore and try out multiple combinations of old and new organizational arrangements. The platform organization is a model that turns upside down our beliefs about what is structural and permanent in the strategy-structure dyad and what is subjective, informal, and ephemeral (Lanzara, 1983) simply because its job is different: to deal with frequent, sudden, and radical changes not just in products, markets, and technologies but in its business identity and in the industries to which it temporarily belongs. Specifically, its purpose is to support managers who face frequent surprises. These surprises are events that appear to be incomprehensible or inconceivable because they represent "cosmology episodes" (Weick, 1993a), in which existing frames, assumptions, and values fall apart, and organizational problem solving and the design of ad hoc initiatives lack a meaningful context. As a result, the platform organization retains simultaneously static and dynamic mechanisms, certainties and doubts, visions and the conditions of their destruction, and ready-made junk routines and the seeds of not-yet-made ones.

Improvising in the Platform Organization

How do managers go about their daily job in the platform organization? How do they recombine structures? Studies of many high-tech firms show that in those industries strategic management consists mainly of a particular form of improvisation: placing bets about what will be the next primary task. Design choices, such as alliances and vertical integration, follow the provisional outcome of such bets. The platform, being easily reconfigurable, is particularly suited to supporting the practice of betting and all that it entails—high flexibility in moving in rapidly to reap short-lived benefits or exiting rapidly when losing or in adapting to new circumstances that require a commitment to a risky move (Ghemawat, 1991). Betting can hardly be planned in advance. Deeper considerations are involved at each turn, especially if the previous bet has been successful: the identity of the business may have changed as a result of a particular move, so past experience is of little use. The platform allows for such opportunistic, semiblind strategic betting: its identity and mission are allowed to drift in order to keep options open for networking with the most appropriate constellation of partners, as dictated by the need of the moment. Because of its fuzziness and intertwined structure, the platform also defies any attempt to use standard approaches to gaining a competitive edge—for example, by pursuing the competitive strategies identified by Porter (1980). On the one hand, the platform organization upsets neat formulations because it looks hybrid, blurred, and often "stuck in the middle." On the other, it can be swiftly set up to respond to a competitor's move in a given industry according to the rules of competitive advantage.

Indeed, one of the striking characteristics of the platform is that it is programmed for perpetual transformation, for generating organizational arrangements and cognitive frames, and for constantly branching out to other, radically different businesses, identities, and industries. The unpredictability caused by strategic betting, the mimetic behavior, and the sedimentation of successive arrangements caused by the ineradicable inertia of preexisting routines and structures all combine to conjure a picture of the platform as a generic context full of junk organizational routines that can be harnessed depending on the needs of the moment. Traditional organizations, even the newer forms, come with a bundle of requirements and expectations that create a context for managerial action. In the platform organization management will have to enact the context while they act, make choices, and envision strategies (Daft and Weick, 1984). How will managers make their daily decisions in such a complex and elusive organizational context? We submit that they will adopt multiple standards in order to move around the redundant parts of the platform. Managers will function according to a hierarchical context (structures and mind-set) in some parts of the organization or as network operators (again organizationally and cognitively) in the network setting. As *bricoleurs*, they will remain creative in the face of surprises because they will be accustomed to operating in chaotic conditions and to pulling order out of the resources and routines at hand (Weick, 1993b). In this perspective, the platform works as a metaorganizational context that creates simultaneous dependencies and belongings. In the platform a manager may operate within the confines and constraints of not just one but many organizational forms at the same time; yet the platform is itself a product of managers' situated rationality and actions while they recombine artfully the arrangements at hand (improvisation) and operate smoothly within them, thereby reproducing the context within which improvisation can continue (Giddens, 1984).

In sum, the platform is far from being a specific organizational structure, in which one can recognize a new or traditional configuration. Rather, its essence can be captured in the virtual organizing scheme, collectively shared and reproduced in action by a pool of human resources—a "habitus," to use Bourdieu's (1977) expression—where structure and the potential for strategic action tend to coincide in highly circumstantial ways, depending on the transitory contingencies of market, technology, and competitors' moves. Organizing principles such as "betting," "opportunistic deployment of partnerships," "pragmatism," and "rapid learning" are rerun in the heads of managers and surface in their acts of improvisation: being shared collectively, they maintain coherence in an organization where structures are continuously eroded.

Summary

Although management and industry observers tend to give a systematic, ex post reconstruction, according to which every step of corporate strategy has precise reasons and justifications and every reorganization is dictated by systematic principles of business reengineering, we submit that the organization of the future, at least in highly dynamic industries, will be characterized by muddling through and improvisation. Surprises and the relevant organizational response, improvisation, have become the main object of our investigation. The study of the consequences of surprises discloses another aspect: the outcome of corporate strategy put in practice in a turbulent environment is a pasted-up organization in which elements of the old are intertwined with trials of the new. The overall picture of the firm of the future turns out to be fuzzy and shapeless, sufficiently responsive to the new. Learning from surprises and improvisation turn out to be the valued core capabilities of its management. In order to capture such emerging organizational features, we cannot rely on traditional models or even on newer ones such as the networked firm. They all suffer from being too tidy and preplanned given the high levels of uncertainty management will be facing. As a different explanation, we have introduced the notion of the platform organization. On the surface the platform looks like a stable pool of junk resources, badly organized according to efficiency criteria but ready to be deployed when strategy requires it. At a deeper level the platform is a collective cognitive scheme that allows managers to improvise effectively—that is, relentlessly to try out new organizational combinations in order to respond to complex, chaotic contexts.

References

Anderson, P., and Tushman, M. L. "Technological Discontinuities and Dominant Designs: A Cyclical Model of Technological Change." *Administrative Science Quarterly*, 1990, 35, 604–633.

Bahrami, H. "The Emerging Flexible Organization: Perspectives from Silicon Valley." *California Management Review*, 1992, 34(4), 33–52.

Bourdieu, P. *Outline of a Theory of Practice*. Cambridge: Cambridge University Press, 1977.

Boynton, A. C., and Victor, B. "Beyond Flexibility: Building and Managing the Dynamically Stable Organization." *California Management Review*, 1991, 34(1), 53–66.

Brown, J. S., and Duguid, P. "Organizational Learning and Communities-of-Practice." *Organization Science*, 1991, 2(1), 40–57.

Burgelman, R. A. "A Process Model of Internal Corporate Venturing in the Diversified Major Firm." *Administrative Science Quarterly*, 1983, 28, 223–244.

Ciborra, C. U. "The Platform Organization: Recombining Strategies, Structures and Surprises." *Organization Science*, 1996, 7(2), 103–118.

Ciborra, C. U., and Lanzara, G. F. "Formative Contexts and Information Technology: Understanding the Dynamics of Innovation in Organizations." *Accounting, Management and Information Technologies*, 1994, 4(2), 61–86.

Daft, R. L., and Weick, K. E. "Toward a Model of Organizations as Interpretation Systems." *Academy of Management Review*, 1984, 9(2), 284–295.

Dosi, G. *Technical Change and Industrial Transformation*. New York: St. Martin's Press, 1984.

Galbraith, J. *Organization Design*. Reading, Mass.: Addison-Wesley, 1977.

Ghemawat, P. *Commitment—The Dynamics of Strategy*. New York: Free Press, 1991.

Giddens, A. *The Constitution of Society: Outline of a Theory of Structuration*. Berkeley: University of California Press, 1984.

Hayek, F. "The Use of Knowledge in Society." *American Economic Review*, 1945, 35, 519–530.

Hedberg, B.L.T., Nystrom, P. C., and Starbuck, W. H. "Camping on Seesaws: Prescriptions for a Self-Designing Organization." *Administrative Science Quarterly*, 1976, 2, 39–52.

Husserl, E. *Ideas*. New York: Collier Books, 1962. (Originally published 1931.)

Knight, F. H. *Risk, Uncertainty, and Profit*. New York: Kelley, 1964.

Lanzara, G. F. "Ephemeral Organizations in Extreme Environments: Emergence, Strategy, Extinction." *Journal of Management Studies*, 1983, 20(1), 73–95.

Lave, J., and Wenger, E. *Situated Learning: Legitimate Peripheral Participation*. Cambridge: Cambridge University Press, 1991.

Lévi-Strauss, C. *The Savage Mind*. Chicago: University of Chicago Press, 1966.

March, J. G. "Exploration and Exploitation in Organizational Learning." *Organization Science*, 1991, 2(1), 71–87.

March, J. G., and Simon, H. A. *Organizations*. New York: Wiley, 1958.

Miles, R. E., and Snow C. C. "Causes of Failure in Network Organizations." *California Management Review*, 1992, 34(4), 53–72.

Mintzberg, H. *Structure in Fives: Designing Effective Organizations*. Englewood Cliffs, N.J.: Prentice-Hall, 1983.

Nelson, R. R., and Winter, S. G. *An Evolutionary Theory of Economic Change*. Cambridge, Mass.: Belknap Press, 1982.

Nonaka, I., and Takeuchi, H. *The Knowledge Creating Company*. New York: Oxford University Press, 1995.

Orr, J. "Sharing Knowledge, Celebrating Identity: War Stories and Community Memory in Service Culture." In D. S. Middleton and D. Edwards (eds.), *Collective Remembering: Memory in Society*. Thousand Oaks, Calif.: Sage, 1990.

Porter, M. E. *Competitive Strategy: Techniques for Analyzing Industries and Competitors*. New York: Free Press, 1980.

Prahalad, C. K., and Hamel, G. "The Core Competence of the Corporation." *Harvard Business Review*, 1990, 68(3), 79–91.

Romer, P. "Increasing Returns and Long-Run Growth." *Journal of Political Economy*, 1986, 94, 1002–1037.

Schumpeter, J. *Capitalism, Socialism and Democracy*. New York: HarperCollins, 1942.

Schutz, A. *The Phenomenology of the Social World*. Evanston, Ill.: Northwestern University Press, 1967.

Scribner, S. "Studying Working Intelligence." In B. Rogoff and L. Lave (eds.), *Everyday Cognition*. Cambridge, Mass.: Harvard University Press, 1984.

Simon, H. A. *Administrative Behavior*. (2nd ed.) New York: Free Press, 1976.

Suchman, L. *Plans and Situated Actions: The Problem of Human-Machine Communication*. New York: Cambridge University Press, 1987.

Thorelli, H. B. "Networks: Between Markets and Hierarchies." *Strategic Management Journal*, 1986, 7, 37–51.

Unger, R. M. *False Necessity*. Cambridge: Cambridge University Press, 1987.

Vera, A. H., and Simon, H. A. "Situated Action: A Symbolic Interpretation." *Cognitive Science*, 1993, 17, 7–48.

Weber, M. *The Theory of Social and Economic Organization*. New York: Free Press, 1964. (Originally published 1947.)

Weick, K. E. *The Social Psychology of Organizing*. (2nd ed.) Reading, Mass.: Addison-Wesley, 1979.

Weick, K. E. "The Collapse of Sense-making in Organizations: The Mann Gulch Disaster." *Administrative Science Quarterly*, 1993a, 38(4), 628–652.

Weick, K. E. "Organization Redesign as Improvisation." In G. P. Huber and W. H. Glick (eds.), *Organizational Change and Redesign*. New York: Oxford University Press, 1993b.

Williamson, O. E. *Markets and Hierarchies: Analysis and Antitrust Implications*. New York: Free Press, 1975.

Williamson, O. E. *The Economic Institutions of Capitalism*. New York: Free Press, 1985.

Winograd, T., and Flores, F. *Understanding Computers and Cognition*. Norwood, N.J.: Ablex, 1986.

Wynn, E. S. "Office Conversation as an Information Medium." Unpublished doctoral dissertation, University of California, Berkeley, 1979.

Zimmerman, D. "The Practicalities of Rule Use." In G. Salaman and K. Thompson (eds.), *People and Organisations*. London: Longman, 1973.

12

The Paths Ahead

Philip W. Yetton and Christopher Sauer

Experience has taught us that the art of successful management lies not in solving problems but in not having them. The most successful companies simply have fewer problems than their competitors. This principle can also serve as an indicator of the usefulness of the new thinking we have been describing in this book. To the extent that it abolishes problems, it is more powerful and successful than traditional thinking. For example, achieving the integration of business and information technology (IT) avoids the problem of alignment; an emergent strategy reduces the problem of environmental change; incrementalism reduces the problem of risk management; and learning respects the value in the status quo. Of course, there are costs: respect for the status quo carries the risk that anachronisms may be retained. However, some costs hardly count at all: for example, incrementalism entails the abandonment of change driven by strategic designs or grand visions, but as these designs have rarely if ever delivered the expected transformation, this is a small sacrifice.

The new way of thinking, like good intentions, is worth little without follow-through. We all know companies that embrace new ideas but change nothing. Along with new thinking, we need to identify new actions because, whatever its shortcomings, managers do currently have ways of implementing the old mind-set. In this last chapter, we not only highlight some of the key contributions from the preceding chapters but also develop from them practical guidance in the form of twelve management rules of thumb. These

rules are listed at the end of each of the subsections under "Replacing Traditional Solutions" below.

To highlight the direction in which the new thinking takes us
and to develop our rules of thumb, we use a familiar template to put
a new spin on the contributions in this book. Readers will recognize it from Chapters One and Two as Scott Morton's (1991)
MIT90s model. The essential feature of this model or schema is that
it portrays organizations as a set of more or less tightly interlocking
elements. The schema and developments of it have proved to be a
powerful organizing framework in the research, teaching, and consulting of the Fujitsu Centre, where we work. It is reproduced in Figure 12.1 for the reader's convenience.

MIT90s Schema

The MIT90s schema is principally a static model, asserting the
importance of a tight fit among the elements of an organization for
high business performance. Each of the elements, such as strategy
and technology, can be realized in a variety of ways. It is therefore
possible to configure different organizational forms appropriate to
different ways of competing. For a firm to change the way it competes, it must transform most or all of the organization. The schema,
being static, does not tell us how to make this transformation.

Because no organization can successfully change all elements at
once, it is necessary to proceed in sequence. The sequence of
change can be traced as a path through the schema. Because different paths constitute different ways of managing organizational transformation, the schema can be used not to specify in detail the
strategy to be adopted or the technology to be implemented but to
define what needs to be managed and in what order. The schema
highlights where management should devote the bulk of its change
effort at any time. The path defines the sequence in which that
emphasis alters. Studying paths to transformation has been the
Fujitsu Centre's major development of the MIT90s schema.

Figure 12.1. Model of Strategic Change and Fit.

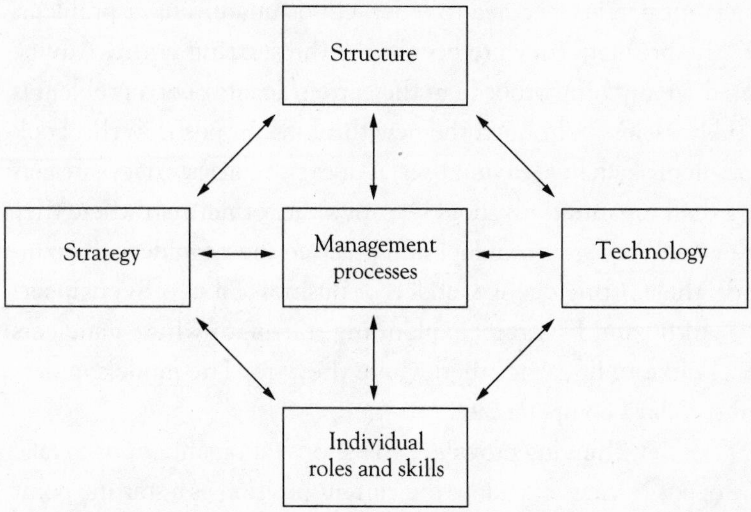

Adapted from Scott Morton (1991, p. 20).

Analysis of paths can tell us much about the nature of the change process—for example, whether it develops bottom-up or top-down. In addition to analyzing the choice among paths, we also focus on choice among configurations, the patterns and logic underlying the fit of the different organizational elements. Choices among different configurations and paths are influenced by the dynamics of the business environment and the risk associated with different steps and paths. These different ways of applying the MIT90s schema are used here to make salient the concerns raised in each chapter and to contrast the traditional and new mind-sets as we develop our guidelines.

Where to Start

We all know the old joke about the man who, when asked whether he knew the way to Rome, replied, "Yes. But I wouldn't start from here." It is, of course, always easier to solve problems if the starting point can be specified to order. Unfortunately, most problems are the problem they are because of the starting point. Advice based on anything other than the current location of a problem is frankly useless. Although the new thinking proposed in this book does imply a change in mind-set, it does not suggest that managers and their organizations should be anywhere other than where they are when they start to adopt and practice the new ideas. By contrast, the existing change models of Business Process Reengineering (BPR) and IT strategic planning start with where managers would like to be rather than where they are. The models undervalue today's competencies.

The new thinking provides two reasons for organizations to take the opposite view and adopt the current position as a starting point for change. First, the new mind-set explicitly values the strengths of the status quo. Most large organizations, despite vast complexity, continue to function precisely because of their embedded competencies. Much of the value of the organization is inherent in its current form. Consequently, the authors in this book stress the importance of the current organization and value it rather than reject it. Second, consistent with the authors' rejection of the idealism of the traditional mind-set, starting from where you are is both realistic and pragmatic.

For many general managers, the new mind-set will not be foreign, and the twelve rules of thumb presented later in this chapter will be welcome because they embody sound business instincts. Of course, there will be need for change. IT practitioners have typically embraced the traditional mind-set, and the new mind-set explicitly enjoins them to change. Those managers who have embraced rationalistic change movements such as BPR will also need to change. Such change will not be easy, for as Daniel Robey (Chapter Nine) spells out, the forces of persistence are strong. Adoption of the guidelines proposed here will be a first step toward deeper change.

Traditional Paths

The two main approaches to IT-based change identified and criticized throughout this book are strategic alignment and technological determinism. They imply incompatible paths. Line managers have adopted the strategic alignment model, in which IT management theory has co-opted the language and content of both the strategy and organization theories of the 1970s and 1980s. In those theories, the first step in organizational transformation is to formulate a vision or strategy, and the second is to restructure the organization to support the strategy. The third step is to put in place whatever is needed, such as new skills, to support and sustain the new dominant design. Because IT has been seen as a support function, it has been considered part of the third step of aligning other support components with the dominant strategy-structure design. This change path is reproduced in Figure 12.2.

The view of change held by many IT professionals is very different. According to technological determinism, the choice of technology is the critical organizational choice. IT professionals build new systems that then change the organization. In this view, the IT professional is a powerful change agent but does not have to confront and manage the multiple and complex links in the schema because those links change automatically in response to the technology. Implicitly, this view assumes that organizational changes occur naturally and without friction. IT professionals have concerned themselves almost exclusively with the technology step and have seen no need for managing other steps (Figure 12.3). Described in this way, our path analysis makes it brutally clear that technological determinism is naïve. No manager today would take it seriously.

Replacing Traditional Solutions

With these incompatible notions identified as operating in the past, how do we move ahead? As is often the case, there are two options.

Figure 12.2. Conventional Model of Strategic Dynamics.

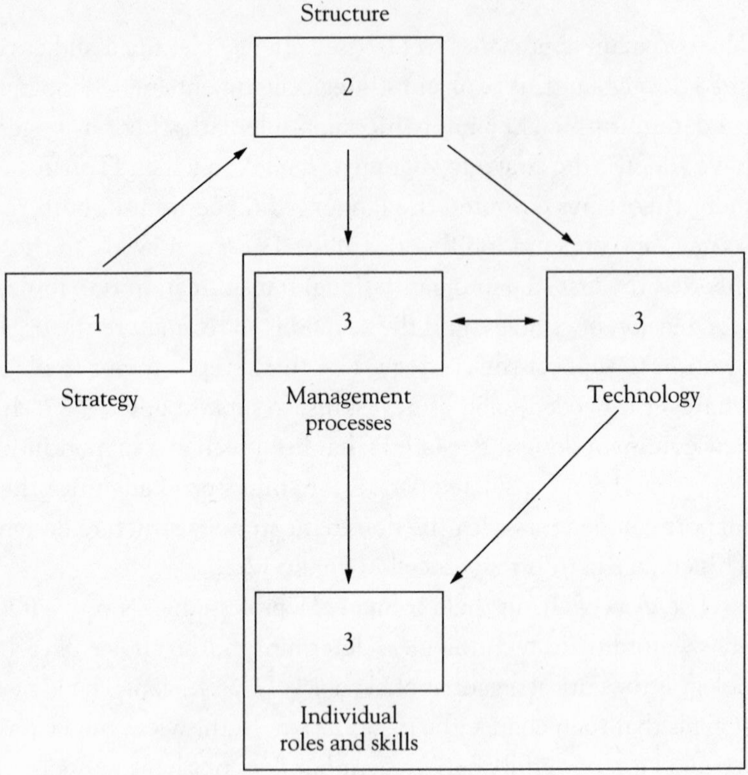

Structure

Adapted from Yetton, Johnson, and Craig (1994, p. 62).

One option is to attempt to reconcile the current differences. Not surprisingly, much recent thinking has implicitly adopted this approach. The other option, which we adopt, is to find a new path or set of paths that will help us manage more effectively in the future than we have in the past. To find this path, we analyze our authors' contributions and then use them to establish twelve rules that will guide organizations in following this new path.

Choice of New Paths

Traditional thinking has assumed a unique best path for organizational transformation whether it be as depicted in Figure 12.2 or

Figure 12.3. Model of Technological Determinism.

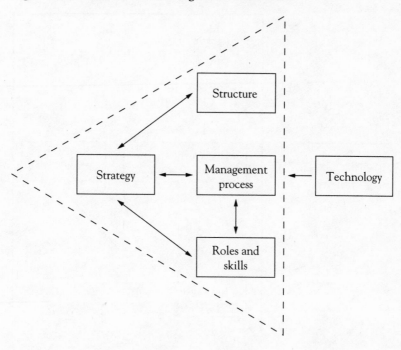

Figure 12.3. The new thinking sees a variety of possible paths to successful IT-based transformation. In Chapter Two, Philip Yetton
describes three case studies in which the paths through the schema
are different both from the conventional wisdom presented in Figure 12.2 and from each other. In the case of the architectural practice, the path began with the tactical adoption of IT, followed by
the partners' acquiring new skills, then by structural change, new
management processes, and, finally, the emergence of new strategic
options that had not been previously considered. This path is reproduced in Figure 12.4. The importance of this contribution is that it
shows that organizations have a choice of potentially effective
paths. Thus, instead of accepting by default the technological-deter-
minist or strategic-alignment path implicit in the latest consultant-
driven IT management product, you must choose your path to
IT-based organizational transformation.

Figure 12.4. Strategic Dynamics at an Architectural Firm.

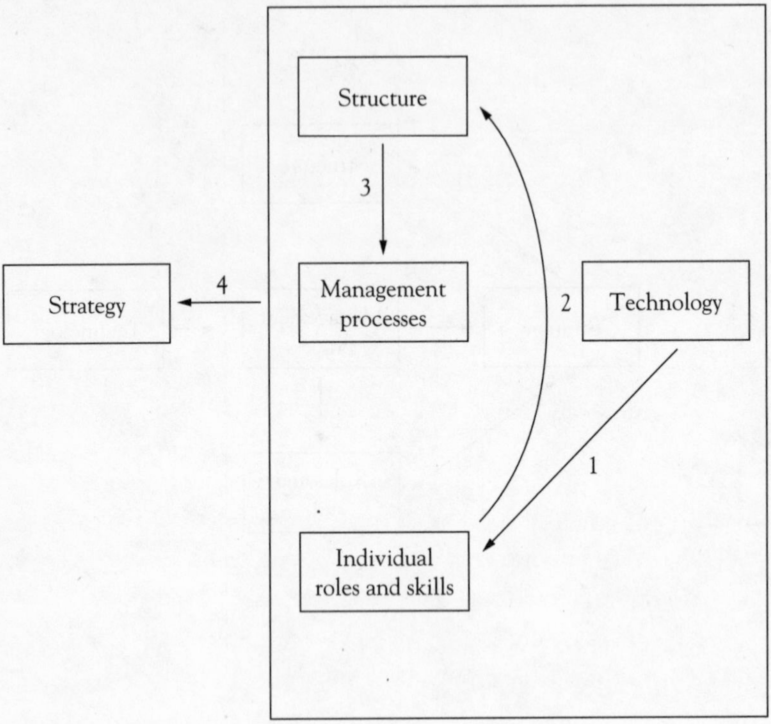

Adapted from Yetton, Johnston, and Craig (1994, p. 63).

In Chapter Three, Janice Burn picks up the issue of the instability of alignment. She finds a complex pattern of leads and lags among three of the elements found in the schema—strategy, structure, and technology. This pattern is shown in Figure 12.5, with the arrows indicating the different paths that could be followed. A simple path can start at any one of the three points and go to each point only once. There are therefore six different simple paths through the schema. If the paths found by Burn reflect different external pressures, such as market or regulatory demands, then we need a better-than-random, one-in-six chance of picking the right path for our current circumstances. These odds are disturbing for

Figure 12.5. Lead-Lag Model of Change.

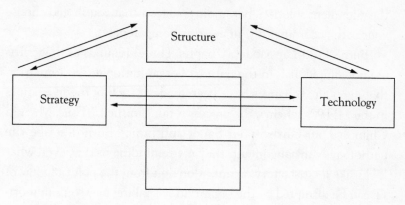

managers. The success of the path in Figure 12.4 suggests that we should look at paths that include all elements of the MIT90s schema, which amounts to 120 simple paths. We clearly need some guidance on how to choose among them.

We have no simple decision rules to guide the choice of paths. The new mind-set's emphasis on improvisation rather than designed and planned action is based on doubt as to whether such simple decision rules can ever be confidently promulgated. The data provided by Burn strongly suggest that the same firm cycles through different paths at different times. As a consequence, it needs to choose the right paths as circumstances change, and it needs the competencies to follow those paths. The skills and management processes necessary to devise and implement a formal positioning strategy that embodies a strategy-to-structure-to-technology path are likely to be different from those needed to undertake a technology-to-structure-to-strategy change path. The former will need strong planning skills, while the latter will require the ability to experiment and respond to the outcomes of experiments. Thus, attention to skills and management processes may be a necessary precursor to following successful paths through strategy, structure, and technology. Consequently, although the emphasis of Burn's research has been on the three components that have dominated the alignment solution, her findings suggest that you should choose your path according to your existing competencies.

Burn's Lead-Lag Model (Chapter Three) reminds us that paths are not simple. It is in the nature of organizational transformation that even after changes have been made at each of the five points in the MIT90s schema, the process is not "finished." Thus, when in Chapter Four Christopher Sauer and Janice Burn describe the pathology of misalignment, they are reminding us that even what looks like a satisfactory organizational fit from the point of view of IT can be disrupted by the organization's taking new steps unmotivated by IT's potential. More generally, they show us that when IT is treated separately from other business considerations, there is a risk of pathological or damaging outcomes. Thus if a new change step is undertaken with little or no consideration of the implications for the fit of IT with the rest of the organization, the path may turn pathological.

The traditional assumption that the business and IT are at some fundamental level separate from each other creates distance and lags; as a result even coherent sequences of steps may fail to deliver improved organizational performance. For example, to provide skills training to take advantage of a new IT system prior to implementation is a coherent sequence, but if the business demands that the training be spread over six months, the training and the application of the skills will be so decoupled that the IT system will usually not deliver the expected benefits. Only if the interlocking of the training step and the new IT step are treated as of primary business importance will the path deliver transformed organizational performance rather than just another new IT system.

We therefore need to create paths by choosing and managing each step so as to sustain or improve the existing organizational fit. Miles and Snow (1984) explain that firms that remain industry leaders for decades do so because they have achieved a tight fit and are able to sustain it because in tight fit the dynamics of change have the self-reinforcing properties of virtuous circles. In other words, the logic by which the organization delivers high performance is so transparent to organizational members that at each step of a change path they can see everything that needs to be done to reestablish the organization's tight fit and to attain a new level of performance that reinforces the change. Thus to choose a successful path you select each step so that the change is reinforced by performance.

In this section we have developed the first three of the twelve rules of thumb:

1. Choose your path to IT-based organizational transformation.

2. Choose your path according to your existing competencies.

3. Select each step so that the change is reinforced by performance.

What It Takes to Change

We have already suggested that path choice should have a basis in the organization's existing competencies. These influence not only the new activities an organization can realistically hope to introduce but also its ability to make successful changes. Chapters Five and Six examine what it takes to choose and manage paths to successful IT-based transformation.

In Chapter Five, M. Lynne Markus and Robert Benjamin focus on just one step—namely, change in roles and skills. Their analysis shows us that as a result of their acceptance of technological determinism IT professionals have traditionally focused almost exclusively on the technology step. Consequently, the roles and skills they have developed have been technical. Thus their influence is restricted to the technology step, yet the value addition of IT comes with change in the other organizational elements.

The skills organizations need to transform themselves through IT include organizational change management. The IT profession can either embrace these skills or try to retain their exclusively technical role. Markus and Benjamin argue that retaining a technical role alone is a losing game because managers are no longer prepared to accept being dependent on IT as change agents and because there is emerging competition from organizational-development (OD) practitioners. The lesson for organizations is to develop the change management skills of key IT professionals. IT professionals will then focus on the need for a path to be created and managed beyond the technology step, which will improve the coordination between the IT step and other steps in the path.

Markus and Benjamin stress that the OD ideology empowers the user. It is explicitly designed to reduce dependence and to build self-sustaining autonomy for the user of a new system. Whether or not IT professionals embrace OD, line managers are increasingly seeking to take control of IT-based change for themselves. So, whether through a rapprochement between business and IT or through line managers' taking control of IT-based change, organizations should break down the barriers between IT and the business and embed IT in business decision making. This chapter's insights are modeled in Figure 12.6 as a strong input into the skills and roles necessary to deliver successful IT-based transformation.

In Chapter Six, V. Sambamurthy and Robert Zmud explore the whole domain of change-related competencies in IT. Their study makes clear the substantial challenge of putting in place what it takes to manage IT-based change successfully. We illustrate this challenge through a deeper analysis of just one of the seven organizationwide categories they identify: line technology leadership, which is a combination of line managers' ownership of IT projects within their domain of business responsibility and the propensity of employees throughout the organization to serve as project champions.

Developing project championship is an issue of role development and requires good, high-level project management and political skills; thus it maps onto the skills/roles element of the MIT90s schema. Line management ownership is more complex to analyze. The simplest interpretation is that it falls within the domain of management processes because, as Yetton explains in Chapter Two,

Figure 12.6. Organizational-Development Model of Change.

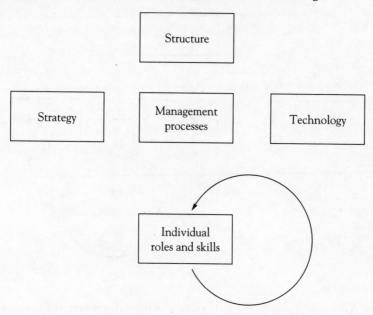

part of the problem of lack of ownership by the line has been the difficulty of managing major IT projects within the normal budget cycle and allocating them to a single budget unit or single manager's responsibility, and similarly for other control systems. So developing line-management ownership certainly involves putting the right management processes in place. But it also involves adoption of an extended role for line managers and further development of their skills in taking increased management responsibility for IT.

If we extend the interpretation, the category of IT management competency that Sambamurthy and Zmud identify as line technology leadership implies the need to put in place appropriate management processes ahead of the technology. Figure 12.7 summarizes this analysis of line-leadership competency. It shows that just this single competency category requires substantial development of management processes and roles and skills, and that they are needed before technology change is undertaken.

Figure 12.7. Two Line-Leadership Competencies.

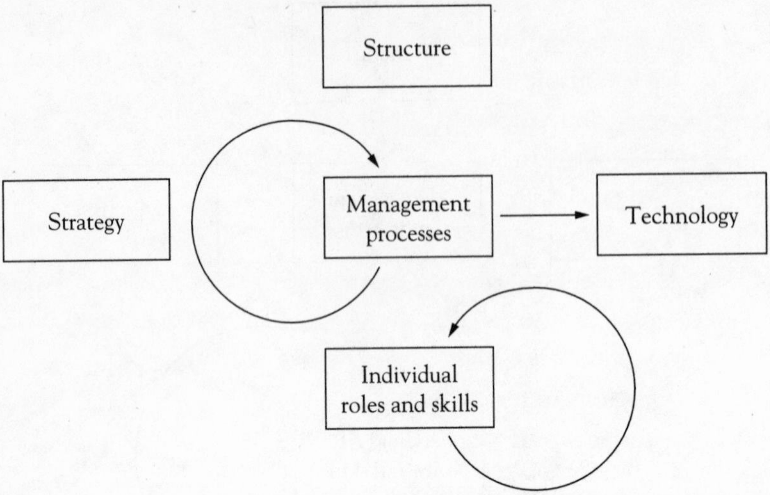

An inspection of the full twenty-nine competencies suggests that although they could be represented within the schema, the patterns would be complex in the extreme. Indeed, Sambamurthy and Zmud's findings remind us powerfully that although it may be possible to resolve the problems around IT-based strategic change in a particular case—that is, to manage a change process well in one particular organization—no general solution exists that would guarantee consistent success. For the time being, therefore, each management team needs to ensure to the best of its ability that the organization develops the full range of IT management competencies. Sambamurthy and Zmud's assessment tool will assist in identifying existing deficiencies.

In this section we have developed the following three rules of thumb:

4. Develop the change management skills of key IT professionals.

5. Break down the barriers. Embed IT in business decision making.

6. Develop the full range of IT management competencies.

Deciding Steps and Paths

IT management competencies are not simply acquired. Although a particular mix of roles, skills, processes, and technologies can be managerially mandated, they do not constitute a competency unless they are exercised in a knowledgeable fashion, which can be achieved only by undertaking paths of IT-based change. The analyses of process change in Chapters Seven and Eight are especially fruitful for developing guidelines to help management decision making in the choice of steps and paths.

In Chapter Seven, Robert Galliers highlights the importance of risk management. In terms of the schema, the trouble with BPR is that it treats risk as a property of the total path to change. Thus, the costs grow cumulatively at each step, but the benefits are not enjoyed until the new organizational design is in place, which does not occur until the whole path has been traversed. Consequently, the organization carries increasing risk as the change continues. If for any reason the benefits are not obtained, nothing offsets the costs. Galliers's emphasis is on the total change process. The whole path must be managed. Inattention to one step will be enough to check and possibly abort the complete path.

The new approach to risk is to partition it into small sequences of change. Ideally, each step will have an independent risk-return balance in which the return both gives an independent incentive to make the step successful and covers the downside to a substantial degree before the initiation of subsequent steps. Considerable advantage thus accrues from limiting the risk to one step at a time.

Jane Craig and Philip Yetton (Chapter Eight) rearrange the geometry of the schema. By partitioning the organizational elements differently, they refocus management attention on the initial steps of a path. Although the emphasis in the BPR literature is on the strategy-structure-technology triangle, the real event of BPR is the building of new core competencies in the triangle encompassing management processes, roles and skills, and technology. In talking of core competencies Craig and Yetton are talking about the abilities that distinguish a business from its competitors. Hence, competing differently requires new core competencies. Their argument is that whereas the traditional mind-set encourages all the management emphasis to be directed to the top triangle in Figure 12.8, the heart of true competitive change is in the bottom triangle. The top triangle tends to have a top-down emphasis, whereas the bottom triangle is usually a bottom-up process.

Both Chapters Seven and Eight recognize existing core competencies as being important and valuable as a basis for developing new ones. Much knowledge, explicit and tacit, is embedded in existing competencies. This knowledge can be tapped only if organizations develop new competencies from the old. This development must take place early in the path. To do so, organizations must innovate bottom-up.

We have drawn out three additional rules of thumb in this section:

7. Develop new competencies from the old.

8. Develop the new competencies early by innovating bottom-up.

9. Limit the risk to one step at a time.

Process of Path Management

Managers choose paths by deciding the sequence of steps to take. At each step, they still have to make the change happen. In Chapter Nine Daniel Robey reminds us of the challenge this process poses. Managing change is a confrontation between the forces of change and the forces of persistence. Robey showcases four theories that explicitly recognize this confrontation: political theory, organizational culture, institutional theory, and organizational learning. By modeling strategic information-systems planning as a horizontal path across the MIT90s schema, we can immediately see why it would be likely to run into cultural resistance. Culture in the

Figure 12.8. Positioning-Versus-Core-Competency Model of Change.

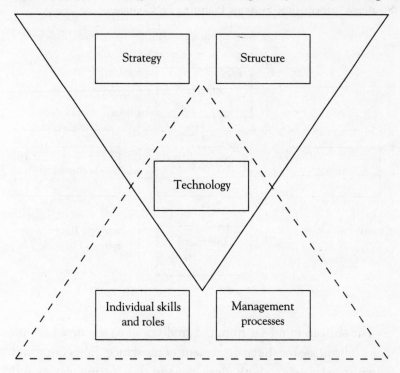

schema consists of structure, management processes, and roles and skills and the links among them (Scott Morton, 1991). Here we see strategic information systems planning running right across the vertical axis of culture without going through two of the elements within which culture is embedded (Figure 12.9). The task of attending to appropriate change in all elements and links of the organization in the face of resistance is the management cross to be borne by the champion of change.

All four theories explored by Robey share one characteristic: they all recognize the power of the status quo and hence the resistance any path of change may encounter and must overcome to be successful. They demonstrate that resistance can exist anywhere within the organization.

**Figure 12.9. Influence of Culture and
Strategic Information-Systems Planning on Change.**

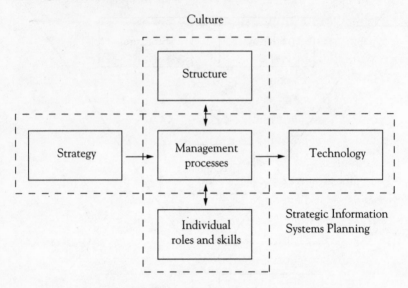

The shift in mind-set from the traditional to the new has one major advantage for the management of resistance. Respecting and valuing the status quo both gives value to the existing players and assumes that they have tacit knowledge that needs to be preserved and that can help in the development of new knowledge in the future. It follows that with the new mind-set organizational members who might be ignored in the plans developed under more traditional thinking are valued as contributors to and carriers of the emergent new competencies.

In common with Robey, Rod Coombs (Chapter Ten) finds that outcomes of IT-based organizational change are unpredictable. Therefore, if planning is the primary process by which an organization manages change, it is likely to experience disappointing results. Thus, managers must adopt a bias for action. Through experimentation, it is possible to learn lessons that are relevant to the specific organizational situation but that would not necessarily be relevant elsewhere.

With the traditional mind-set, senior managers attempted to reallocate power to meet their own objectives; in the process, they created powerful winners and losers and engendered dangerous resentment from the losers, who responded frequently in covert ways that often blocked senior management's change path. The new mind-set advocates empowerment for all players. Coombs's characterization of power as a relational phenomenon rather than as the property of one agent reminds us that the successful management of change at any point in the schema requires negotiation and political bargaining.

Claudio Ciborra's picture of the future (Chapter Eleven) is as uncertain as, and even more turbulent and chaotic than, the past. He excites and should scare us with the challenge of the shapeless platform organization. Current theories about how to cope with dynamic environments either allocate the risk across units, as is the case with Miles and Snow's (1992) "network organization," or assume there is a stable core, as with Boynton and Victor's (1991) dynamic stability—a combination of frequently changing products and slowly changing processes—and with Bahrami's (1992) dualistic organization, which consists of a stable "bedrock" and temporary arrangements of project teams and multifunctional groups. These three theories fall short as models for managing the relentless switching between the sharply different technology life cycles at Olivetti as described by Ciborra.

Ciborra is not describing a process that could be construed as the path of an organization through the schema. Instead, we interpret him as describing at a metalevel the shift from one particular form of the schema to another form. Rather than exploring different paths, he analyzes choices among different end states. The issue becomes how to reduce the cycle time—that is, the elapsed path time—for building a new organization. This reduction in time is likely to require, at minimum, parallel paths through the schema to fast track development. More likely, it will require latent competencies that can almost instantaneously be made manifest in a new organization.

Ciborra's emphasis on experimentation and improvisation draws out a lesson implicit in much of the rest of the book. The new thinking recognizes that outcomes are emergent. Successful managers of change paths are quick to recognize and seize opportunities. If the platform organization becomes widespread, the time in which opportunities emerge and can be seized will be compressed.

In this section we have developed the final three rules of thumb:

10. Adopt a bias for action; learn lessons by doing.

11. Engage in negotiation and political bargaining to ensure success.

12. Recognize and seize opportunities.

Steps to the Future

This book has presented and developed leading edge thinking about the management of IT-based organizational transformation. It is fresh thinking that breaks with the past rather than extending it. The consistency and coherence of the assumptions embedded in the new thinking suggest that it heralds a new beginning. In this concluding section we try to encapsulate the essence of the new thinking by summarizing its perspective on the past, present, and future. The future, we suggest, will require the nature of organizational thinking to change yet again.

The Past

The past that the contributors to this book reject is heroic in more than one sense. First, it embraced an idealism in its assumptions about the organizational world. Organizations were supposed to function as smoothly as machines in pursuit of universally accepted goals. Because IT was seen as a discrete part of the machine, the assumption was that, once implemented, it would have certain well-defined effects. Organizational outcomes therefore could be highly predictable. The status quo was a product of history that held little or nothing of essential value for transforming the organization. The knowledge necessary to produce improved outcomes was well defined and explicit; in other words, the future could be designed independently of the present, and it would be created by a deterministic technology.

Second, the past was heroic in the central place it gave to the visionary designer. Management practice was centered on strategic positioning. What mattered for IT was the grand strategic design and the organizational structure. Strategy and structure would determine competitive success and failure. They were therefore the key elements of the organization to which IT had to be aligned. Moreover, in regard to organizational transformation, it was assumed that paths to change started with strategy and proceeded through structure before IT was involved. In contrast, IT professionals thought that technology was where the management of change started and finished because they believed that technology had only to be implemented for all other organizational change to follow automatically. Heroism lay in clever technological design. Nobody treated the existing core competencies (management processes, roles and skills, and technology) and change to them as a high priority.

Traditional thinking was idealistic not realistic. It was perhaps appropriate in a business world that was relatively stable and where complexity could be made tractable by divisional organization. In consequence, the world could be known and would remain unchanged long enough for plans to be drawn, systems to be designed, and technology to be implemented.

Although the reality has been quite different, organizations have retained the traditional mind-set and have had many problems with IT as a result. In reality the business world has been turbulent, not stable. Divisional organization does not make complexity tractable in relation to IT, hence the failure of the federal structure. The world cannot be known well enough for all the important thinking to be done at the time of strategy formulation, structural design, and IT planning. Complexity, turbulence, resistance, and time lags conspire to create a world in which much of what is important in IT-based organizational transformation occurs in the bottom triangle of Figure 12.8, and the dynamics often require it to take place ahead of the strategy step. In summary, then, past experience has been less successful than expected because management attention has been focused on the wrong places, which has led to the pursuit of inappropriate paths to transformation. We have misjudged the nature of the world in which we have had to manage IT.

The Present

The present is characterized by a more realistic assessment of organizations than in the past and a corresponding pragmatism. Today we are beginning to know where to focus management attention, and we have some alternative paths to transformation. Our thinking is closer to the new mind-set. Organizations are recognized as consisting of multiple constituencies whose competitive interactions yield unpredictable outcomes. IT is just one element of the organization that interacts with others. Organizations deliver performance through their special mix of resources including their competencies, which include much knowledge that is valuable but not readily extricated from the organization. Competitive advantage emerges through the learning that transforms existing competencies into new ones. Outcomes frequently emerge rather than being planned.

The realities that have been the undoing of traditional solutions are rendered more manageable by the new thinking. Developing new core competencies based not on dreaming but on a firm understanding of what the organization can do is central. Strategic opportunity emerges based on the new competencies. The problem of developing a clever strategic design dissolves. Learning is the engine of change, and the new paths are more bottom-up than top-down. We no longer need to incur high risks by following top-down paths that attempt to anticipate the future in detail yet involve lags and delays that undermine the business design. By managing steps rather than whole paths, we can increase the independence rather than the interdependence of steps and hence further reduce the problem of risk.

The redirection of management attention has a further benefit: it reduces the problem of the separation of business and IT. In the process of discovering what the organization can do, in playing a winning game in which IT is employed in gaining achievable business benefits, business managers and IT professionals inevitably get closer than they have been and discover shared interests and opportunities. The problems of alignment begin to disappear, and IT becomes more manageable.

How easy is it for organizations to develop new ways of thinking? In this chapter we have spelled out some implications for management. Some of the taken-for-granted trade-offs have to be challenged. For example, partitioning risk into independently justifiable steps will require the discarding of attractive-looking change options that require several dependent steps for their benefits to be gained. Discarding these options will go against the grain, but attractive options have been deceptive in the past. The organizational maturity engendered by the new thinking involves both recognizing the true difficulties of managing interdependent paths and passing over the promise of glittering prizes.

Nevertheless, we believe that the evident managerial good sense of the new thinking makes it accessible to and usable in a wide range of firms. We already have a number of successful examples, such as the architects Flower and Samios (see Chapter Two). They can be emulated. They do not require superhuman management; they need only do a few important things better than their competitors, not everything. For example, in the case of the Australian Stock Exchange, which is described briefly in Chapter Two, the technology step was high-risk and required attentive management, but according to the CEO the rest of the reorganization was "just standard management." The new thinking is therefore a realistic alternative to the conventional wisdom of IT management and is accessible to a wide range of organizations, not just a tiny elite.

The Future

The extreme view of the future presented by Claudio Ciborra in Chapter Eleven is a fearsomely turbulent world in which change is rapid and for which entirely new organizational forms such as the platform organization are required. As the cycle time for market change—and hence organizational change—shortens, the requirements for successful change will become more demanding. This scenario is already real in a few industries. Others will follow at different rates. As industry conditions change, we should watch for new organizational forms such as the platform organization. The platform organization emphasizes choice among organizational configurations and the ability to rapidly implement them. Whereas first-order competencies may be sufficient for the present, the future will require second-order abilities—the ability to choose among and switch competencies.

To be able to inhabit such worlds and survive, organizational members will no longer be able to rely on slowly attaining a deep understanding of the logic underlying the key dynamics of the organization. Because there will be many such logics, understanding more than one representation of the organizational configuration will be part of every member's cognitive equipment. Whereas the schema we have used so far has linear links and hence understands organizational configurations only through those links, the future will require a fractal configuration in which the image of the whole is, to use Coombs's expression, "inscribed" in every part. Only then will it be possible to make choices and changes at the necessary speed.

However, it is extremely unlikely that organizations will be able to make the transition to such advanced capabilities without having mastered new ways of thinking. On the principle of one step at a time, adopting the new mind-set is today's step.

References

Bahrami, H. "The Emerging Flexible Organization: Perspectives from Silicon Valley." *California Management Review*, 1992, 34(4), 33–52.

Boynton, A. C., and Victor, B. "Beyond Flexibility: Building and Managing the Dynamically Stable Organization." *California Management Review*, 1991, 34(1), 53–66.

Miles, R. E., and Snow, C. C. "Fit, Failure and the Hall of Fame." *California Management Review*, 1984, 26(3), 10–28.

Miles, R. E., and Snow, C. C. "Causes of Failure in Network Organizations." *California Management Review*, 1992, 34(4), 53–72.

Scott Morton, M. S. (ed.). *The Corporation of the 1990s: Information Technology and Organizational Transformation*. New York: Oxford University Press, 1991.

Yetton, P. W., Johnston, K. D., and Craig, J. F. "Computer-Aided Architects: A Case Study of IT and Strategic Change." *Sloan Management Review*, 1994, 35(4), 57–67.

Index

A

Acer Computer, 104

Actor-network theory, 206, 237–239. *See also* Social theories

Adaptive mode, 71, 72, 74. *See also* Planning modes

Adhocracy, 66, 67, 68–69, 77, 258; in Hong Kong organizations, 75, 76. *See also* Organizational structures

Advocacy, change, 135, 138–139

Airline reservation systems, 5, 177, 201

Alignment. *See* Fit; Lead-Lag Model; Strategic alignment

Alignment conflict, 103–105

Alignment confusion, 103, 104–105

Allen, T. J., 57–58, 87

American Airlines SABRE, 5, 201

American Hospital Supply/Baxter, 27, 201

Analyzer type, 62, 63, 64, 74. *See also* Strategy, external IT

Anderson, P., 269, 274

Applegate, L. M., 210, 227

Architectural firm (Flower and Samios) case example, 5, 41, 42–46, 286

Argyris, C., 127, 140

Attewell, P., 211, 212–213, 227

Audit. *See* Organizational Cultural Audit

Australian Department of Veterans Affairs (DVA), 41, 47–49

Australian Graduate School of Management, Fujitsu Centre, 40–41, 53, 280

Australian Stock Exchange (ASX), 41, 46–47, 301

Automation: and informating of processes, 4–5; and support role of IT, 4

Azevedo, A., 219, 228

B

Bahrami, H., 259, 263, 275, 297, 302

Baker, B.S.H., 179, 180, 185

Bancroft, N. H., 117, 140

Banking industries, Hong Kong. *See* Hong Kong banking organizations

Barki, J., 151, 162

Barley, S., 212, 227

Barney, J. B., 17, 18, 20, 21, 143, 162

Baselines, new versus traditional views of, 15–16

Bashein, B. J., 116, 132, 140

Baxter, S., 175, 185

"Because-of" motives, 267

Bedrock, 259, 297

Benjamin, R. I., 12, 113–114, 115, 116, 134, 140, 142, 289–290

Benson, J. K., 216, 227

Betting, 258, 272, 273. *See also* Impro-
    visation
Bjørn-Andersen, N., 128, 141
Block, P., 119, 125, 140
Bloomfield, B., 243, 244, 245, 255, 256
Boddy, D., 135, 140
Bourdieu, P., 273, 275
Boynton, A. C., 7, 21, 32, 53, 259,
    275, 297, 303
Brancheau, J., 152–153, 162
Bricolage, 258, 262, 271. *See also*
    Improvisation
Brown, C. V., 145, 161
Brown, J. S., 265, 275
Brynjolfsson, E., 27, 53
Buchanan, D., 135, 140
Burgelman, R. A., 261, 275
Burn, J. M., 24, 25, 55, 60, 87, 89,
    91–92, 104–105, 111, 147, 286,
    287–288
Business, traditional versus new
    thinking about, 16–17
Business deployment competencies,
    149, 150; effectiveness of, 155
Business planning model, 71, 72.
    See also Planning modes
Business process change. *See* Process
    change
Business Process Reengineering
    (BPR): assumptions of, 189–191;
    beliefs of, 174–180; centrality of
    business process and IT in, 174–
    177; criticisms of, 165, 166, 169–
    170, 173–180; design versus imple-
    mentation in, 191, 192–194; failure
    rates of, 116; and IT-based organi-
    zational transformation, 10–11,
    51–52, 188, 282; IT-driven, in case
    example, 47; marketing of, 171;
    and new technologies, 210; obliter-
    ation as first step in, 178–179; and
    organizational memory, 166–167,
    178–179, 224; and organizational
    transformation, 293–294; profit
    maximization objective of, 173;
    radical change in, 171, 177–178,
191, 196–199; risks in, 169–170,
    173–180, 192; roots of, 172–173,
    187–188; social theory perspective
    on, 247–248; and strategy, 194–
    196; theoretical framework for,
    188–189, 192–194, 201–202; theo-
    retical framework for, alternative,
    199–201, 202–203; unitary, de-
    terministic strategic change in,
    179–180. *See also* Process change

C
Callon, M., 237
Capital resources acquisition, 5
Case Western Reserve University,
    Wetherhead School, 135
Cash, J. I., 29, 53, 210, 227
Caston, A., 145, 163
CATWOE (customers, actors, trans-
    formation process, worldview,
    owner, environment), 183
Cause-effect model, 14–15
Champy, J., 10, 20, 41, 51, 54, 188,
    191, 193, 197, 203, 210, 224, 227
Chandler, A. D., Jr., 190, 203
Change, force of, 206
Change management, 12, 71,
    115–118; change advocacy strate-
    gies of, 135, 138–139; failures
    of, 116–117; human aspects of,
    116–117, 123–124; human resource
    perspective on, 117; and IT cultural
    change, 133–134; IT versus organi-
    zational development perspective
    on, 120–121; IT specialist role in,
    131–140; IT technological-impera-
    tive worldview and, 118–119,
    122–125; organizational develop-
    ment perspective on, 117, 120–
    121, 126–131; and transforma-
    tional paths, 289–290, 291. *See also*
    Business Process Reengineering;
    Organizational development; Orga-
    nizational transformation
Checkland, P., 178, 180, 183, 185
CHESS, 46, 47

Cheung, H. K., 104–105, 111
Ciborra, C. U., 12, 100, 146, 147, 201, 203, 207–208, 257, 259, 269, 275, 297–298, 302
Classical school of strategy, 172, 173
Collaboration: with external networks, 149, 151; infrastructure versus human issues in, 138–139
Collis, D. J., 17, 20, 146, 161
Compeau, D., 123, 141
Competencies: action-oriented guidelines for, 160–161; building on existing, 20; and Business Process Reengineering, 194, 195–196, 293–294; and choice of transformational path, 289; in complex environments, 260–261; core, 293–294, 295; future needs and, 159–160; IT management, 143–161; IT management, categories of, 149–153; IT management, effectiveness of, 153–156; IT management, organizational role of, 146–149; IT management, and organizational transformation, 156–159, 290–292; IT specialist, for organizational change, 113–114, 115–140, 289–290, 291; monitoring of, 157–158, 161; in networked organization paradigm, 145; of platform organizations, 207, 258; and positioning approach, 195–196; research needed on, 158–159; strategy for enhancing, 161; and transformational paths, 289–292. See also Improvisation; Knowledge resources
Competition. See Environment, competitive/complex
Complexity. See Environment, competitive/complex
Computer-aided design (CAD), 42–46
Computer-aided software engineering (CASE), 212, 214
Computerized tomography, 212

Computing, frameworks of, 250–252
Conservatism, 83–85
Consultants: external versus internal, 128–129; roles of, 119; social theory perspectives on, 244–245
Content expertise, versus process expertise, 127–128
Contracting out. See Outsourcing of IT
Contradiction, logic of, 205–206, 209; institutional theory and, 217, 220–222, 225–226; versus logic of determination, 205–206, 217, 226–227; managerial implications of, 225–227; organizational culture and, 217, 218–220, 225–226; organizational learning and, 217, 222–224, 225, 226; and paradoxical consequences, 213–215; political theory and, 216–218, 225; theories that employ, 215–224
Conventional model of strategic dynamics, 35–37. See also Strategic dynamics
Coombs, R., 206–207, 231, 243, 247, 255, 256, 296–297, 302
Cooper, D., 243, 256
Cooper, R., 115, 116, 141
Copeland, D. G., 5, 20, 143, 162, 177, 185
Cost-benefit analysis of IT, failure of, 30–32
Costs: for IT-enabled change projects, 116; maintenance, 29–30
Covin, D. P., 83, 88
Craig, J. F., 5, 21, 41, 42, 52, 53, 54, 152, 166, 187, 200, 203, 293–294, 303
Creative destruction, 262
Credibility, IT specialist: and change management role, 130–131, 135; crunches of, 135, 136–137; and traditional role, 124–125, 132
Cronin, M. J., 147, 161
Croson, D. C., 29, 54
Cross-specialists, 133

Cultural change, IT, 133–134. *See also* Change management; Organizational culture
Customer network competencies, 149, 150, 151
Cycles of change, 56, 83–85, 86–87; and stagnation, 99–102. *See also* Lead-Lag Model

D

Daft, R. L., 265, 273, 275
Danieli, A., 244, 256
Data-center utility competencies, 151, 153; effectiveness of, 155
Davenport, T. H., 10, 20, 39, 51, 54, 57, 87, 152, 161, 171, 174, 175, 178, 185, 188, 197, 199, 203
Davidow, W. H., 151, 161
Davis, G. B., 185
de Gues, A., 179, 185
Decision making, rational versus improvisation, 266–268
Defender type, 62, 63, 64, 74. *See also* Strategy, external IT
Delayed type, 62, 64, 65, 66. *See also* Strategy, external IT
Delivery type, 62, 64, 65, 66. *See also* Strategy, external IT
Denver International Airport (DIA), 213–214
Dependent type, 62, 64, 65, 66. *See also* Strategy, external IT
Design-school mind-set, 16–17. *See also* Business Process Reengineering; Strategy
Desktop computing, 210
Determinism. *See* Technological determinism
Differentiation, 6, 14; alternatives to, 50, 166; and IT demands, 37–38; and market segmentation, 34–35, 36
Digital telephony, 131
Dilemma, 213. *See also* Paradoxical outcomes
Disciplinary concept of power, 236–237, 248–250. *See also* Social theories

Discrete-entity model, 13–15
Divisionalized Form, 66, 67, 68–69, 77, 166; in Hong Kong organizations, 75, 76. *See also* Organizational structures
Documentation, compulsive, 214
Dosi, G., 269, 275
Doty, D. H., 91, 111
Double bind, 213. *See also* Paradoxical outcomes
Downsizing, and outsourcing, 48, 130
Drafting, 44, 46. *See also* Computer-aided design
Drive type, 62, 64, 65, 66. *See also* Strategy, external IT
Drucker, P. F., 139, 141
Du Pont, 124
Dualistic organizational systems, 259, 297
Duguid, P., 265, 275
Dumais, S., 215, 228
Duncan, R., 222, 227
Dutton, J., 146, 160, 163
DVA. *See* Australian Department of Veterans Affairs
Dynamic alignment. *See* Lead-Lag Model
Dynamic improvement approach, 166, 199–201, 202–203
Dynamic stability model, 259, 297

E

E-mail use, 214
Eagleson, G., 194, 203
Earl, M. J., 62, 64, 67, 87, 152, 170, 185, 161
Eccles, R., 29, 39, 53, 54
Elam, J. J., 223, 229
Electronic communications, ironies of, 214–215
Electronic data interchange (EDI), 98, 101
Emergencies, improvisation in, 263–264
End-user self-sufficiency: and IT cultural change, 134; and IT specialist role, 123–124, 130–131;

and training, 123–124. *See also*
Sociotechnical movement
Engine of recombination, improvisation as, 207–208, 257–258,
262–268. *See also* Improvisation
Enterprise models, 268
Entrepreneurial mode, 71, 72. *See also*
Planning modes
Entrepreneurship, organicity and,
83–85
Environment, competitive/complex:
flexible organization and, 258–261,
268–270; improvisation and, 262–
268; platform organization and,
270–274, 297–298; and pressures
for IT-involved organizational
change, 115–116, 302; and pressures for process change, 187; and
role of information technology,
1–3; strategic alignment in, 89–90,
106
Environmental analysis, 182
ESPRIT, 221
European Economic Community,
221
Evolutionary school of strategy, 172,
173
Experimentation, 12, 223–224, 296.
See also Improvisation
Expertise, organizational development versus IT specialist view of,
127–128
External network competencies, 149,
150, 151; effectiveness of, 155

F

Facilitator, organizational
development, 120–121, 126–131. *See
also* Organizational development
Factory portfolio, 71, 73, 74. *See also*
Portfolios, IT systems
Federal structure: limitations of,
39–40, 50–51; and recombination,
262; strategic alignment in, 7–9,
37–40
Feedback loops, multiple, 184
"FINAC" case study, 80–81

Financial-services sector, 241–242
Fiol, C. M., 222, 227
Fit: external and internal, 91–92;
models of, 34–40, 56–60, 91–92;
theory of organizational, and
Business Process Reengineering,
185–186. *See also* Integration of
IT; Outsourcing of IT; Strategic
alignment
Flores, F., 266, 277
Flower, J., 42, 43, 44
Flower and Samios, 5, 41, 42–46, 106,
301
Ford, J. D., 216, 227
Ford, L. W., 216, 227
Foucault, M., 236
Frameworks of computing, 250–252
Freeman, J., 195, 203
Friedman, A. L., 122, 141
Fuerst, W. L., 18, 21, 143, 162
Fujitsu Centre, Australian Graduate
School of Management, 40–41, 53,
280

G

Galbraith, J., 265, 275
Galliers, R. D., 152, 165, 169, 180,
182, 185, 293
Gash, D. C., 117, 124, 141, 142
Gattiker, U. E., 123, 141
Geographical information systems,
212
Ghemawat, P., 272, 275
Giddens, A., 236, 273, 275
Gill, T. G., 223, 227
Glick, W. H., 91, 111
Globalization: and alignment conflict,
103–105; and alignment confusion,
103, 104–105; and strategic alignment, 102–105, 110
Goldman, S. L., 151, 161
Granovetter, M., 179, 185
Griffiths, P., 6, 21
Grint, K., 170, 186
Groupware, 122, 123–124, 131
Growth model. *See* IT infrastructure
Guimaraes, T., 144, 153, 161

H

Habitus, 273

Hall, G., 193, 194, 203

Hamel, G., 160, 162, 194, 200, 203, 259, 276

Hammer, M., 10, 20, 41, 51, 54, 57, 87, 116, 141, 165, 178, 186, 188, 191, 193, 197, 203, 210, 224, 227

Hannan, M., 195, 203

Hardware capacities, 153. *See also* Data-center utility competencies

Harianto, F., 151, 162

Hartwick, J., 151, 162

Hayek, F., 264–265, 266, 275

Hedberg, B.L.T., 258, 275

Henderson, J. C., 7, 21, 58, 60, 87, 91, 111, 144, 153, 162, 190, 203

Hierarchies, improvisation in, 265

High-tech firms: improvisation in, 271–272; organizational structures of, 207–208, 258–261, 269–270

Hofman, J. D., 131, 142

Hong Kong banking organizations, 24; Organizational Cultural Audit, framework of, 60–74; Organizational Cultural Audit, results of, 74–76; strategic alignment stagnation in, 96–97

Hopper, M. D., 5, 21

Hoverston, P., 227

Huber, G. P., 91, 111, 211, 227

Huff, A., 146, 160, 163

Hull, R., 247, 250, 256

Human resource (HR) management, 5; and change management, 117; and contradiction, 220–221; and management initiatives, 248

Husserl, E., 266, 275

"HWS" case study, 81–82

Hypocrisy, 213. *See also* Paradoxical outcomes

I

Iacono, S., 221, 227

IBM, 258

Implementation: and design, in Business Process Reengineering, 191–192, 192–194; IT role in, 191–192; strategy focus versus, 169–170, 191

Improvisation, 207–208, 257–258; and choice of transformational path, 287, 298; in emergencies, 263–264; as engine of recombination, 262–268; in hierarchies, 265; and market behavior, 264–265; versus planned decision making, 266–268; in platform organizations, 268–274

"In-order-to" motives of action, 267

Incrementalism: in dynamic improvement model, 200–201, 202–203; versus obliteration/radical change, 178–179, 197–198, 200

Industry life cycle, 98–99

Informated organization framework, 250–252

Information technology (IT): and business strategy, 57–60; as disrupter of power distributions, 234–235; false prophesies about, 28–34, 52; linkages of, 57–60; new, 51, 210; new, and IT specialist roles, 113, 116, 122–123, 124–125, 131; new mind-set in, 13–19; new mind-set in, perspective on the future, 302; new mind-set in, perspective on the past, 298–300; new mind-set in, perspective on the present, 300–301; new mind-set in, practice of, 284–298; performance problems of, 9–10, 27–28; as pliable tool, 234; power in, 233–235, 248–250; representational properties of, 206–207, 239–240; role of, in global competitive environment, 1–3; role of, in organizational transformation, 1–3, 10–11; role of, in process change, 191–194; role of, traditional thinking about, 3–5. *See also* Organizational transformation, IT-based; Outcomes; Outsourcing of IT; Packaged information technologies; Strategic alignment; Strategic planning; Traditional IT

Information technology (IT) management: competencies of, 143–161; competencies of, categories of, 149–153; competencies of, effectiveness of, 153–156; competencies of, and organizational transformation, 156–161, 290–292; competencies of, role of, 146–149; cultural change of, 133–134; in networked organization paradigm, 145; new paths to, 284–298, 300–302; new versus traditional approaches to, 11–19, 298–300; and organizational processes, 231–255; in platform organizations, 271–273; practical guidelines for, 284–298; successful practices in, case examples of, 40–50, 52. *See also* Integration of IT; Organizational transformation, IT-based; Outsourcing of IT; Strategic alignment; Strategic planning; Traditional IT management

Infrastructure. *See* IT infrastructure; Organizational infrastructure; Organizational structures

Innovation: cyclical model of, 83–85, 86–87, 99–100; and flexible structure, 258–261; technological and organization, as mutual process, 252–253. *See* Cycles of change; Organizational transformation, IT-based

Innovation-consolidation cycle, 106–108

Institutional theory: and logic of contradiction, 206, 217, 220–222, 225–226; managerial implications of, 225–226

Instrumental approach, 231–232, 251–252. *See also* Technological determinism

Integration of IT, 6, 14, 89; in case examples, 41–47; and informated organization framework, 251–252;

innovation-consolidation cycle for, 106, 107; and process change, 166; versus strategic alignment, 106–108

Interest groups, 216–218

Intranet, 210

Irony, 213. *See also* Paradoxical outcomes

IT-based organizational transformation. *See* Organizational transformation, IT-based

IT infrastructure: competencies of, 150–151, 152–153, 155; growth of, four-stage model of, 67, 70, 71; and organizational infrastructure, 76–83. *See also* Lead-Lag Model

IT managers, 40; and IT cultural change, 133–134; and IT management competencies, 160–161; and will to collaborate, 138–139. *See also* Competencies

IT planning competencies, 150, 152; effectiveness of, 155. *See also* Planning modes

IT planning model, 71, 73–74, 75–76. *See also* Planning modes

IT specialists: behavioral skill acquisition for, 135; as change advocates, 135, 138–139; change-management skills for, 131–140; client dependence on versus independence, 130–131; credibility of, 124–125, 130–131, 132, 135, 136–137; as facilitators, obstacles to, 129–130; resistance of, to change-management skill acquisition, 132–133; resistance of, to new technologies, 124–125; role of, in change management, 131–139; role of, traditional, 119, 123–124; versus senior line managers, 32–33; technological-imperative worldview of, 118–119, 122–125; worldview of, versus organizational development worldview, 120–121, 126–131

IT strategic planning. *See* Strategic planning

Italy, rescue organizations network in, 263–264
Ives, B., 3, 21, 151, 162

J

Jacobs, G. C., 7, 21, 32, 53
Johnston, K. D., 5, 21, 41, 42, 54, 303
Jones, D. T., 115, 142
Jones, J. W., 144, 153, 163
Jones, M., 187, 203

K

Kalakota, R., 27, 54
Keen, P., 27, 30, 54, 190, 203
Keil, M., 116, 123, 130, 132–133, 139, 141
Kennedy Airport, 214
King, J. L., 221, 227
Kling, R., 13, 21, 211, 221, 227
Knight, F. H., 264, 275
Knights, D., 242, 247, 252, 256
Knowledge resources: in new IT, 15, 17–18, 20; and organizational learning, 166–167, 226; in traditional IT, 5–6, 15. See also Competencies; Organizational learning
Koch, S., 215, 228
Kossek, E. E., 117, 141
Kotter, J. P., 134, 141
Kraut, R., 215, 228

L

Lanzara, G. F., 263, 269, 271, 275
Larwood, L., 123, 141
Latour, B., 237
Lave, J., 265, 275
Lead-Lag Model, 24, 56, 76–83; cyclical change model and, 83–85, 86–87, 99–100; and external change, 78–80; implications of, 85–86; IT-lag change and, 81–82; IT-lead change and, 80–81; and IT management competencies, 148–149; as path to transformation, 286–288; and stagnation, 95–102, 109–110

Learmonth, G. P., 3, 21
Learning organizations, 223–224
Leavitt, H. J., 175, 176, 186, 210, 228
Lévi-Strauss, C., 258, 271, 275
Levinson, E., 116, 134, 140
Lindblom, C., 200, 204
Line managers: and change management skills, 132; failure of, to take hands-on control, 23, 33–34; IT executives as, 133–134; and IT management competencies, 150, 151–152, 291, 292; learning gap and, 32–33; and will to collaborate, 138–139
Line technology leadership competencies, 150, 151–152; effectiveness of, 155
Lisburn, D., 175, 185
Logic of contradiction, 205–206, 209; institutional theory and, 217, 220–222, 225–226; versus logic of determination, 205–206, 217, 226–227; managerial implications of, 225–227; organizational culture and, 217, 218–220, 225–226; organizational learning and, 217, 222–224, 225, 226; and paradoxical consequences, 213–215; political theory and, 216–218, 225; theories that employ, 215–224
Logic of determination, 209–211; versus logic of contradiction, 205–206, 217, 226–227; and paradoxical outcomes, 211–213. See also Technological determinism
Logical incrementalism, 178. See also Incrementalism
London Stock Exchange, and Taurus, 27–28
Lotus Notes, 123
Lucas, H. C., Jr., 210, 228
Lyles, M. A., 222, 227

M

Machine Bureaucracy, 66, 67, 68–69, 71, 74, 77; in Hong Kong

organizations, 75, 76; in public authority case example, 78–80. *See also* Organizational structures
Macintosh system, 42, 44
Magill, S. L., 145, 161
Maintenance costs. *See* Costs
Majchrzak, A., 116, 141
Malone, M. S., 151, 161
Management. *See* Information technology management; Traditional IT management
Manchester (England) School of Management, Programme on Information and Communication Technology (PICT) research project at, 232, 235; theoretical perspectives of, 235–241; theoretical perspectives of, applications of, 241–248
March, J. G., 224, 228, 265, 275, 276
Market decision making, improvisation and, 264–265
Market segmentation strategy, 34–35, 36, 196–197
Markus, M. L., 12, 113–114, 115, 116, 118, 123, 124, 125, 128, 130, 132–133, 139, 140, 141, 211, 214, 228, 289–290
Martin, E. W., 144, 153, 162
Martinez, E. V., 116, 142
Mason, R. O., 143, 162,
Massachusetts Institute of Technology, 57–58
Mata, F. J., 18, 21, 143, 162
Matrix organization, 268
McFarlan, F. W., 62, 71, 87, 190, 204
McGee, J., 36, 54
McKenney, J. L., 5, 20, 27, 28, 54, 143, 162, 177, 185
McWhinney, W., 119, 142
Mechanistic organizations, 83–85
Merchant, K., 33, 34, 54
Meyer, J. W., 220, 228
Microsoft, 258
Miles, R. E., 36, 54, 62, 64, 87, 189, 190, 204, 258, 259, 276, 288–289, 297, 303

Millar, V. E., 9, 21
Miller, D., 91, 111
Mills, Q. F., 210, 227
Mind-sets: importance of, 18–19; new, 13–19, 287–302; new versus traditional, 19–29
Mintzberg, H., 62, 66, 71, 74, 88, 166, 172, 179, 186, 190, 200, 204, 256, 276
Misalignment, 92; analysis of, 94–95; in case study, 92–94
MIT90s framework, 35, 188–189; new paths in, 284–298; and path analysis, 280–281; traditional paths in, 283, 284, 285; reconfigured, 192–194, 199
Moad, J., 125, 142
Monitoring, of IT management competencies, 157–158, 161
Montgomery, C. A., 17, 20, 146, 161
Mrs. Fields Cookies, 223
Multidivisional form, 268
Multiple-constituency perspective, 13–14, 18
Mumford, E., 117, 142, 170, 186
Murray, F., 242, 247, 252, 256

N

Nagel, R. N., 151, 161
Nance, W. D., 124, 142
National Health Service (NHS), 242–243
NCR, 260
Nelson, D. L., 211, 228
Nelson, R. R., 149, 162, 265, 276
Networked organization: in high-tech firms, 258–259; IT management competencies in, 146–161; paradigm of, 145, 297; and recombination, 262, 268; social theory perspective on, 246–247
Networks, external, 149, 150, 151
Neutrality, 128–129
Niederman, F., 152–153, 162
Nohria, N., 29, 53
Nolan, R. L., 29, 53, 54, 62, 67, 88

Nonaka, I., 270, 276
Nystrom, P. C., 258, 275

O

Obliteration, 178–179. *See also*
Business Process Reengineering; Radical change
Olfman, L., 123, 141
Olivetti, 259–260, 269, 297
Olson, M. H., 151, 162, 185
Opportunistic deployment of partnerships, 273
Organicity, entrepreneurship and, 83–85
Organizational Cultural Audit, 60–74; business planning component of, 71, 72; cross-alignment dimension of, 71–74; external business-strategy component of, 61, 63; external dimension of, 61–66; external IT strategy component of, 64–66; framework of, 61, 62; internal dimension of, 66–71; IT infrastructure component of, 67, 70, 71; IT planning component of, 71, 73–74; organizational configuration classifications in, 66–67; organizational infrastructure component of, 67, 68–69; results of, in Hong Kong study, 74–76, 78–83. *See also* Lead-Lag Model; Strategic alignment
Organizational culture: IT, changing of, 133–134; and logic of contradiction, 206, 217, 218–220, 225–226; managerial implications of, 225–226, 294–295, 296
Organizational development (OD), 117; applied to IT-based organizational change, 139–140, 290, 291; implications of, for organizational change, 130–131; inhibiting factors in, 121, 128–130; promoting factors in, 120, 128–130; worldview of, 126–131; worldview of, versus IT worldview, 120–121
Organizational identity, 260, 261, 269–270

Organizational infrastructure: and IT infrastructure growth, 76–83; in Organizational Cultural Audit, 67, 67–69. *See also* Lead-Lag Model
Organizational learning, 166–167; and dynamic improvement approach, 200–201; and logic of contradiction, 206, 209, 217, 222–224, 225, 226; managerial implications of, 225, 226; versus obliteration approach, 178–179
Organizational memory, 222–224, 225, 226. *See also* Organizational learning
Organizational structures: classifications of, 66–67, 68–69; efficiency perspective on, 268–269; flexible, 258–261; impact of, on planning mode, 76, 77; IT impact on, 211–215; and IT infrastructure growth, 76–83; and strategy, 190. *See also* Lead-Lag Model; Networked organization; Platform organization
Organizational transformation, IT-based, 1–3; Business Process Reengineering approach to, 10–11, 51–52; challenge of, 10–11; competencies for, core, 293–294, 295; competencies for, IT management, 113, 114, 143–161, 290–292; competencies for, IT specialist, 113–114, 115–140, 289–290, 291; future of, steps to, 298–302; in integration case examples, 41–47; logic of contradiction view of, 211–227; logic of determination view of, 209–211; IT specialist blockage of, 124–125; new mind-set and, 12–19, 279–302; outcomes of, 209–227, 231–255; in outsourcing case example, 41, 47–50; path analysis and, 280–281; paths to, new, 284–298; paths to, traditional, 283, 284, 285; pressures for, 115–116; process change and, 165–167, 169–185, 187–203,

293–294, 295; social theories applied to, 231–255; strategic alignment and, 35. *See also* Business Process Reengineering; Change management; Competencies; Outcomes; Process change;

Orlikowski, W. J., 124, 131, 142, 212, 214, 228

Orr, J., 265, 276

Outcomes: causal variables in, 212–213; comparative research on, 211–213; joint IT/organization, 205, 206–207, 231–255; paradoxical, 205–206, 209–227. *See also* Paradoxical outcomes; Performance

Outsider status, 128–129

Outsourcing of IT: in case example, 41, 47–50; and IT specialist role, 130

Ownership, of costs versus benefits, 31–32

Oxymoron, 213. *See also* Paradoxical outcomes

P

Packaged information technologies: and change-management role of IT specialists, 122–124, 133; and end-user self-sufficiency, 122–123, 130–131; and end-user training, 123–124; use of, in architectural firm case example, 43

Paradoxical outcomes, 12–13, 205, 213–215; examples of, 213–215; institutional factors and, 217, 220–222; and logic of contradiction, 215–227; organizational culture and, 217, 218–220; organizational learning and, 217, 222–224; political interests and, 216–218. *See also* Contradiction, logic of; Outcomes

Partnership framework of computing, 250

Paths: analysis of, 280–281; choice of, 284–289; new, 284–298; process of managing, 294–298; traditional,

283, 284, 285. *See also* MIT90s framework

Pennings, J. M., 151, 162

Penrose, E., 146, 162

People issues: in change management, 116–117, 123–124; in collaboration, 138–139; and management initiatives, social theory perspective on, 245–248; and process change, 174–177, 192–194

People's Republic of China, 105

Performance: and logic of contradiction, 205–206; organizational, and IT management, 143–144; problems with, 9–10, 27–28; as reinforcer of change, 289. *See also* Outcomes

Persistence, forces of, 206, 215–224; managerial implications of, 225–227, 294–296. *See also* Contradiction, logic of

PEST analysis, 182

Pettigrew, A. M., 179, 186

Pfeffer, J., 14, 21

Phenomenology, 266–267

Planning modes, 71, 72, 74; influences on, 75–83. *See also* IT planning competencies

Platform organization, 207–208, 268–270; characteristics of, 270–271; improvisation in, 257–258, 271–274; as path to transformation, 297–298; and role of IT management competencies, 147

Political theory: and logic of contradiction, 206, 216–218, 225; managerial implications of, 225. *See also* Power

Poole, M. S., 216, 228

Porter, M. E., 3, 21, 166, 182, 186, 188, 190, 204, 272, 276

Portfolios, IT systems, 71, 73–74; and Lead-Lag Model, 80–83

Positioning model, 166, 190–191, 195–196, 199, 202, 299; alternative to, 199–203, 294, 295

Power: disciplinary concept of,
236–237, 248–250, 296–297; in
information systems, traditional
views of, 233–235; organizational
development view of, 128; and
social theories, 235–241. *See also*
Political theory
Practical thinking, 265
Pragmatism, 273
Prahalad, C. K., 160, 162, 194, 200,
203, 259, 276
Preiss, K., 151, 161
Privatization, in outsourcing case
example, 48
Process adaptiveness competencies,
150, 152; effectiveness of, 155
Process change, 165–167, 169–185,
187–203; developing alternative
future scenarios for, 181, 182–183;
dynamic improvement approach to,
166, 199–201, 202–203; essence of,
170–171; expense of, 171; holistic
approach to, 165–166, 180–185;
IT role in, 191–194; and MIT90s
model, 188–189, 192–194, 199,
293–294, 295; as path to transformation, 293–294, 295; preparation
for, 181, 182; and root definitions,
183–184. *See also* Business Process
Reengineering
Process consulting skills, 132
Process expertise, 127–128
Process informating, 4–5
Process innovation/invention versus
process improvement, 197, 199
Processor architecture, 153. *See also*
Data-center utility competencies
Processual school of strategy, 172–173
Product life cycle, short, 259–260
Product-market strategies, and IT
management competencies, 146
Professional Bureaucracy, 66–67,
68–69, 77; in Hong Kong organiza-
tions, 75, 76. *See also* Organiza-
tional structures
Profit maximization objective, 173,
179–180

Programme on Information and
Communication Technology
(PICT) research project, 232,
235; theoretical perspectives of,
235–241; theoretical perspectives
of, applications of, 241–248
Prospector type, 62, 63, 64. *See also*
Strategy, external IT
Prusak, L., 36, 39, 54
Public authority (PHA) case study,
78–80

Q

Quality assurance controls, 153. *See
also* Data-center utility competencies
Quality programs, and Business
Process Reengineering, 194
Quinn, J. B., 166, 178, 186, 200, 204

R

Radical change, 171, 177–178, 191,
196–199. *See also* Business Process
Reengineering
Rapid learning, 273
Rational decision making, improvisa-
tion versus, 266–268
Rationalistic mind-set, 13–15
Rea, D., 243, 256
Reactor type, 62, 63, 64. *See also*
Strategy, external IT
Recombination, improvisation as
engine of, 207–208, 257–258,
262–268. *See also* Improvisation;
Platform organization; Resource-
based view
Reengineering. *See* Business Process
Reengineering; Process change
Representational properties of IT,
239–240. *See also* Social theories
Rescue organizations network,
263–264
Resistance: and forces of persistence,
215–224; of IT specialists, to
change-management skill acquisition, 132–133; of IT specialists, to
new technologies, 124–125. *See
also* Status quo

Resource-based view (RBV), 17–18;
and IT management competencies,
146, 160; and platform organiza-
tion, 207. *See also* Improvisation;
Platform organization
"ResourceCo" case study, 92–94;
analysis of, 94–95, 106
"Right stuff," 12–13
Riley, P., 116, 140
Risks, in Business Process Reengineer-
ing, 169–170, 173–180, 192
Robey, D., 14, 118, 124, 125, 141,
205–206, 209, 211, 212, 219, 222,
223, 224, 228, 229, 282, 294, 295
Rockart, J. F., 116, 142, 143, 144, 153,
162, 171, 186
Rodriguez-Diaz, A. G., 224, 228
Romer, P., 262, 276
Roos, D., 115, 142
Root definitions, 183–184
Rosenthal, J., 193, 194, 203
Rowan, B., 220, 228
Ruhleder, K., 214–215, 229
Rule, J., 211, 212–213, 227
Rumelt, R., 34, 54, 190, 204

S
SABRE, 5, 201
Sahay, S., 212, 228
Sambamurthy, V., 114, 143, 144,
145, 149, 152–153, 157, 162, 163,
290–292
Sauer, C., 1, 9, 10, 21, 24, 25, 89, 279,
288
Saunders, C. S., 144, 153, 163, 222,
229
"SBC" case study, 82–83
Scacchi, W., 13, 21
Scarbrough, H., 174, 175, 186
Scenarios, alternative future, 182–183
Schein, E. H., 132, 134, 142, 218, 229
Schumpeter, J., 262, 276
Schutz, A., 266, 267, 276
Schwarz, R. M., 127–128, 142
Scope of projects, 33–34
Scott, W. R., 220, 229
Scott Morton, M. S., 10, 21, 27, 28,

35, 54, 57–58, 87, 88, 188, 204,
210, 229, 280, 295, 303
Scribner, S., 265, 276
SEATS, 46–47
Security controls, 153. *See also* Data-
center utility competencies
Sein, M., 123, 141
Self-assessment, for monitoring
IT management competencies,
157–158, 161
Self-disciplining, 236–237. *See also*
Social theories
Self-renewing organizational "tents,"
258
Self-sufficiency. *See* End-user self-
sufficiency
Senn, J. A., 177, 186
Sense-making, 261
Shapeless organizations. *See* Platform
organization
Sheather, S., 194, 203
Short, J. E., 143, 162, 171, 174, 175,
185, 186
Shrivastava, C. S., 146, 160, 163
Silicon Valley, 263
Silver, M. S., 119, 142
Simon, H. A., 265, 266, 267, 276
Simple Structure, 66, 68–69, 77; in
Hong Kong organizations, 75, 76.
See also Organizational structures
Situatedness, 264–265
Skills. *See* Competencies; Training
Slevin, D. P., 83, 88
Sloan School of Management, Massa-
chusetts Institute of Technology,
57–58
Smart machine, 218
Smircich, L., 218, 229
Snow, C. C., 36, 54, 62, 64, 87, 189,
190, 204, 258, 259, 276, 288–289,
297, 303
Social shaping, 237. *See also* Actor-
network theory; Social theories
Social theories, 232–233; actor-net-
work, 237–239; application of,
241–248; contemporary European,
235–241; and disciplinary concept

of power, 236–237; and IT management, 250–255; managerial
implications of, 254–255; and
representational properties of IT,
239–240

Sociotechnical movement, 165, 174,
175. *See also* End-user self-sufficiency

Soft systems approach, 165–166, 179,
180–185, 253

Soh, C., 130, 141

Specialism, 6, 14

Spender, J. C., 146, 163

Stagnation, 95–96; analysis of,
98–102; avoidance of, 109–110;
in case examples, 96–98; cyclical,
96–97; deliberate policy of, 97,
102; and industry life cycle,
99–100; and IT inability to lead
business, 97–98

Stanton, S. A., 116, 141

Star, S. L., 214–215, 229

Starbuck, W. H., 258, 275

Status quo: obliteration of, 178–179;
and resistance to change, 294–295,
296; traditional versus new views
of, 15–16, 298–299; valuing of,
166–167, 178–179, 296. *See also*
Organizational learning

Status symbols, 221–222

Stein, E. W., 223, 229

Stock exchange systems: Australian,
46–47; London, 27–28

Strassmann, P. A., 9, 21, 27, 54

Strategic alignment, 6–9, 23–25;
concept of, 56–57; conflict in,
103–105; confusion in, 103,
104–105; cyclical change model
and, 83–85, 86–87, 99–100; effective management of, 56; federal
structure and, 7–9, 37–40, 50–51;
globalization and, 102–105, 110;
integral approaches versus, in case
examples, 41–47, 49; Lead-Lag
Model of, 56, 76–83; limitations of,
for IT-enabled organizational trans-

formation, 55, 60; living with,
108–110; longitudinal study of,
60–74; management difficulties of,
91–92; misalignment and, 92–95;
model of, 57–60; and organizational fit, 91–92; outsourcing approach versus, in case example,
47–50; path of, 283, 284; pathology of, 24, 89–111; pathology of,
avoiding the pitfalls of, 108–110;
pathology of, sources of, 105–108;
practice of, 56–57; stagnation and,
95–102, 109–110; and traditional
IT management, 34–40. *See also*
Lead-Lag Model

Strategic business units (SBUs), 1–2;
integration and, 89

Strategic dynamics: conventional
model of, 35–37; as path to transformation, 285, 286; in successful
practice, 44–45, 285, 286. *See also*
Dynamic improvement approach

Strategic information systems (SIS),
5, 11

Strategic management, 179–180, 190

Strategic planning, 6–7; as learning,
179; and organizational transformation, 282; and positioning
approach, 190–191

Strategic portfolio, 71, 73. *See also*
Portfolios

Strategic role of IT: and organizational transformation, 10–11; traditional thinking about, 4–5. *See
also* Organizational transformation;
Strategic alignment; Strategic
planning

Strategy: Business Process Reengineering and, 194–196; dynamic
formulation of, 199–201; focus on,
versus implementation, 169–170,
191; schools of, 172–173; and
structural adaptation, 190, 195–
196; unitary, deterministic view
of, versus incremental views,
179–180

Strategy, external business: classifi-
cations of, 61, 63, 64; Lead-Lag
Model and, 78–83. *See also* Lead-
Lag Model; Strategic alignment

Strategy, external IT: and Lead-Lag
Model, 80–83; in Organizational
Cultural Audit, 64–66. *See also*
Lead-Lag Model; Strategic
alignment

Strategy-structure fit, 34–40. *See also*
Fit; Lead-Lag Model; Strategic
alignment

Structural adaptation, and strategy,
190, 195–196

Suchman, L., 268, 276

Supplier network competencies, 149,
150, 151

Support portfolio, 71, 73, 74. *See also*
Portfolios

Support role of IT, traditional
thinking about, 4; and technical
specialism, 6

Surprises, 262–263

Swanson, E. B., 211, 229

SWOT analysis, 182

Systemic school of strategy, 172, 173

Systems approach. *See* Soft systems
approach

Systems development techniques,
social theory perspective on, 245

Systems-rationalist model, 13–15

T

Takeuchi, H., 270, 276

Tapscott, D., 145, 163

Technical framework of computing,
250

Technical mastery, internal, 42–43

Technological determinism, 14,
209–211, 246; and instrumental
approach, 231–232; and IT worldview, 118–119, 122–125; versus
logic of contradiction, 205–206,
217, 226–227; and paradoxical
outcomes, 211–213; path of, 283,
294

Technology leadership competencies,
150, 151–152; effectiveness of, 155

Temporary survival, and flexible organization, 259, 297

"The organization is the IT and the
IT is the organization" framework,
250–252

Thorelli, H. B., 258, 276

Time horizons, 33–34

Tinkering, 258, 262. *See also*
Improvisation

"TRADEP" case study, 97–98;
analysis of, 98–102, 107–108

Traditional IT: current solutions in,
34–40; false assumptions in, 28–34;
implications of, to change management, 123–125; inhibiting factors
in, 121, 122–123; mind-set of, versus new mind-set, 12–19; power in,
233–235; promoting factors in, 120,
122–123; separation of, from business, 5–6, 106–108, 109; strategic
role of, 4–5; strategy-structure fit
models in, 34–40; support role of,
4, 5; technological worldview of,
118–119, 122–125. *See also* Information technology; Technological
determinism

Traditional IT management, 5–9,
123–125; current solutions in,
34–40; new approaches versus,
11–19, 283–298; paths in, 283,
284, 285; problems and failures of,
28–34; replacing with new, options
in, 283–284. *See also* Information
technology management; Strategic
planning; Strategic alignment;
Technological determinism

Training: cross-, 133; end-user,
123–124; for IT specialist change
management skills, 135. *See also*
End-user self-sufficiency

Transformational leadership, 197

Turnaround portfolio, 71, 73, 74. *See
also* Portfolios

Tushman, M. L., 269, 274

U

Unger, R. M., 269, 276
Ungson, G. R., 222, 229
United Kingdom: hospital doctors in, 236–237; National Health Service, 242–243
University of Lancaster, 165–166
"USINC" case study, 97; analysis of, 98–102, 107

V

Value-added partnerships, 149, 150, 151
Value-chain, 182
Van de Ven, A. H., 216, 228
Vaverek, K. A., 222, 229
Venkatraman, N., 7, 21, 55, 58, 60, 87, 88, 91, 111, 143, 157, 163, 177, 186, 190, 203
Vera, A. H., 266, 276
Victor, B., 259, 275, 297, 303
Videoconferencing, 113, 131
Virtual corporations, 210
Voice mail, 131
von Simson, E., 39, 54
Vurdubakis, T., 245, 256

W

Wade, J., 193, 194, 203
Walsh, J. R., 222, 229
Walton, R. E., 123, 134, 142
Ward, J., 6, 21
Waters, J. A., 172, 179, 186
"WBC" global bank case study, 103–104, 106–107
Weber, M., 266, 276
Webster, J., 123, 141
Weick, K. E., 261, 264, 265, 271, 273, 275, 276, 277

Weir, M., 117, 142
Weiss, A., 222, 227
Wenger, E., 265, 275
Westpac, CS90, 28
Wetherbe, J. C., 152–153, 162
Wetherhead School, Case Western Reserve University, 135
Whinston, A., 27, 54
Whisler, T. L., 210, 228
Whitmore, P., 6, 21
Whittington, R., 172–173, 179–180, 186
Williamson, O. E., 268, 269, 277
Willmott, H., 242, 247, 248, 252, 256
Winograd, T., 266, 277
Winter, S. G., 149, 162, 265, 276
Wishart, N. A., 223, 224, 228, 229
Womack, J. P., 115, 142
World Wide Web: and IT specialist role, 113, 116, 122, 131; and organizational competencies, 147; and organizations, 210
Wynn, E. S., 265, 277

Y

Yates, J., 116, 142
Yetton, P. W., 1, 5, 21, 23–25, 27, 41, 42, 52, 53, 54, 89, 90, 152, 157, 166, 187, 200, 203, 279, 285, 290–291, 293–294, 303

Z

Zimmerman, D., 268, 277
Zmud, R. W., 7, 21, 32, 53, 114, 143, 144, 145, 149, 152–153, 157, 162, 163, 290–292
Zuboff, S., 4, 21, 174, 186, 215, 218, 229
Zwass, V., 223, 229